Peter Lely
A Lyrical Vision

THE COURTAULD Gallery

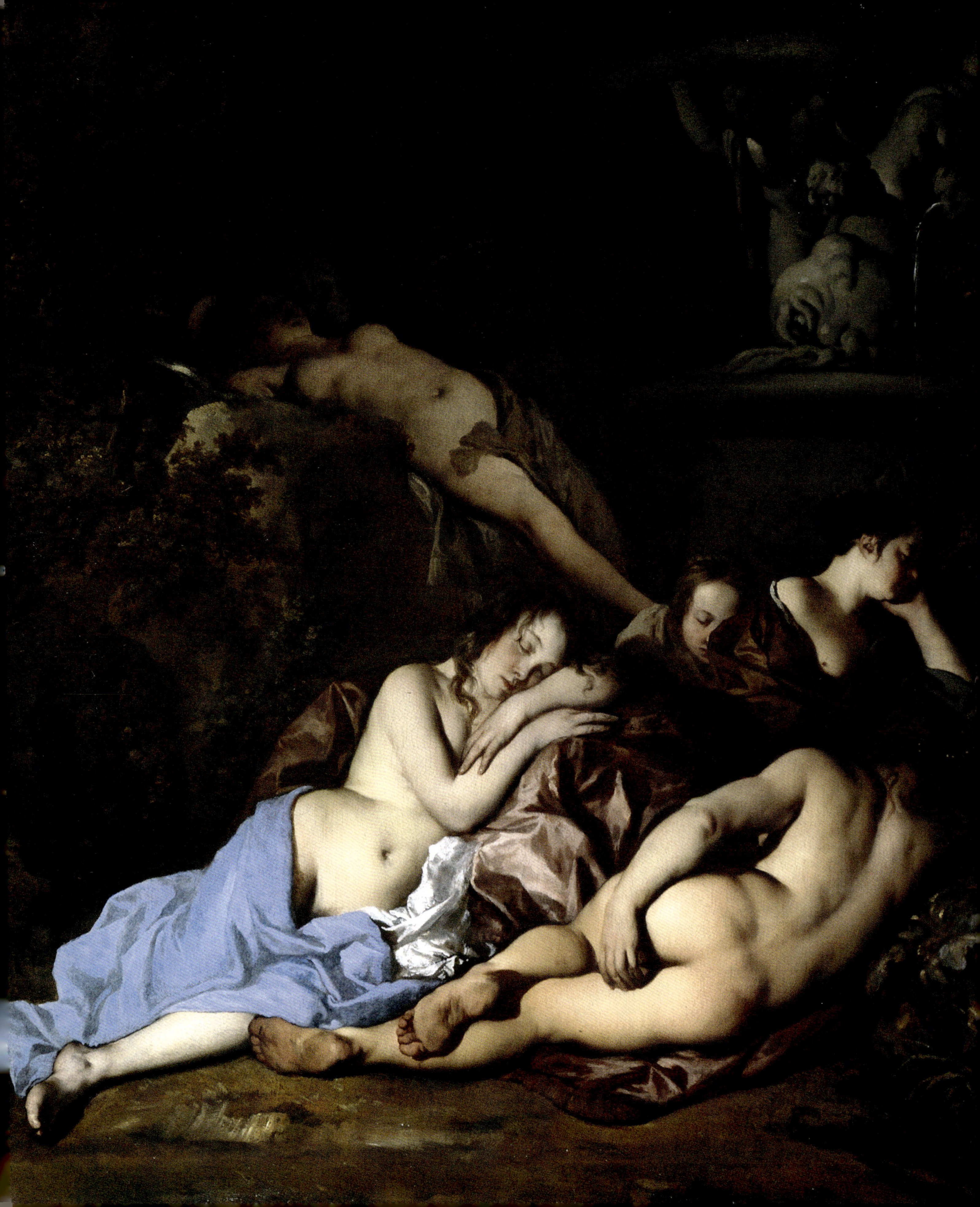

Peter Lely
A Lyrical Vision

EDITED BY
Caroline Campbell

CONTRIBUTORS
Diana Dethloff
Karen Hearn
David A.H.B. Taylor

THE COURTAULD GALLERY
IN ASSOCIATION WITH
PAUL HOLBERTON PUBLISHING
LONDON

First published to accompany the exhibition
Peter Lely: A Lyrical Vision

The Courtauld Gallery, London
11 October 2012 – 13 January 2013

The Courtauld Gallery is supported by
the Higher Education Funding Council for
England (HEFCE)

The Paul Mellon Centre *for Studies in British Art*

ISBN 978 1 907372 40 7

British Library Cataloguing in Publication Data

A catalogue record for this book is
available from the British Library

Produced by Paul Holberton publishing
89 Borough High Street, London SE1 1NL, UK
www.paul-holberton.net

Designed by Philip Lewis

Origination and printing by E-graphic, Verona, Italy

FRONT COVER detail, cat. 7
BACK COVER cat. 9
FRONTISPIECE detail, cat. 9
PAGE 11 detail, cat. 12

Contents

Foreword

THIS EXHIBITION AIMS to contribute to our understanding of seventeenth-century art in Britain through a focused examination of Peter Lely's relatively little known group of 'subject pictures'. Often drawing on pastoral themes and suffused with Lely's knowledge of the art of the Venetian Renaissance, these frequently complex and ambitious compositions form an intriguing strand in the history of seventeenth-century British art, otherwise dominated by portraiture. The exhibition is organised around *The Concert*, one of the largest and most beguiling paintings of the artist's career. Along with a second subject painting, now known to depict *Reuben presenting Mandrakes to Leah*, *The Concert* was bequeathed to The Courtauld Gallery in 1947 as part of the major collection assembled by Viscount Lee of Fareham. Lee sold another of his paintings by Lely, this one a portrait of an unknown lady, to Samuel Courtauld, the great collector of Impressionism who joined Lee and Sir Robert Witt in establishing The Courtauld Institute of Art in 1932. Now also part of the Gallery's permanent collection, this portrait became one of Courtauld's most cherished possessions, inspiring several poems and one of his few art historical writings.

Peter Lely: A Lyrical Vision has been organised by Caroline Campbell, who was until very recently The Courtauld Gallery's Schroder Foundation Curator of Paintings. I wish to thank her unreservedly for her commitment to all aspects of this project, even after having taken up the many responsibilities of her new curatorial role at The National Gallery, London. This foreword gives me the happy opportunity to thank her in print for the enormous contribution she made to the success of the Gallery over the seven years of her curatorship. On behalf of The Courtauld I also wish to extend warm thanks to the scholars who, alongside Caroline, contributed to the catalogue: Diana Dethloff, Karen Hearn and David Taylor. Diana, with Catharine MacLeod, is preparing a new catalogue raisonné of Peter Lely's work and we are especially indebted to her for having made her extensive knowledge so freely available.

Particular thanks are due to those individuals and institutions that have allowed us to exhibit cherished works from their collections. For private owners the loan of pictures of this calibre and scale can be extremely difficult, and I wish to thank them most warmly for their support. Amongst the museums and galleries that have supported us I want to thank our colleagues at Tate and, most especially, Dulwich Picture Gallery, from whose collection we have so generously been permitted to borrow what are quite possibly Peter Lely's two finest works.

As a university art museum, The Courtauld Gallery has championed a distinctive type of exhibition which is highly focused in character and aims to shed new light on particular episodes in the history of art. Especially where their subject matter extends beyond the narrow pantheon of internationally recognised names, these exhibitions rely fully on the financial support of others. We would not have been able to organise *Peter Lely: A Lyrical Vision* without the very generous assistance of our principal sponsor, Mr James Stunt, whose enthusiasm and personal affinity for Peter Lely's work recalls that of Samuel Courtauld. James Stunt has formed one of the world's very finest private collections of portraits by Lely and in so doing has encouraged others to look again at the exceptional qualities of this artist. The Courtauld also wishes to acknowledge the generous contribution of the Paul Mellon Centre for Studies in British Art, which supported this project with a research grant as well as assisting with the costs of the catalogue. Finally, and as so often before, I have the pleasure of acknowledging the irreplaceable role that the Friends of The Courtauld play in supporting the Gallery's exhibition programme, alongside so much else that makes The Courtauld what it is.

ERNST VEGELIN VAN CLAERBERGEN
Head of The Courtauld Gallery

Exhibition Supporters

LEAD SPONSOR
James Stunt

SPONSOR
The Friends of The Courtauld

The Courtauld Gallery also wishes to acknowledge the support of:

The Paul Mellon Centre for Studies in British Art

The Government Indemnity Scheme, administered by Arts Council England

Curator's Acknowledgements

This exhibition could not have happened without the help of many people. Firstly, I thank Diana Dethloff and Kate Stonor, who implanted in my consciousness the idea that a Lely subject picture exhibition might work well at The Courtauld. Diana – who has written one of the catalogue essays – has been endlessly enthusiastic and generous in sharing her immense knowledge about Lely, both as an artist and as a collector. Kate undertook technical examinations of all the Lelys in the collection as part of her Andrew W. Mellon Fellowship at The Courtauld. Subsequently, she conserved *Reuben presenting Mandrakes to Leah* (with the help of a Woodmansterne Art Conservation Award), and we had many discussions – sometimes with Diana– in front of the picture. I would additionally like to thank Karen Hearn and David Taylor for kindly sharing their scholarship on Lely, and for contributing essays to the catalogue, as well as Catharine MacLeod, who has offered wise advice.

The project would not have got off the ground without the enthusiastic backing of our generous supporters: James Stunt, the exhibition's lead sponsor, and the Friends of The Courtauld. James' passion for Lely is probably unmatched by any man or woman. He is a dedicated collector who is assembling an impressive group of Lelys, which are set to rival the Windsor Beauties. He has been unswervingly and unhesitatingly committed to this exhibition. The Friends of the Courtauld, chaired by Lucía Halpern, are also to be thanked for their unstinting kindness towards the Gallery. I am grateful to the Paul Mellon Centre for Studies in British Art, to its Director Brian Allen and the incoming Director Mark Hallett, for awarding me a research grant and a publication grant towards this exhibition and the catalogue which accompanies it.

Without loans, an exhibition would not exist, and I thank all those individuals and institutions who have made these possible, including those from collectors who wish to remain anonymous. The Courtauld is indebted to the Government Indemnity Scheme, administered by Rhiannon Davies and her colleagues. It is my pleasure to acknowledge the help of the following:

Caroline Arscott, James and Claire Birch, Sue Bond, Jane Brehony, Xavier Bray, Stephanie Buck, Aviva Burnstock, Hugh Belsey, Maryellen Cetra, Penelope Curtis, Louisa Dare, Anne Dary, Emma Davidson, Wilma Day, Emmanuelle Delapierre, Ian Dejardin, Sara Denham, Cynthia De Souza, Brett Dolman, Jill Dunkerton, Jane Eade, Kate Edmondson, Rachael Fenton, Lucy Findlay, Susan Foister, Sacha Gerstein, Kerstin Glasow, John Goodall, Bendor Grosvenor, Ingrid Guiot, Fergus Hall, Henrietta Hine, Matthew Hirst, Paul Holberton, Antony Hopkins, Rica Jones, Larry Keith, Kate Knight, Alastair Laing, Chloe Le Tissier, Katharine Lockett, Philip Lewis, Helen Martin Leake, Belinda Moore, Philip and Catherine Mould, Charles Noble, Laura Parker, Mary Peskett Smith, Sophie Plender, Laura Popoviciu, Charlotte Proctor-Smith, Anne Puetz, François Ribemont, Annie Roper, Nicole Ryder, Xavier Salomon, Olivia Savatier-Sjöholm, Cyrille Sciama, David Solkin, Deborah Swallow, Hannah Talbot, The Lord Tollemache, Malene Wagner Bahamonde, Betsy Wieseman, Joff Whitten, Joanna Woodall, Paul and Seth Woodmansterne, Barnaby Wright.

At The Courtauld Gallery I would like to thank all my former colleagues, but particularly Graeme Barraclough, Julia Blanks, Sandra Boks, Jack Kettlewell, Rachel Sloan, and Ernst Vegelin van Claerbergen. Graeme has ably conserved two of the paintings in the exhibition, and has been endlessly helpful. Julia has managed the loans and the installation of the exhibition with her customary aplomb, and Jack and Graeme together have installed it beautifully. Rachel Sloan has curated a fascinating display of drawings by Lely and from his collection, with the help of Naomi Lebens. I also wish to acknowledge the considerable role which Sandra Boks has played in this project. Sandra, the Gallery's intern from The Courtauld's MA in Curating the Art Museum, compiled research dossiers on all the pictures in the exhibition, made numerous translations from Dutch texts, and has provided assistance in many ways. I am grateful to the staff of many London research libraries, but particularly the Witt and Book Libraries at The Courtauld and the National Gallery Library, for all the help they have offered me. I am very appreciative of the work of Karin Kyburz, who ordered all the images for the catalogue.

Nicholas Penny has kindly permitted his Curator of Italian Paintings before 1500 to continue working on a topic so peripheral to her new collection as Peter Lely, and has also expressed real enthusiasm for the subject. I remain particularly indebted to Ernst Vegelin van Claerbergen, who has been unwavering in his commitment to this project, and has shown deep forbearance with a curator no longer on the premises.

CAROLINE CAMPBELL

Samuel Courtauld Society

DIRECTOR'S CIRCLE

Anonymous
Andrew and Maya Adcock
Farah and Hassan Alaghband
Apax Partners
I C Carr
Christie's
Coller Capital Ltd
Mark and Cathy Corbett
Nicholas and Jane Ferguson
The Garcia Family Foundation
Sir Nicholas and Lady Goodison
James Hughes-Hallett
Nick Hoffman
Daniella Luxembourg, London
John A. McLaren/AkzoNobel
Charles and Tineke Pugh
Derek and Inks Raphael
Paul and Jill Ruddock
Sotheby's
Nicolai and Katja Tangen
Elke and Michael von Brentano
Niklas and Catherine Zennström

PATRONS' CIRCLE

Anonymous
Agnew's
Lord and Lady Aldington
Joan and Robin Alvarez
Felix Appelbe
Jean-Luc Baroni Ltd
Philip and Cassie Bassett
John and Cynthia Beerbower
Douglas Blausten
The Lord Browne of Madingley
Tania Buckrell Pos
Mr Damon Buffini
David and Jane Butter
Julian and Jenny Cazalet
Mr Colin Clark
Colnaghi
Samantha Darell
Roger and Rebecca Emery
Eykyn Maclean Ltd
Mr Sam Fogg
GAM
David Gibbons
Lucía V. Halpern and John Davies
Paula and Schuyler Henderson
Joanna Hewitt
Jennifer Hicks
Andrew Hochhauser QC
Amanda Hochman
Philip Hudson
Nicholas Jones
Daniel Katz Ltd
Klein Solicitors Ltd
Norman A. Kurland and Deborah A. David
Helen Lee and David Warren
Lefevre Fine Art
Stuart Lochhead and Sophie Richard
Mark and Liza Loveday
Dr Chris Mallinson
Janet Martin
Mr Jay Massey
Clare Maurice
The Honourable Christopher McLaren
Lillian McNeila
Chiara Medici-Terzaghi
Norma and Selwyn Midgen
John and Jenny Murray
Mr Morton Neal CBE and Mrs Neal
John Nicoll and Laurence Colchester
Mrs Carmen Oguz
Mr Michael Palin
Lord and Lady Phillimore
Marie-Christine Poulain and Read Gomm
Leslie Powell
Charles Rose
Lady Jennifer Rose
Mrs Janice Sacher
Mr Adrian Sassoon
Stephanie Schleiffer, Haunch of Venison
Philip Searl
Richard and Susan Shoylekov
William Slee and Dr Heidi Bürklin-Slee
Marjorie Stimmel
Sir Angus Stirling
Mrs Philippa Thorp
Johnny Van Haeften
Erik and Kimie Vynckier
The Rt. Hon. Nicholas & Lavinia Wallop
George and Patricia White
Lynne Woolfson

ASSOCIATES

Mrs Kate Agius
Lord Jeffrey Archer
The Hon Nicholas Assheton CVO, FSA
Mr Dominique and Ms Brit Axelroud
Mrs James Beery
John G. Bernasconi
Sarah Boardman
Henry and Maria Cobbe
Mr Oliver Colman
Prisca and Andrew Cox
Emma Davidson
Richard Deutsch
Simon C. Dickinson Ltd
Mr Andrew P Duffy
Ben Elwes Fine Art
Sibylla Jane Flower
David and Diana Frank
Jane Gordon-Clark
Mrs Katherine Gyngell
Edward Harley
Michael and Morven Heller
Richard Lambert
Annick Lapôtre
Virginia Morck
Philip Mould Ltd
Martin Randall
The Lady Ridley of Liddesdale
Anna Somers Cocks
Rex De Lisle Stanbridge
Mr Robert Stoppenbach
Peter Stormonth Darling
Professor Deborah Swallow
Dr John Sweetman
Yvonne Tan Bunzl
Diana and John Uff
The Ulrich Family
The Weiss Gallery

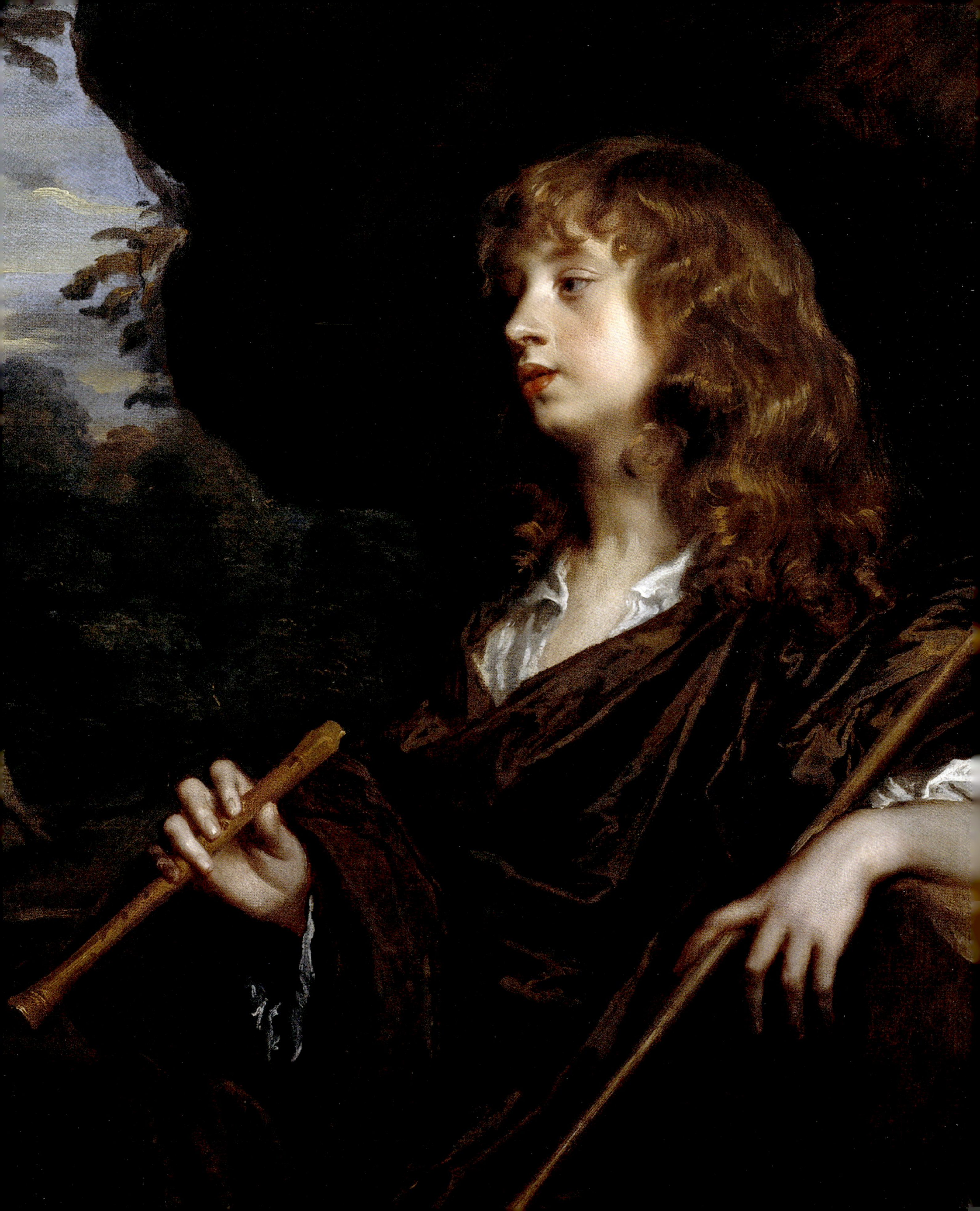

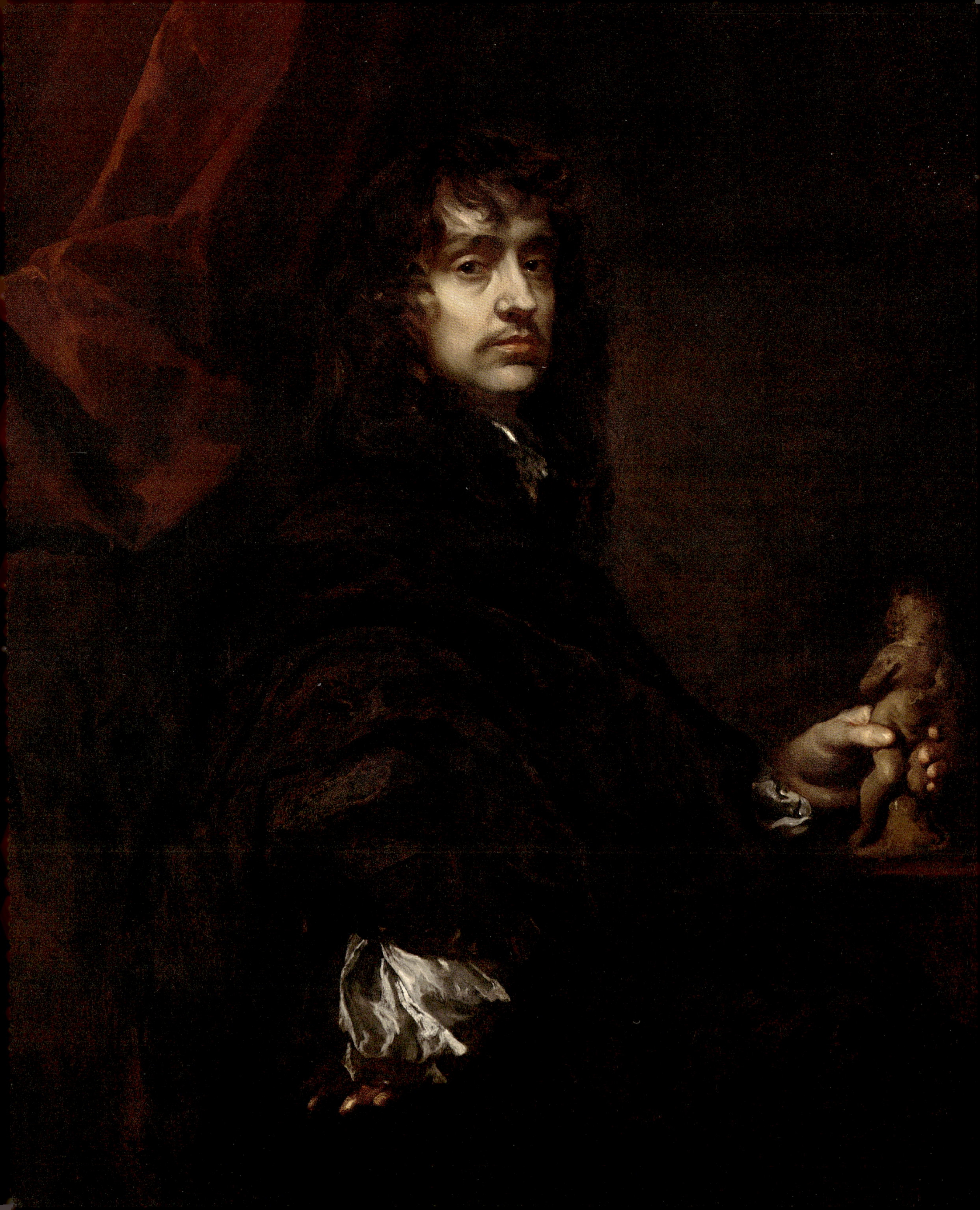

Becoming Peter Lely

CAROLINE CAMPBELL

THE PAINTER NOW FAMILIAR as Sir Peter Lely (fig. 9) is one of the outstanding artists to have worked in seventeenth-century England. In a popular sense Lely's modern reputation is dependent on his portraits of the Restoration court with its cast of beauties, mistresses and aristocratic rakes. This exhibition aims to look beyond these familiar and often formulaic images at the inventive and brilliant paintings that first captivated his London patrons. Lely was born Pieter van der Faes to Dutch parents in the German province of Westphalia in 1618. His father Johan, a captain of an infantry company in the service of the Elector of Brandenburg, was then stationed in the garrison town of Soest. Lely's mother was from Utrecht; his father's family was from The Hague. He gained his name from the fact that a lily was carved into the gable of the house where his father had been born.[1]

Lely's upbringing was cosmopolitan; his training with Frans Pietersz. de Grebber in 1630s Haarlem was both thorough and in tune with the latest pictorial fashions in the Netherlands.[2] As a result, Lely learnt to paint narrative and religious pictures as well as portraits in de Grebber's workshop. But Lely's reputation has primarily been formed by the hundreds of portraits which he – with the ever-increasing involvement of his studio – produced in London over a period of more than thirty years. Lely was indisputably the outstanding artistic personality of Restoration England. Following the Restoration of Charles II he became Principal Painter to the King, and it is therefore through Lely's eyes that we see the glittering, sometimes corrupt but always lively world of the court of Charles II (see fig. 14). His subjects included the king's "idol'd mistresses", such as Nell Gwyn (fig. 1) and Barbara Villiers, Lady Castlemaine, perhaps represented in fig. 6, who was one of his most important patrons, besides the king's brother, the future James II, and his first wife Anne Hyde, Duchess of York (who commissioned the celebrated series of 'Windsor Beauties' now in the Royal Collection at Hampton Court).

Detail of fig. 9

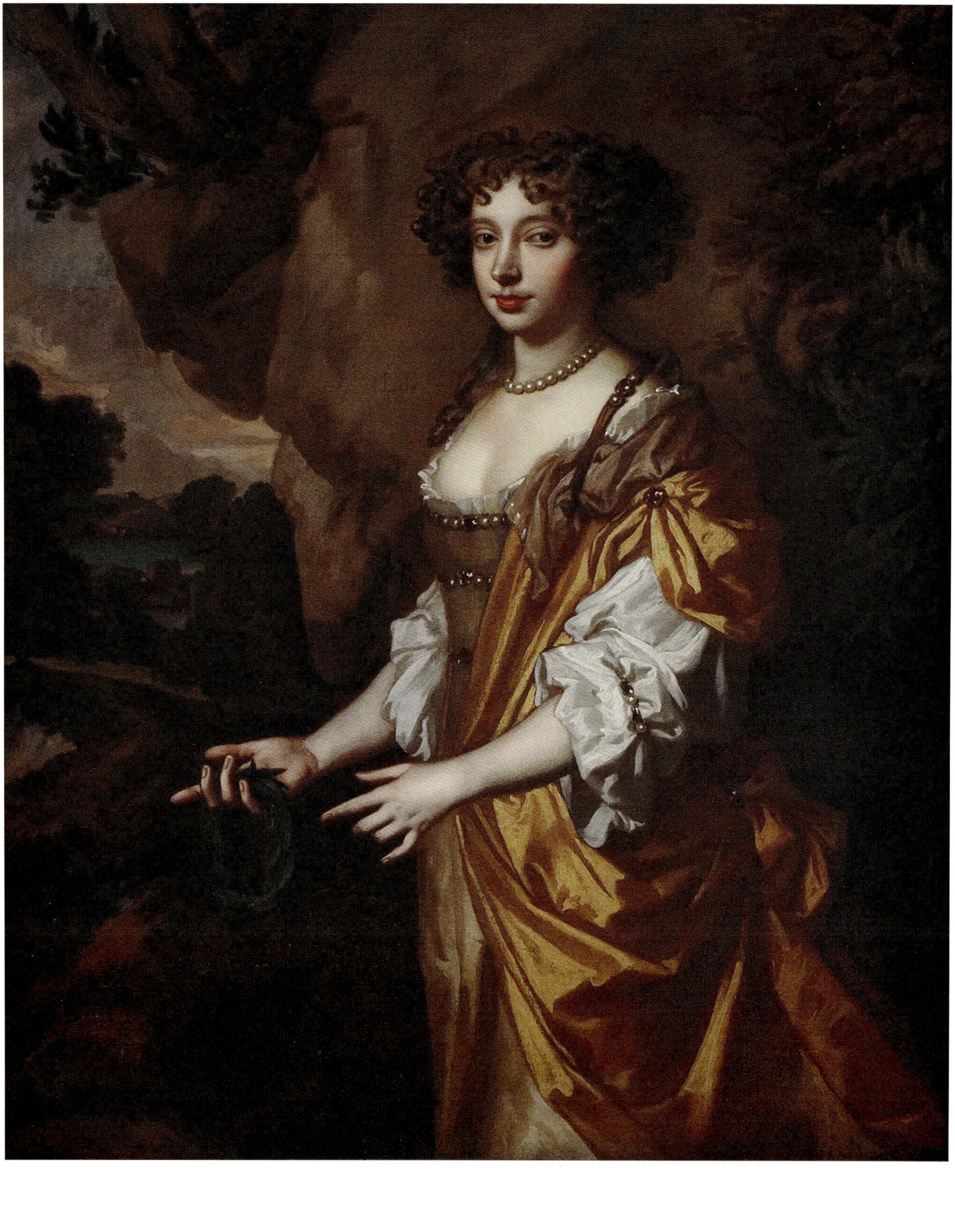

FIG. 1
Peter Lely (1618–1680)
Nell Gwyn, *c.* 1668–80
Oil on canvas, 126.4 × 102.9 cm
Collection of James Stunt

FIG. 2
Peter Lely (1618–1680)
Lady Mary Fane (1639–1681), *c.* 1662
Oil on canvas, 137 × 103 cm
Collection of James Stunt

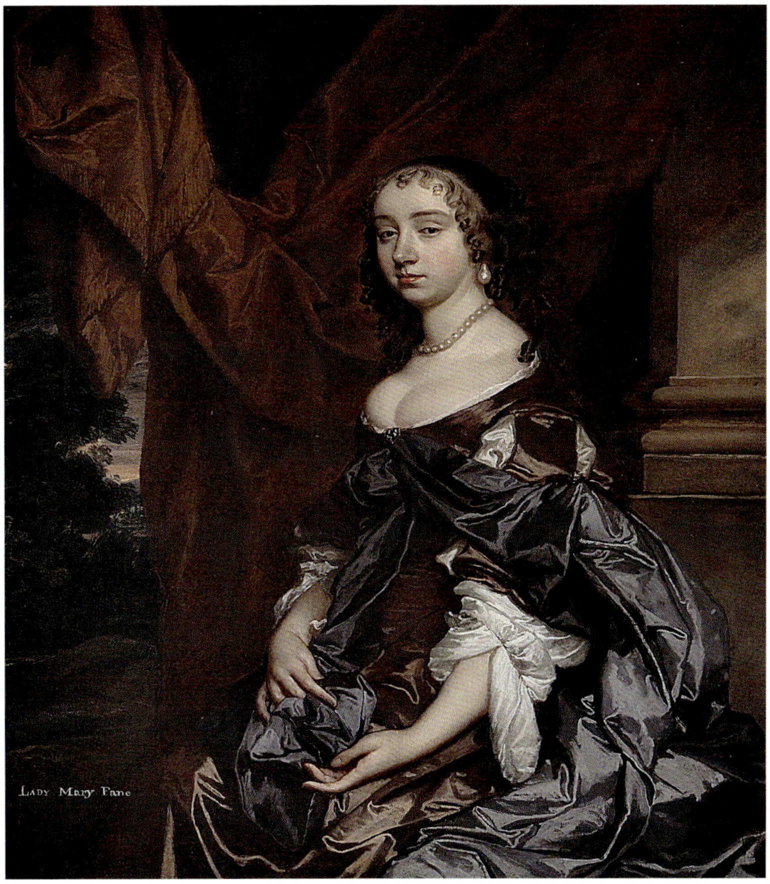

Country houses and museums alike are full of paintings by Lely or which can be associated with his manner. Lely's talent – and perhaps later his undoing – was the ability to convey what appeared to be a convincing and lively likeness of his sitter, but using pictorial stocks-in-trade which were obvious and could seem hackneyed. Lely sought to refashion his sitters according to a pictorial ideal, which for women (see fig. 2) was apparently based on the features of Barbara Villiers. A number of contemporary writers asserted that it could be difficult to recognise someone from Lely's portrait of them. As the poet John Dryden commented, Lely "drew many graceful pictures, but few of them were like".[3] Others criticised their similarities: "… Mr Walker the Painter swore Lilly's pictures was all Brothers & Sisters".[4] Lely worked hard (reportedly from 9 am until 4 pm daily)[5] and ran a large and efficient studio, which trained a large number of imitators, some of whom painted in a bastardised and simplified fashion that might be termed the Lely manner. Their work is characterised by bold contrasts of light and shade on drapery, and an extraordinary homogeneity of their sitters' features. It was easy to buy studio copies of Lely's work: seventeen of Charles II alone were found in the artist's studio at his death.[6]

Lely made an immense impact on English portraiture – perhaps more than his celebrated contemporary Van Dyck. Indeed, it is not until the career of Gainsborough that he finds a serious rival in terms of influence. Like both these painters, he did not wish to be viewed by posterity merely as the recorder of the great and the good of his age. It is of course the great irony that this is exactly what happened to all three of them, at least in England. Lely was neither the first nor the last Dutch artist to live and work in England, but he was perhaps the one whose reputation in his adopted country was most enduring, although he maintained close contacts with the Netherlands (including with his family) and the Dutch art world throughout his life, as Karen Hearn demonstrates elsewhere in this volume. Lely became a naturalised Englishman in 1662, and long before that date had embedded himself fully into the local artistic scene, joining the Painter-Stainers' Company in 1647, within four years of his probable arrival in London. This implies his early intention to remain in England: the life of the superstar international court artist was not one for him, as it had been for both Rubens and Van Dyck. At any rate, it would not have been possible in view of the changed relations between England and her Continental neighbours in the 1640s and 1650s, occasioned by the Civil Wars which convulsed the British Isles and by the establishment of the Commonwealth.

Lely's career could, however, have been very different. It was by no means inevitable when he came to England either that he should spend the rest of his life in Britain or that he should become a portraitist. His early ambition was to be a painter of narrative subjects, by far the most prestigious career for an artist trained in Holland, and particularly in Haarlem. He devoted himself to the production of what were called 'subject pictures', inspired by classical mythology, the Bible or contemporary literature. It is this genre of work that the present exhibition aims to explore.

It is not clear exactly when Lely came to London, although it is thought to be some time in the first half of the 1640s. His Dutch biographer, Arnold Houbraken, writing between 1717 and 1719, thought that he had left Holland in the train of Prince William of Orange, who married Princess Mary in London in 1643.[7] Houbraken got the year wrong (Mary and William were wed in May 1641), but the date he assigned to Lely's arrival is that inscribed on one of his rare landscape drawings, now in the British Museum (fig. 13). Two of Lely's earliest English portraits, which are probably of Sir George Booth, later Lord Delamere (fig. 3) and his second wife Anne (fig. 50), were probably painted in 1644, when

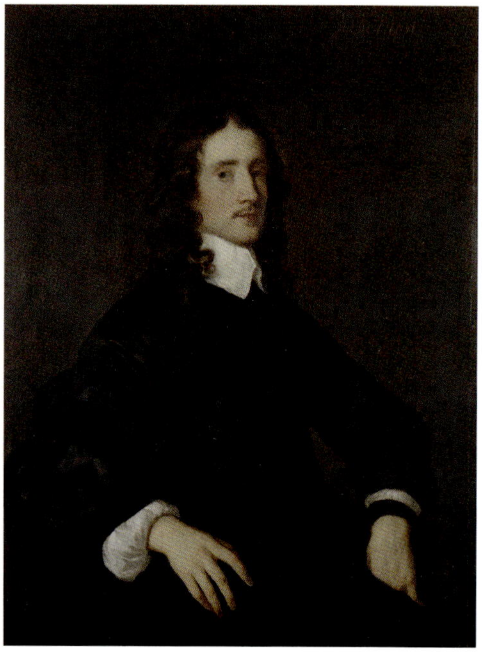

FIG. 3
Peter Lely (1618–1680)
Portrait of a Man
(probably Sir George Booth, later Lord Delamare),
c. 1644–45
Oil on canvas, 102.9 × 77.5 cm
The Bodleian Library, University of Oxford

FIG. 4
Titian (Tiziano Vecellio; active *c.* 1506–76) and workshop
The Vendramin Family, venerating a Relic of the True Cross, begun *c.* 1540–43, completed *c.* 1550–60
Oil on canvas, 206.1 × 288.5 cm
The National Gallery, London

the couple were married.[8] Lely was certainly well established in the city by 1647, when he was commissioned by the Earl of Northumberland to paint Charles I (Syon House, Northumberland collection) and three of his children (fig. 52).

It seems that Lely planned to deal in pictures as well as paint them when he first arrived in London. Lely lodged in the house of George Geldorp, a fellow Dutchman (fig. 20), and like Geldorp he appears to have been active as a dealer (see further Diana Dethloff's essay in this volume). The 1640s were certainly interesting times to be involved with the sale and acquisition of Old Master pictures. There was an established market for Dutch small landscapes with figures, and it was this sort of picture that Lely intended to make himself. Lely probably knew some Italian Renaissance art in the Netherlands, but it was in London that he became exposed to it, and to the work of Van Dyck. Both made a lasting impression on him and his art.

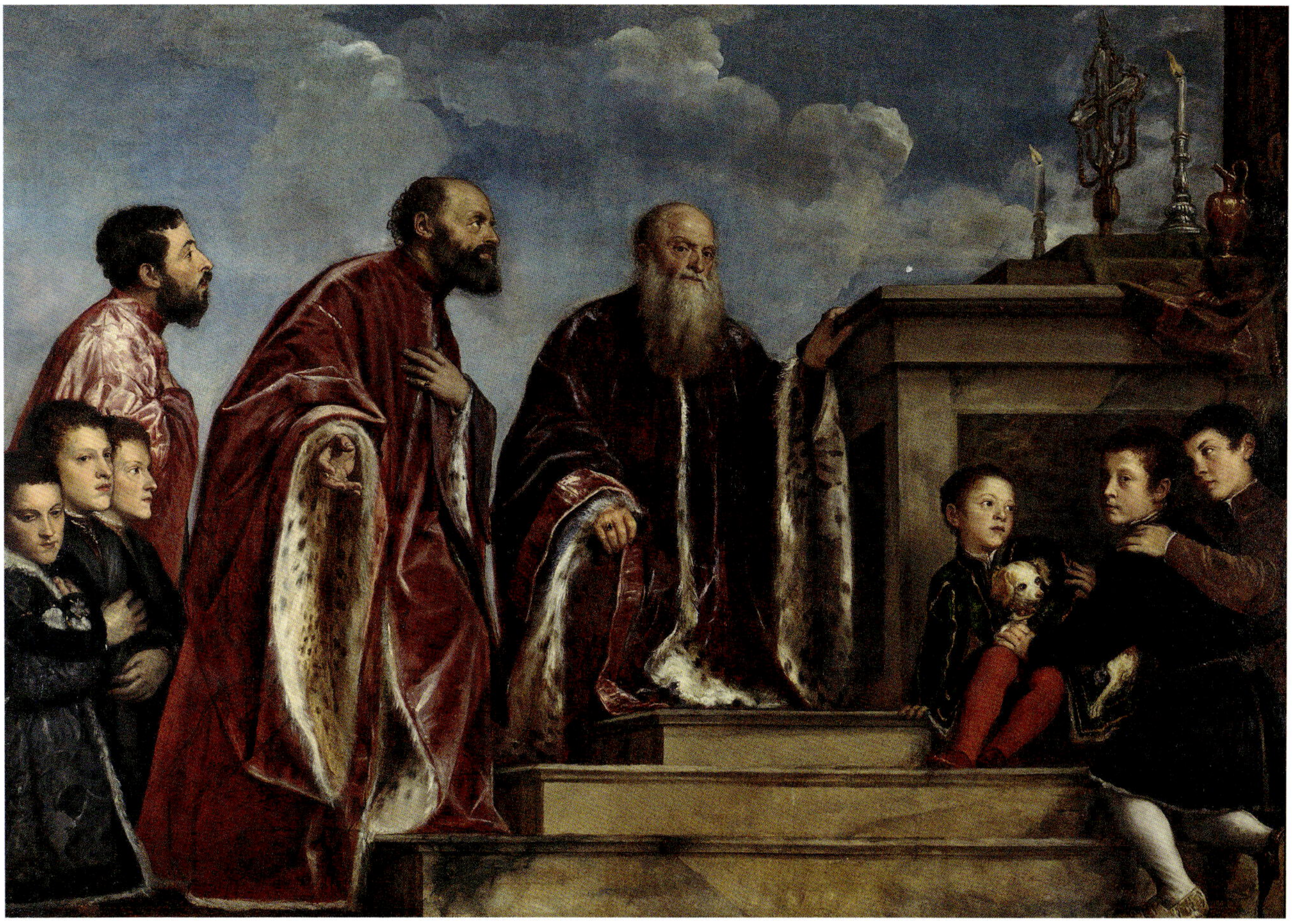

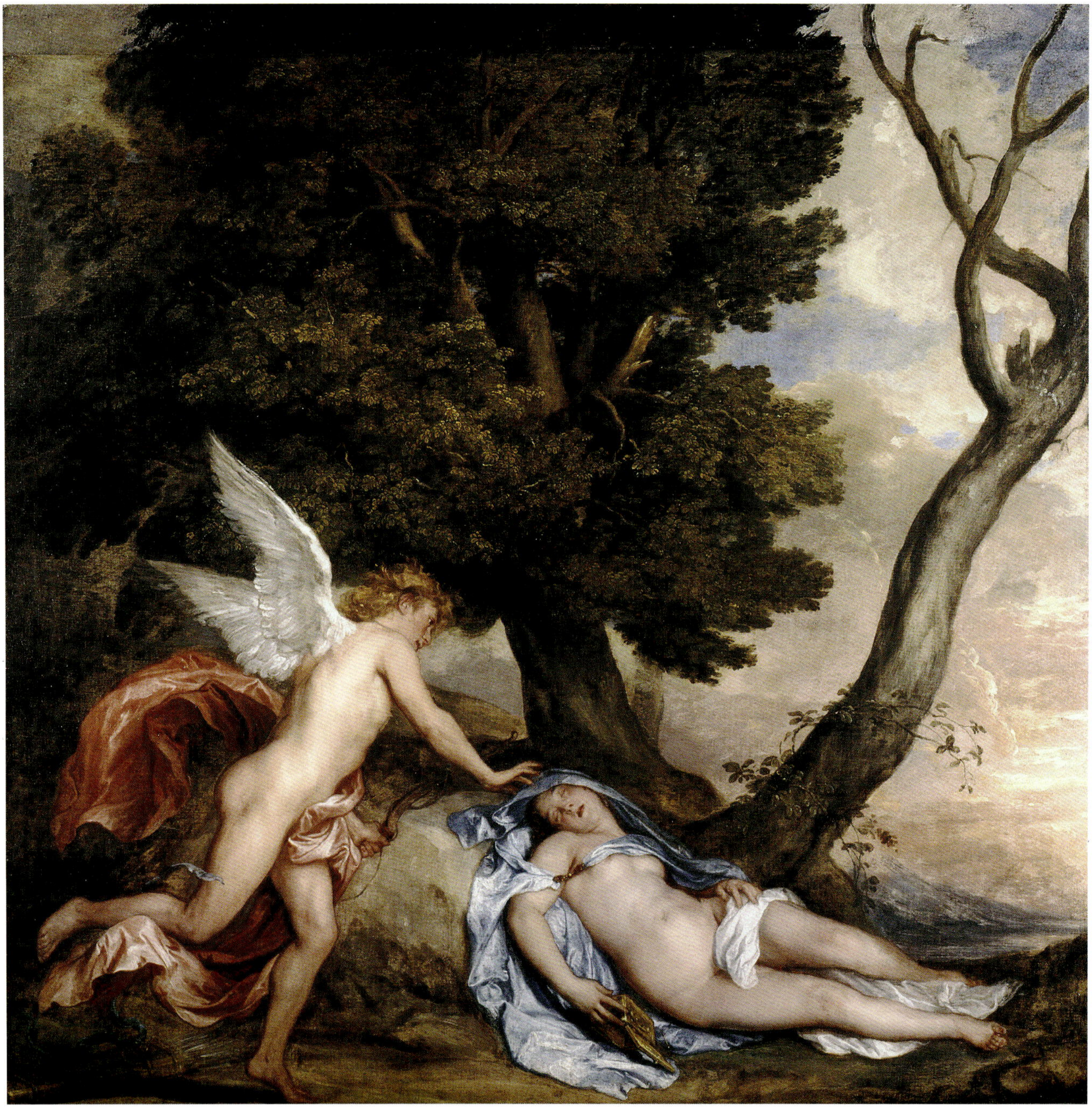

FIG. 5
Anthony van Dyck (1599–1641)
Cupid and Psyche, 1639–40
Oil on canvas, 200.2 × 192.6 cm
The Royal Collection

London in the middle of the seventeenth century was one of the best places in Europe to see Italian Renaissance painting, and particularly that made in Venice in the decades after 1500. This was largely the result of the extraordinary collections formed by the Stuart dynasty and leading members of their courts. Henry, Prince of Wales, bought the earliest group of Venetian paintings in England; this taste was shared by his younger brother, the future Charles I. Many of the most important English peers, both Laudians and Puritans, Royalists and Parliamentarians, were active purchasers in this field. British collectors including the Earl and Countess of Arundel, the 1st Duke of Buckingham, the Marquess (later Duke) of Hamilton and the 10th Earl of Northumberland amassed extensive holdings of the works of Titian, Giorgione and their contemporaries. Among these paintings was an astonishing group of Titians, including the *Venus del Pardo* (Paris, Musée du Louvre) and *Jacopo Pesaro presented to Saint Peter* (Antwerp, Koninklijk Museum voor Schone Kunsten), both owned by Charles I; *The Flaying of Marsyas* (Kroměříž, Archbishop's Palace), *The Bravo* (Vienna, Kunsthistorisches Museum), *The Death of Actaeon* and *The Vendramin Family, venerating a Relic of the True Cross* (fig. 4; both London, The National Gallery). Northumberland's collection, which included this last painting (formerly owned

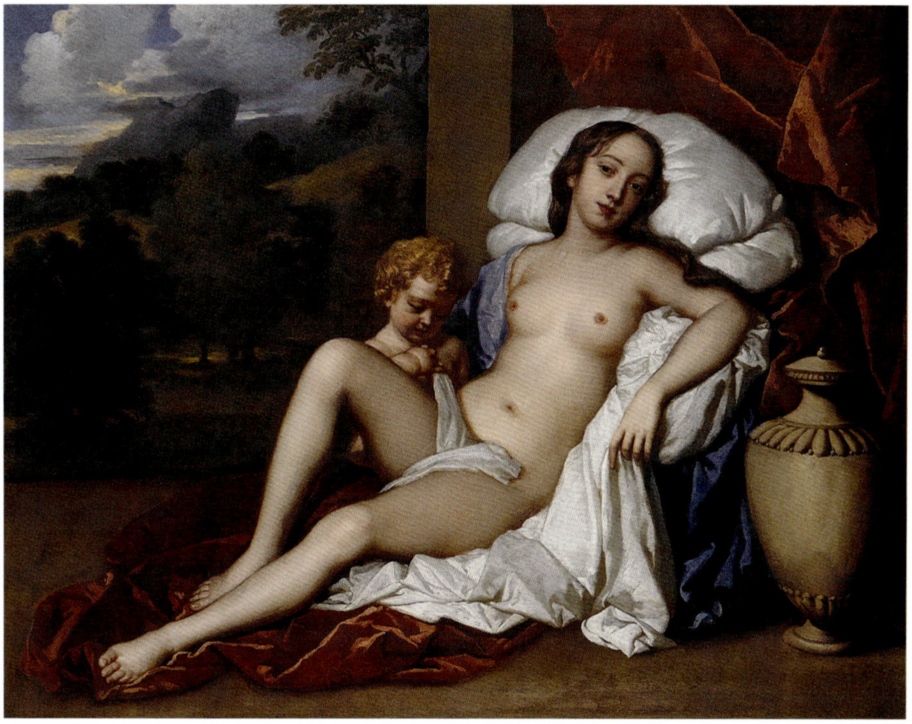

FIG. 6
Peter Lely (1618–1680)
Portrait of a Lady and Child as Venus and Cupid, c. 1665
Oil on canvas, 123.2 × 157.5 cm
Private collection

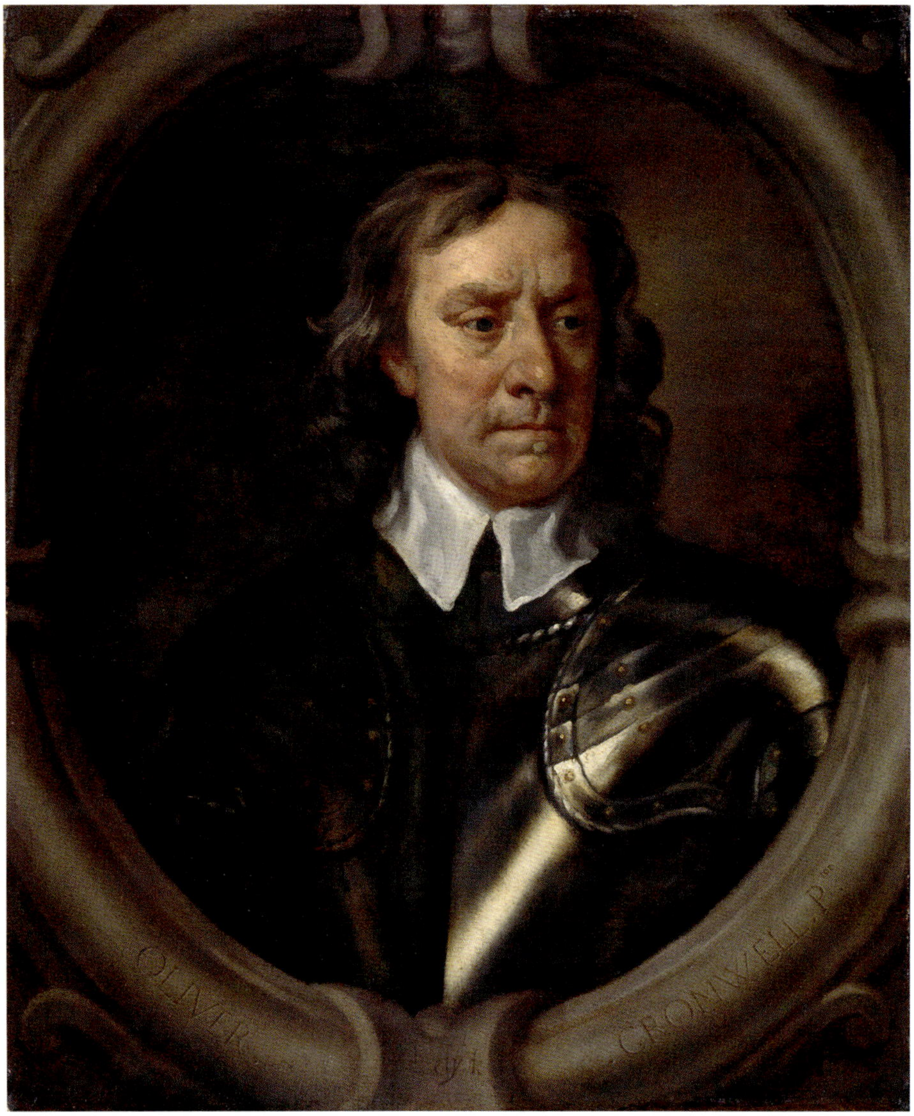

FIG. 7
Peter Lely (1618–1680)
Oliver Cromwell, 1653–54
Oil on canvas, 77.5 × 62.9 cm
Birmingham Museums and
Art Gallery, Birmingham

by Van Dyck) and other Titians, as well as works by Mantegna, Correggio, Rubens and Van Dyck, must have been particularly open to Lely, as the earl was one of the young artist's most significant patrons and advocates. But during the 1640s all these paintings were, at certain points, accessible to artists as a result of the forced sales and sequestrations of the Civil War. These swept an unbelievable quantity and quality of artworks on to the open market, including all of Charles I's celebrated collection, which was sold in Old Somerset House on the site of this exhibition. Following the Somerset House sales Lely was to buy Van Dyck's most Titianesque painting, the extraordinarily beautiful *Cupid and Psyche* (fig. 5), which places the god and his lover in an idealised landscape setting.

Lely, like Van Dyck before him and Manet after him, found deep inspiration in these Venetian Arcadian visions of contemporary musicians, scarcely clothed women (or nymphs), gods and demi-gods among shaded woody groves. Lely owned several pictures in this vein, including possibly the *Lovers in a Landscape* now in the National Gallery (fig. 41), which he and his contemporaries believed was by Giorgione. His most ambitious subject pictures of the late 1640s and early 1650s, such as *The Concert* and *Nymphs by a Fountain* (cat. 7 and 9), show the impact which they and other Venetian pictures made upon him. Even the long rectangular format of *The Concert* (cat. 7) and *Reuben presenting Mandrakes to Leah* (cat. 4) can be explained by the similar dimensions of paintings such as Titian's *The Vendramin Family, venerating a Relic of the True Cross* (fig. 4).

Like many successful painters and particularly those with an active portrait practice, Lely had the ability to charm if he wished. The diarist and Navy official Samuel Pepys, who was presumably not the object of such an offensive, considered him "a mighty proud man . . . and full of state",[9] and Houbraken records his jealousy of his younger rival Godfrey Kneller.[10] It is notable that he steered a very careful course through the turbulent waters of the English Civil Wars and their aftermath. In London in the late 1640s he was particularly associated with the 'Protestant Earls', members of the nobility who had objected to the high absolutism of Charles I. Lady Dysart (fig. 43), the other significant patron of Lely's in these years, was both a vocal Cromwellian and an alleged member of the Royalist organisation the 'Sealed Knot', dedicated to the Restoration of Charles II.

Lely himself appears to have had shared loyalties or at least to have shaped his loyalties according to circumstance. He had portrayed Charles I and several of his children for the Earl of Northumberland (including fig. 52), but as his friend the Royalist poet Richard Lovelace remarked, through Lely's portrait of Charles I and his second son (Syon House, Northumberland collection) one could see the King's "clouded majesty". Lely also notoriously painted Oliver Cromwell (fig. 7), who is reported to have asked Lely to portray him as he was – "pimples warts & every thing as you see me",[11] rather than as he would like to be. Cromwell's apocryphal comment should be viewed with some caution,[12] as he was just as conscious of image-making as any king. It should further be remembered that Lely, with his friend Geldorp and Sir Balthasar Gerbier, petitioned Parliament in 1653 to commission a series of paintings of its greatest achievements. These were to be placed in Whitehall Palace, a complex which included the Banqueting House with its ceiling by Rubens celebrating the achievements of the Stuart monarchy and the divine right of kings.[13]

Yet Lely was also careful to maintain connections with the young king, Charles II, during his exile, and those closely associated with him, such as Aubrey de Vere, Earl of Oxford (fig. 8), shown wearing a breastplate and with a sword, and to return those pictures he had acquired from Charles I's collection, including Ter Brugghen's *Laughing Musician with Bass Viol* (fig. 12) and Van Dyck's *Cupid and Psyche* (fig. 5), immediately after the restoration of the monarchy in 1660. His reward, although it was as much a recognition of his status as England's pre-eminent painter, was his appointment as Principal Painter to Charles II in October 1661. Lely was to hold this post until his death in 1680. It was perhaps in his official capacity that in the mid 1660s Lely produced a famous series of drawings of the annual Grand Procession of the Order of the Garter, the illustrious chivalric order fully restored by Charles II. Two of these drawings are in the Witt Collection at The Courtauld.[14] A Florentine visitor to London in 1667–68, Lorenzo Magalotti, also recorded that the king had commissioned from Lely a pastoral scene on a life-size scale, in which the beauties of the Court were to be depicted as nymphs.[15]

Lely never left England following his brief trip to Holland with his friend Hugh May in the mid 1650s. Much of his London life was spent in Covent Garden, close to the grand residence of his early patron, the Earl of Northumberland, and to Somerset House on the Strand. In 1650 he moved to a house in the north-east corner of the Piazza (near the modern rear entrance to the Royal Opera House), where he lived and worked until his sudden death in his studio on 30 November 1680. He was buried in the church of St Paul's, Covent Garden, where in 1674 Ursula, the mother of his three children and latterly his wife, had been laid to rest after her death in childbirth (baby Peter shortly followed his mother to the grave). Lely's house had a relatively small frontage for a building in this fashionable location,[16] but the studio was carefully designed, with light sources coming from a number of angles. He liked to work six feet from the window, with light from behind his left shoulder, and his subject placed an equal distance – also six feet – from both the painter and the light source.[17] The rest of the house was carefully appointed, perhaps echoing Lely's awareness of the lavish lodgings Van Dyck had maintained at Blackfriars, adorned with his marvellously rich collection of Old Master and contemporary paintings, drawings and prints (including figs. 10, 15 and 16). Three years before his death, Lely assessed his collection, and concluded "that at a very moderate rate sett upon them they

FIG. 8
Peter Lely (1618–1680)
Aubrey de Vere, Earl of Oxford, and his Countess (née Anne Bayning),
c. 1647–59, probably 1656–59
Oil on canvas, 131.4 × 155.6 cm
Collection of James Stunt

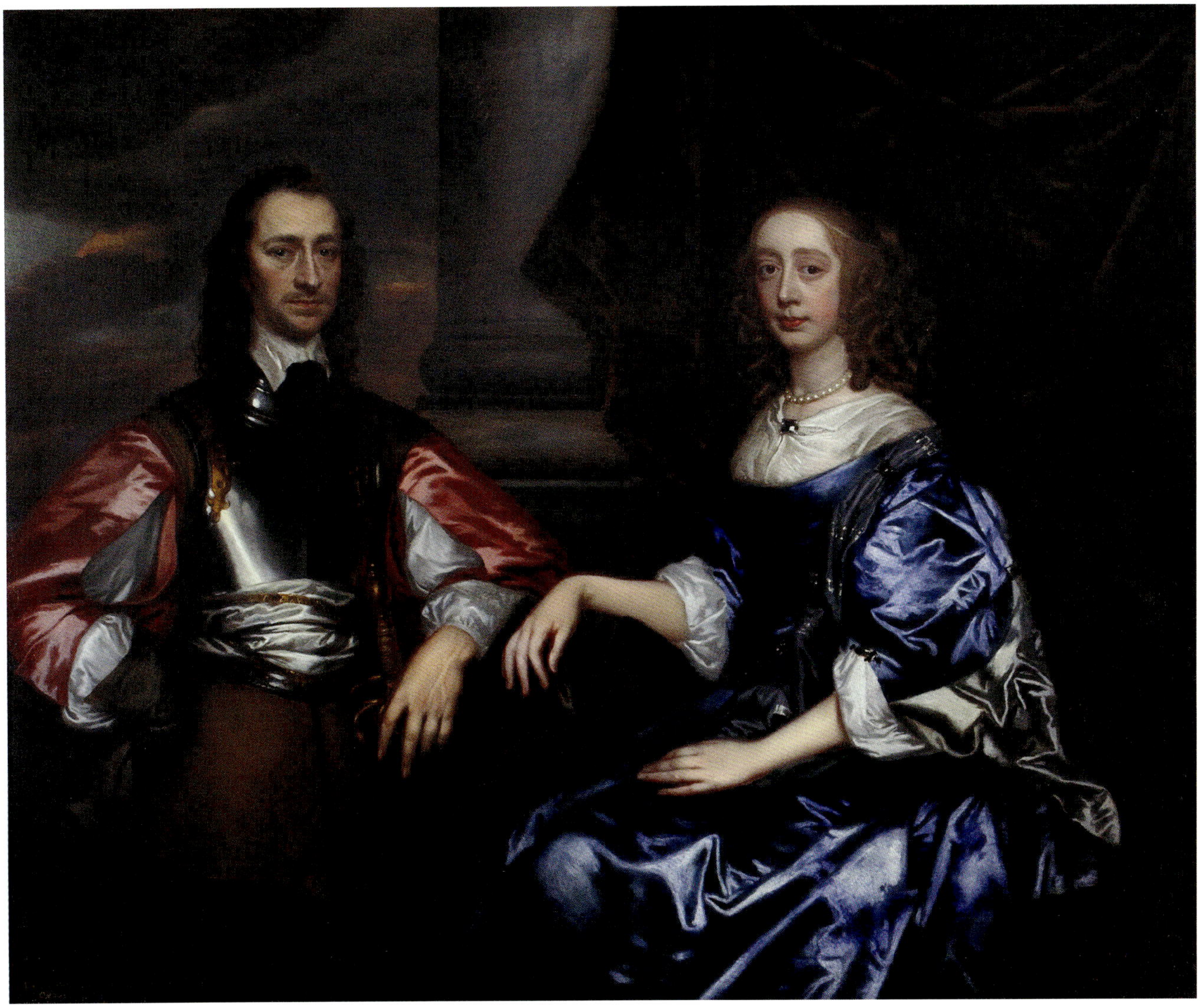

came to about £10,000".[18] The collection was sold following Lely's death to provide a living for his two surviving children, John and Anne. Despite his success, and material prosperity, including a house at Kew and land in Lincolnshire, Lely was not an astute businessman – as his friend Roger North confessed – and he left an estate encumbered by considerable debts and legacies. In the years following Lely's death, from 1681 to 1694, the painter's entire studio effects and the collections were sold off, raising nearly £9,000. Lely's "loving friend" and most active executor, Roger North, "stampt every individual paper"[19] (save those he believed to be by Lely himself) with the *PL* mark, which has itself become a mark of value. The extent and quality of the prints and drawings owned by Lely is extraordinary: according to North these totalled around ten thousand items. Lely was particularly assiduous in forming a collection of Italian sixteenth-century drawings and prints, and objects he owned today constitute a central part of the primary British collections of prints and drawings, including those of the British Museum, the Ashmolean and Fitzwilliam Museums, Chatsworth and The Courtauld (see figs. 15 and 16). Some of Lely's collection subsequently passed to the pre-eminent eighteenth-century English artist-collectors, Jonathan Richardson the Elder and Sir Joshua Reynolds.

The works of art which Lely collected were important for his own artistic production. Lely was a pictorial magpie, picking up ideas and motifs from any number of sources, but uniting them in a fashion which combined the Italian Renaissance and the Dutch Classicist movement of the seventeenth century but in a more Baroque and showy manner. Although Lely's style was indebted to Van Dyck, it was quite his own. In this exhibition and catalogue we are attempting to show the richness of Lely's subject pictures, and how they shaped his development as a portraitist. Lely's narrative pictures are his least known works, but also among the most ambitious, sensitive and beautiful pictures he ever produced. For far too long Lely has only been regarded as a portraitist. The time has come to redress the balance of his posthumous reputation. He emerges as an artist of outstanding invention and skill, both a chronicler of his age and a painter who could transport those who viewed his works to paradisical realms of dream and imagination.

NOTES

1 Oliver Millar, *Sir Peter Lely 1618–80*, exh. cat., National Portrait Gallery, London, 1978–79, p. 9.

2 Albert Blankert, Jeroen Giltaij and Friso Lammertse, eds., *Dutch Classicism in Seventeenth-Century Painting*, exh. cat., Boijmans Van Beuningen Museum, Rotterdam, and Städelsches Kunstinstitut, Frankfurt am Main, 1999–2000, pp. 116, 228.

3 Quoted by Oliver Millar in London 1978–79, p. 25. Dryden's comment is found in the 'Preface' to *Sylvae* (1685).

4 British Museum, Add. MS 22950, f. 41.

5 Arnold Houbraken, *De groote schouburgh der Nederlantsche konstschilders en schilderessen,* 's Gravenhage (1718–21), ed. J. Swart, C. Boucquet and M. Gaillard, 3 vols., 1753, II, p. 43.

6 'Editorial: Sir Peter Lely's Collection', *Burlington Magazine*, LXXXIII, no. 485, August 1943, pp. 185–91, at p. 188.

7 Houbraken 1718–21 (1753), II, p. 43.

8 Millar in London 1978–79, pp. 34–35, nos. 2 and 3.

9 *The Diary of Samuel Pepys*, entry for 25 March 1667 (new style), http://www.pepysdiary.com/archive/1667/03/25/index.php (accessed 29 June 2012).

10 Houbraken 1718–21 (1753), II, pp. 47–48.

11 George Vertue 'Notebooks: I', *The Walpole Society*, XVIII, 1929–30, p. 91.

12 See Millar in London 1978–79, p. 47.

13 Diana Dethloff, 'Lely, Sir Peter (1618–1680)', *Oxford Dictionary of National Biography*, Oxford, 2004; online edn, May 2009, http://www.oxforddnb.com/view/article/16419 (accessed 14 May 2012).

14 For this series, see Millar in London 1978–79, pp. 80–87, nos. 86–116. The Courtauld drawings are nos. 102 and 113.

15 Millar in London 1978–79, p. 15.

16 Dethloff 2004.

17 BM, Add. MS. 22950, f. 15.

18 Diana Dethloff, 'The Executors' Account Book and the Dispersal of Sir Peter Lely's Collection', *Journal of the History of Collections*, VIII, 1996, pp. 15–51, at p. 15.

19 Dethloff 1996, p. 20.

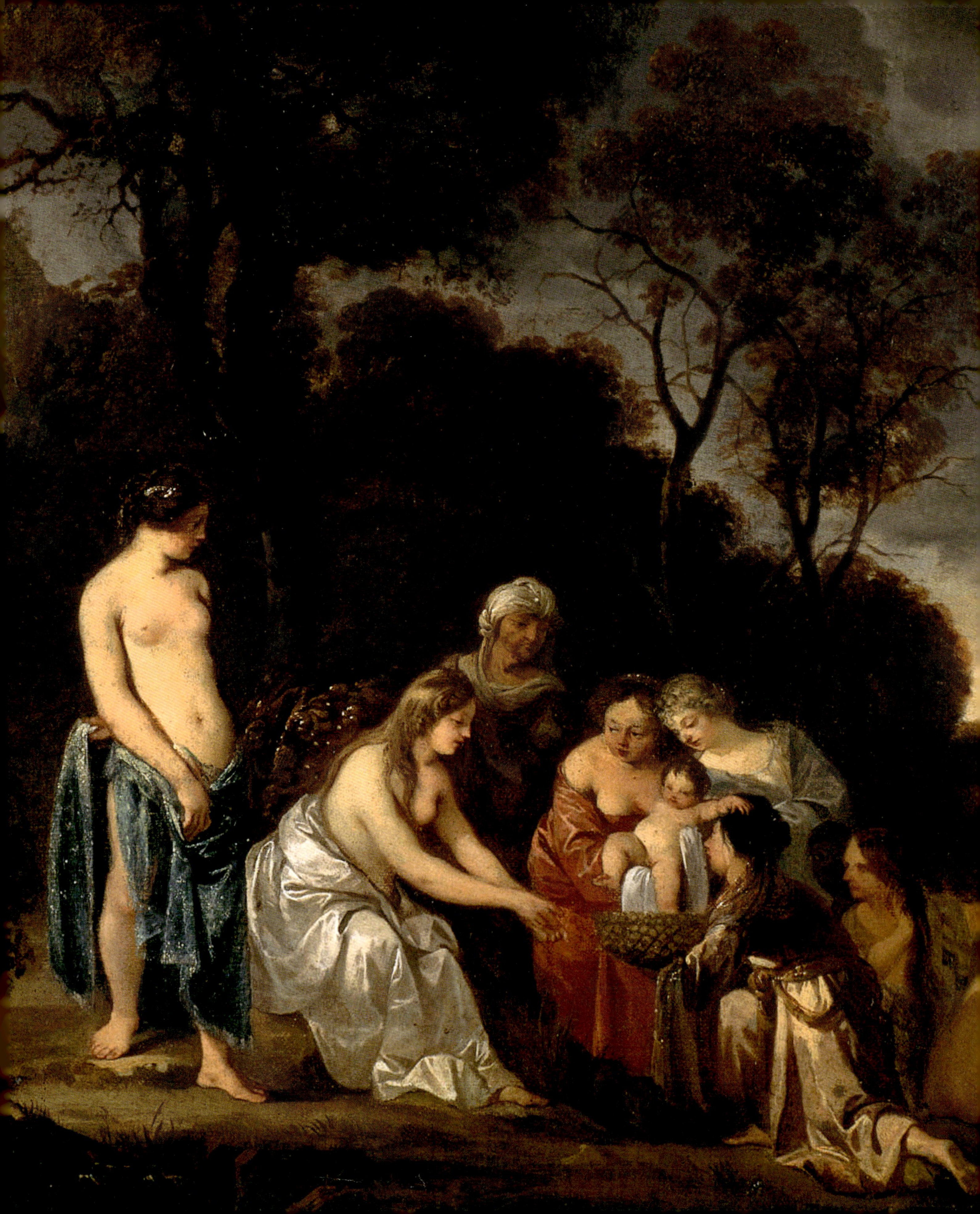

Lely and Holland

KAREN HEARN

Cat. 1 (detail)

WHEN PIETER VAN DER FAES, whom we know today as 'Peter Lely' (fig. 9), arrived in London near the start of the 1640s, he was in his early twenties. He had been trained as a painter in the Dutch city of Haarlem, which was a significant commercial and artistic centre, and had now crossed the sea to a new country and an unfamiliar society – one that was, moreover, in the first stages of the political, social and financial turmoil that became the English Civil War(s).

However, in spite of its timing, the brave step that he was taking was perhaps not such a surprising one. Throughout the sixteenth and seventeenth centuries, royal, aristocratic and even gentry clients in Britain had become accustomed to employing overseas-born and -trained artists, particularly to produce portraits, which was the main form of painting that they required. The German Hans Holbein II (1497/98–1543), principal painter to King Henry VIII, was perhaps the most celebrated of these early incomers. In that officially Protestant country – which adhered to the Second Commandment's prohibition of bowing down before images – religious imagery (and indeed, until well into the seventeenth century, almost any narrative picture) was highly problematic. The training system for English artists does not seem to have resulted in work that satisfied elite patrons there. At the same time, well-trained painters, who were capable of making far more sophisticated products than the local practitioners, were turning up there, particularly from the Northern and Southern Netherlands (the present-day Netherlands and Belgium, respectively). They came either as religious refugees, to escape persecution in continental Europe, or as economic migrants, seeking opportunities in a fresh and comparatively welcoming market across the North Sea.

A number of artists from the Northern Netherlands had travelled to England (which, after the accession of James VI of Scotland to the English throne in 1603 as James I, was to become the united kingdom of Britain). These included Cornelis Ketel (1548–1616), trained in Gouda and Delft, who had lived and worked in England between 1573 and 1581; Gerrit van Honthorst, (1592–1656) from Utrecht, who visited England briefly in 1628 and while he was there portrayed Charles I; Adriaen Hanneman (*c.* 1601–1671) active there between 1626 and about 1637; Jan Lievens (1607–1674) from Leiden, who resided in London 1632–35; Cornelis van Poelenburgh (*c.* 1586–1667), from Utrecht, who had worked in Italy and who painted small Italianate landscape scenes with classical figures for Charles I (similar to those later produced by Lely) and who was in London from 1637 to 1641; and, from the city of Haarlem itself, Hendrick Gerritsz. Pot (*c.* 1580–1657), who worked briefly in London in 1632, again for Charles I.

Many more artists travelled to England from the Southern (predominantly Catholic) Netherlands, especially from the great trading port and artistic centre of Antwerp. The most significant of these would be Anthony van Dyck (1599–1641), who spent most of the final nine years of his short life in England, working for Charles I and for the leading nobility (see fig. 10) until his death in London in December 1641. Indeed, it may have been Van Dyck's death – and the ensuing vacancy for a royal painter – that encouraged Lely to look towards England.

When Pieter van der Faes was born, on 14 September 1618, western Europe was riven by political tensions, and was about to suffer even greater upheaval, with the imminent outbreak of the Thirty Years' War.[1] Pieter's parents both came from the Northern Netherlands (which by then were predominantly Protestant). His mother, Abigael van der Vliet (died 1661) was from Utrecht, while the affluent family from which his father Johan van der Faes (1592–*c.* 1643) sprang had become well established at The Hague during the later sixteenth century.[2] Johan had been born in The Hague in a house described as 'In de Lelye' on the western side of the Noorteynde (Noordeinde) – a house that had a lily carved on its gable – and himself became known by the name 'Lely'.[3] At some early stage his son Pieter seems also to have adopted this motif as his name – 'Pieter Lely'.

The early eighteenth-century artist and writer Arnold Houbraken stated that Pieter was born in Soest, which is presumed to be Soest in Westphalia rather than Soest near Utrecht in the Northern Netherlands.[4] Pieter's father was captain of a unit of infantrymen in a Dutch regiment in the service of the German Elector of Brandenburg and, during the first decades of the seventeenth century, as records show, the regiment was stationed in various locations in Westphalia, including Soest.

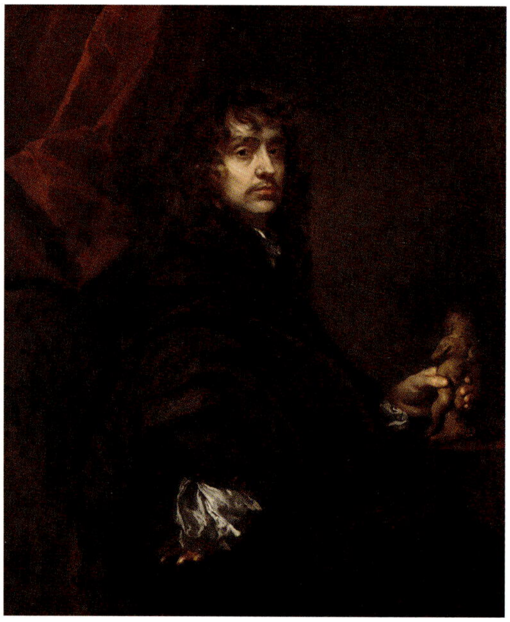

FIG. 9
Peter Lely (1618–1680)
Self-portrait, *c.* 1660
Oil on canvas, 108 × 87.6 cm
National Portrait Gallery, London

Little is known of Pieter's early years, but in the 'finders' book' of the Haarlem Guild of Saint Luke – the guild of painters – it was noted on 6 October 1637 that the artist Frans Pietersz. de Grebber was to be asked to enrol all the pupils whom he had not yet registered, or for whom he had not yet paid the relevant dues. These included "Pieter lelij".[5] Of this entry, Friso Lammertse and Jaap van de Veen have observed, "It seems probable that Lely was studying with de Grebber at the time, but this is not necessarily the case. De Grebber still had to pay fees for no fewer than sixteen apprentices. In view of the number, there must have been pupils among them who had already left the studio."[6]

Frans Pietersz. de Grebber (1573–1649) was a member of the extensive Catholic De Grebber dynasty of Haarlem artists, although few works by him survive today. In 1616 he visited Rubens in Antwerp while acting as an intermediary in the exchange of works of art between Rubens and the English ambassador to The Hague, Sir Dudley Carleton. De Grebber was much in demand as a teacher, and surviving records indicate that he had many pupils.[7] According to Houbraken, Lely trained with Frans Pietersz. for only two years.[8] A full apprenticeship could, however, last as long as

FIG. 10
Anthony van Dyck (1599–1641)
Lady Elizabeth Thimbleby and her sister, Dorothy, Viscountess Andover, 1637
Oil on canvas, 131.1 × 149 cm
The National Gallery, London.
Bought, 1977

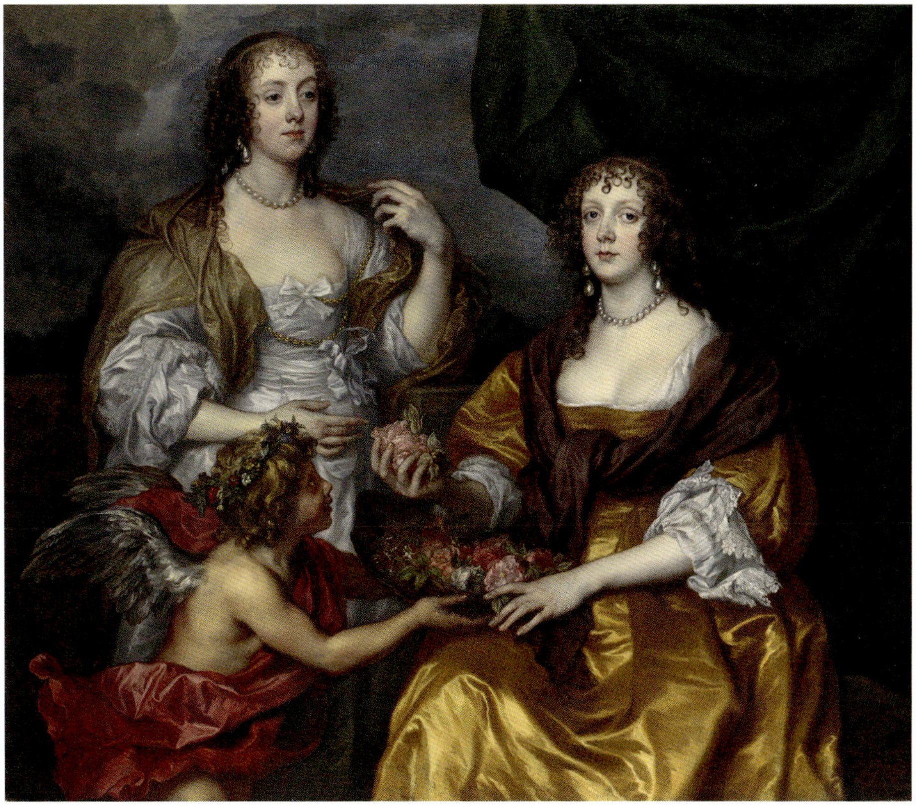

seven years. Frans's 1611 portrait of Job Claesz. Gijblant – who was the uncle and guardian of the woman the painter Frans Hals had recently married – is traditional in style and handling (Haarlem, Frans Hals Museum, inv. no. 65–95). De Grebber is now particularly known for two large portraits of Haarlem civic militia groups, *The Banquet of the Saint Hadrian Civic Guard*, 1600 (Haarlem Town Hall), which comprises 29 male figures, and *The Officers and Men of the Saint George Civic Guard*, 1619 (Haarlem, Frans Hals Museum) depicting 46 gentlemen.[9]

Many more works survive from the hand of De Grebber's son, Pieter (*c.* 1600–1652/54), who is categorised as a 'Haarlem classicist', and there are interesting parallels between some of his paintings and those of Peter Lely. He too studied in Haarlem under his father Frans, and then with the celebrated painter and printmaker Hendrick Goltzius. Around seventy works by Pieter de Grebber survive: some are portraits but most are narrative images of religious subjects (fig. 11) and often involve a number of small full-length figures; there are also more than twenty drawings.[10] Pieter de Grebber's earliest dated works are a *Mother with Three Children* (Houston, Museum of Fine Arts) and a *Charity* (Haarlem, Frans Hals Museum), both of 1622.[11] In 1638 he was commissioned to produce a number of large paintings for the palace of the Stadholder Frederick Hendrik at Honselaersdijk (many of which are now lost), and again, in 1647, paintings for the Oranjezaal in the new palace Huis ten Bosch, by Frederick's widow Amalia van Solms.[12] In 1632 De Grebber had become a member of the Guild of Saint Luke in Haarlem, and in 1642 he was elected its Dean. Like the painter Salomon de Bray, Pieter is said to have played a prominent part in Haarlem musical life, translating Latin poetry and setting the results to music. In Dutch homes and communities, music played a significant part in social interaction, and this is reflected in seventeenth-century Dutch images – indeed it appears that more than ten per cent of the Dutch paintings of this period have a musical theme.[13] Contemporary theory saw a congruence between the 'sister arts' of painting and music. Surviving early works by Lely (see cat. 5, 6, 7, 8 and figs. 45, 47, 48, 49) indicate that in London he, too, would depict a number of these musical subjects.

Haarlem was proud of being one of the very oldest cities in the Netherlands. Its recent history had been dramatic. Besieged by Spanish forces in 1572–73 and then occupied by them, and partly torched in 1576, it had been liberated only in 1577. In April 1581 the Catholics were prohibited from celebrating Mass, and, although clandestine churches soon sprang up, the Church as a major source of artistic patronage largely disappeared. Haarlem developed a distinctive artistic tradition which arose partly through the migration of Flemish (Southern Netherlandish) artists, with many other refugees, to the Northern Netherlands. They emigrated because of the harsh control of the ruling Spanish authorities in the south, and because the blockade of Antwerp there had greatly damaged the region's maritime trade.[14] The arrival in Haarlem of these wealthy and entrepreneurial craftsmen and merchants resulted in a period of immense material growth, and by 1600 many new buildings were being commissioned. In 1618 there was an almost wholesale change in the city's government – a 'political upheaval'; it was taken over by wealthy traders, particularly brewers. Like their predecessors, the new post-1618 elite commissioned individual and group portraits. The years between 1620 and 1645 are generally considered to have seen the peak of Haarlem's prosperity,[15] although during this period a number of key merchants left the city for nearby Amsterdam, and in 1635–36 a severe outbreak of plague killed more than 7,000 Haarlem inhabitants – almost one fifth of its population.[16]

The refugees from Flanders included the artist and writer Karel van Mander (1584–1606), the oldest member of the group known as

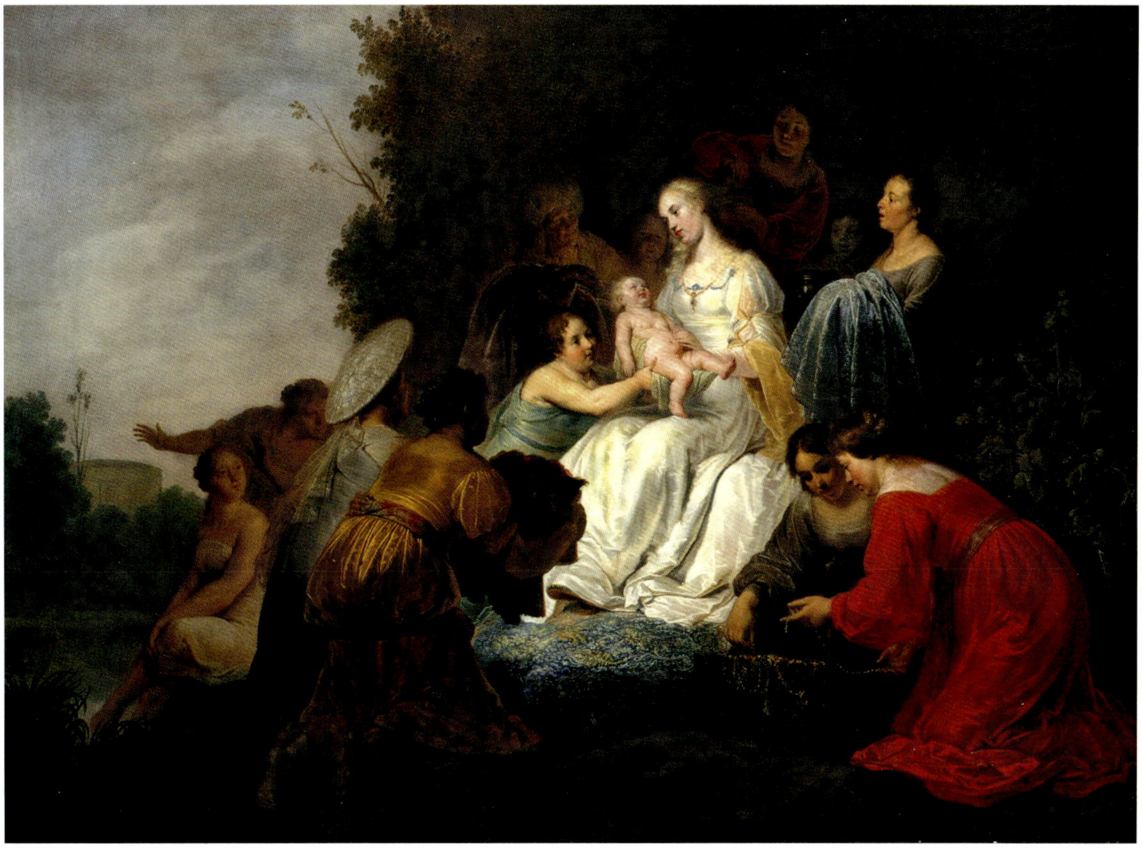

FIG. 11
Pieter de Grebber (*c.* 1600–1652/54)
The Finding of Moses, 1634
Oil on canvas, 169.5 × 228.5 cm
Gemäldegalerie Alte Meister, Dresden

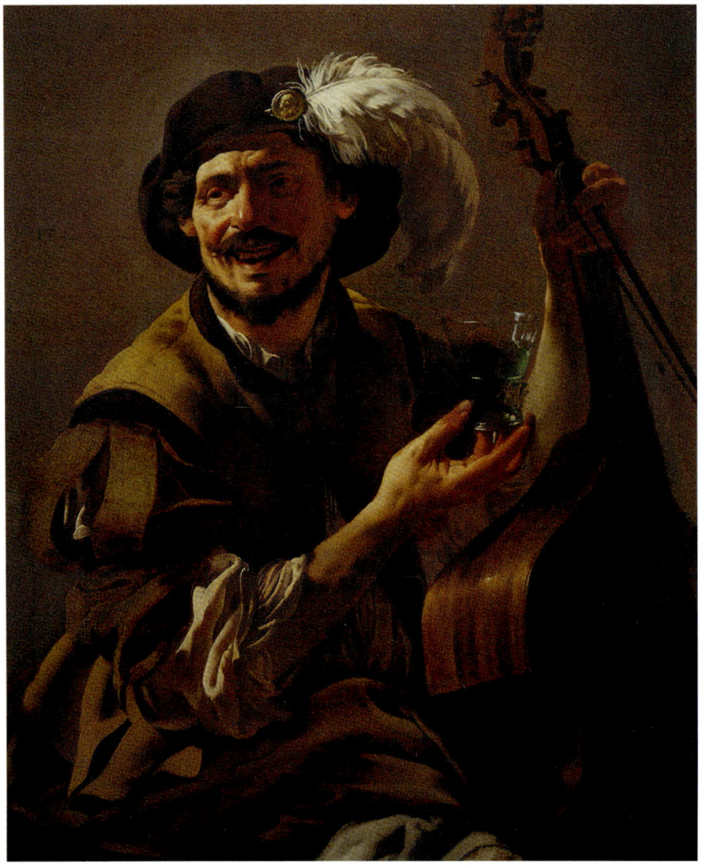

FIG. 12
Hendrick ter Brugghen (1588–1629)
Laughing Musician with a Bass Viol and a Glass, 1625
Oil on canvas, 104.6 × 85.2 cm
The Royal Collection

the 'Haarlem Mannerists'. He is best known today as the author of *Het Schilder-Boeck*, published in Haarlem in 1604, a substantial book which, according to its title page, was intended for "painters, lovers of art and poets, also all ranks of people", and included biographies of Netherlandish and German artists in emulation of Vasari's *Lives of the Italian Artists*.[17] In the late sixteenth century, with Cornelis van Haarlem and the printmaker and painter Hendrick Goltzius, Van Mander apparently set up a short-lived informal academy there.

A subsequent influence on painting in Haarlem were the group of Utrecht artists who travelled to Rome and saw the work of Caravaggio, particularly Hendrick ter Brugghen (*c.* 1588–1629; see figs. 12 and 46), Gerrit van Honthorst and Dirck van Baburen (1595–1624). Caravaggio's use of strong lighting to heighten the drama and immediacy of a scene, and his introduction of life-sized, individual, half-length genre (rather than portrait) figures, were among the elements adopted by the Utrecht 'Caravaggisti', and which were in turn introduced to painting in Haarlem. A number of their paintings depicted single sitters with musical instruments, such as Ter Brugghen's *Flute Player* from 1621 (Kassel, Staatliche Gemäldegalerie, inv. no. 179), *Man playing a Lute* from 1624 (London, National Gallery, NG 6347) and his *Laughing Bravo with a Bass Viol and a Glass*, signed and dated 1625 (fig. 12). The last work was bought by King Charles I, then sold by the Commonwealth after his execution; it was subsequently acquired by Lely, in whose possession it was reported on 18 May 1660.[18]

One of Van Mander's last pupils in Haarlem was Frans Hals (died 1666), who joined the Guild of Saint Luke in 1610. Hals became the leading Haarlem portraitist and painted some of the most powerful militia group portraits of his time. These included the 1616 *Banquet of the Officers of the Haarlem Militia Company of Saint George* (Haarlem, Frans Hals Museum); over the following half century he was to paint a further eight immense life-size animated group portraits. In the 1620s and 1630s Hals also specialised in the Caravaggists' format of half-length single-figure genre scenes, depicting musicians, drinkers, actors and children.[19] It is interesting to note that when Horace Walpole saw the group of six paintings by Lely of single individuals playing musical instruments (see cat. 5 and 6) in the Craven collection at Coombe Abbey in 1768, he identified them, somewhat surprisingly, as "by Francis Halls".[20] In the middle and latter years of his career, *c.* 1630–50, Hals concentrated principally on portraiture. His leading position remained unchallenged, although a younger group of portraitists had now emerged – Johannes Cornelisz. Verspronk (before 1603–1662), Pieter de Grebber and Pieter Claesz. Soutman (*c.* 1585–1657); the latter two were also the foremost history painters in Haarlem in the years between 1630 and 1650. Leading Haarlem genre painters of the next generation included the talented Judith Leyster (1609–1660), who was enrolled in the Guild of Saint Luke in 1633, although after her marriage in 1636 to Haarlem fellow-artist Jan Miense Molenaer (*c.* 1610–1668) she effectively ceased to paint.[21] Molenaer, like Willem Buytewech (1591–1624), specialised in multiple-figure scenes in interiors – of so-called 'merry companies' – scenes that both revel in the depiction of prosperity yet are implicitly concerned about the moral consequences of wealth.[22]

During the decade of the 1640s, Haarlem was comparatively stable and prosperous, so there was no obvious economic imperative for Lely to leave the city.[23] However, as indicated above, a considerable number of successful artists were already active and well established there. Lely may have decided that there would be more opportunities open to him elsewhere. Attempts have been made to identify works that Lely might have painted while he was still working in the Netherlands,[24] but very few references have been found to him, or to his works, in the Dutch archives.[25]

The circumstances in which Lely decided to migrate to London are unclear. In 1695 Richard Graham wrote that Lely went to England in 1641 – the year in which Anthony van Dyck died, on 9 December – and began working there as a landscape painter before switching to painting portraits.[26] Bainbrigg Buckeridge, echoing Graham, stated that "Coming over to England in the year 1641, [Lely] for some time followed the natural bent of his genius, and painted landskip with small figures, as likewise historical compositions; but at length finding face Painting more encouraged here he turned his study that way, wherein, in a short time, he succeeded so well that he surpassed all his contemporaries".[27]

Early in the eighteenth century, more than seventy years after the event, Arnold Houbraken wrote that Lely had travelled to London with the young William of Orange, who had sailed there to marry the eldest daughter of Charles I, Mary, and to accompany her back to the Netherlands. However, partly because Houbraken mistakenly gave the date of this event as 1643, rather than 1641, his account has been assumed to lack credibility in its detail. By

FIG. 13
Peter Lely (1618–1680)
Landscape with small figures; rocky banks with trees on left, buildings in middle ground to right with hills in distance, 1643
Brush and grey wash, with faint areas of brown wash (?), 15.5 × 21 cm
The British Museum, London

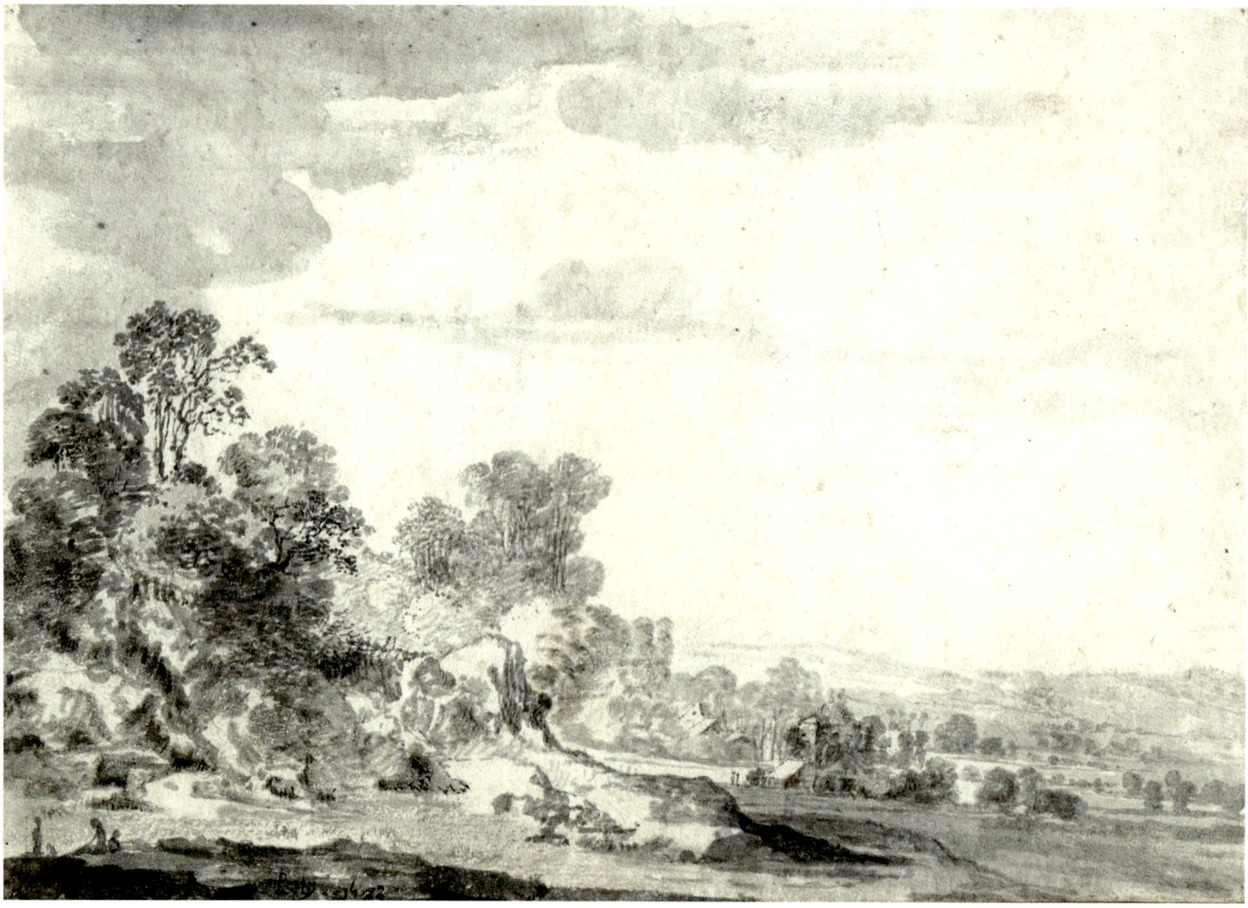

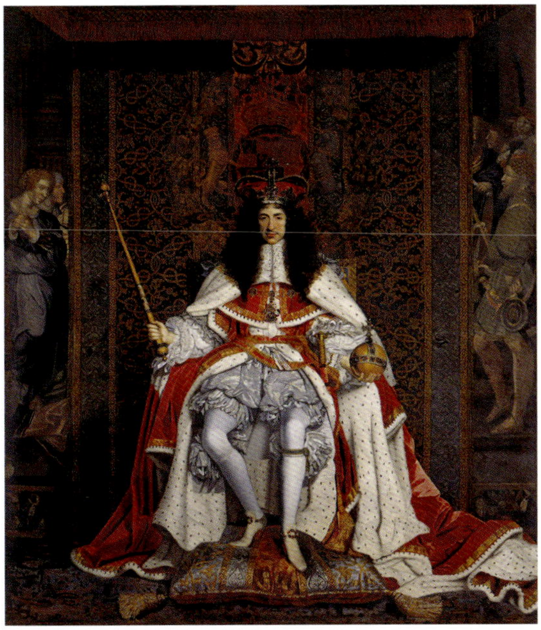

FIG. 14
John Michael Wright (1617–1694)
King Charles II, c. 1661–62
Oil on canvas, 281.9 × 239.2 cm
The Royal Collection

stating that by the time Lely was "in his 25th year" he had gained a great reputation, Houbraken effectively reiterated the date 1643. According to the engraver and art history enthusiast George Vertue (who also was writing many decades later) Lely initially worked in London for the Flemish painter, dealer and entrepreneur George Geldorp (died 1665; see fig. 20); Vertue's source was apparently the Dutch marine painter Isaac Sailmaker (1633–1721), who had lived and worked in Geldorp's house at the same time.[28]

It is, however, generally accepted that Lely was in England by 1643, the date inscribed on a signed drawing, *Landscape with small figures*, now in the British Museum (fig. 13). He must have maintained links with his family back in The Hague, where he still owned property and where, as the main seat of the Dutch court, many exiled British royalists, including the young Charles II, would shortly be residing. A posthumous inventory of the possessions of Odilia van der Faes, Lely's wealthy aunt, made on 12 April 1652, indicated that he inherited a quarter of her estate, which included the house 'in de Lelye'.[29] References in the Dutch archives to Lely as a property owner in The Hague recur in February 1665, May 1674 and December 1679.[30]

Lely is known to have travelled back to the Dutch Republic only once when, in the summer of 1656, he was accompanied by a friend, the English architect Hugh May (1621–1684), who had lodged in Lely's Covent Garden house since the early 1650s.[31]

Lely's Dutch origins did not impede his progress in London. He became a freeman of the London Painter-Stainers' Company – the local equivalent of the Haarlem Guild of Saint Luke – in 1647. In 1658, towards the end of the Commonwealth years, the royalist historian and writer William Sanderson listed "Lillie" among what he called the "English Modern Masters" in his book on painting past and present: "Those now in *England* are not less worthy of fame then any forraigner; and although some of them be strangers [that is, foreigners] born, yet for their affection to our *Nation* we may mixe them together. Our Modern Masters comparable with any now beyond Seas ...".[32] Lely was granted naturalisation by the British Parliament on 16 May 1662.

Meanwhile, in 1660, the exiled Charles II (fig. 14) had been restored to the British throne. Following the execution of his father Charles I in 1649, the younger Charles had lived in exile on the Continent, particularly in the Netherlands. It was from The Hague, on 24 May 1661, that he and his entourage set off for their journey back to Britain, embarking at Scheveningen on 2 June. At a farewell dinner on the eve of Charles's departure, it was announced that the States of Holland had decided to present the young king with "a number of rare objects". The importance that they attached to this project to curry favour with Charles is indicated by the fact that the immense sum of 600,000 guilders was set aside to cover the costs of the dinner, of travel for the appointed Dutch envoys and for "suitable gifts and presents".[33] These were to include an "exquisitely embroidered bed" – evidently a grand State Bed, with such accessories as a "canopy, chairs, a fire screen, tapestries and all the accoutrements of a suite". It was also decided to send a gift of paintings – especially Italian 'Old Master' paintings, since it was understood that that was the type of work that Charles favoured. This was to become known as the 'Dutch Gift', and one of the advisers chosen for the project was Gerrit Uylenburgh (*c.* 1625–1679), an Amsterdam-based landscape-painter and art dealer, and kinsman by marriage to the painter Rembrandt van Rijn. Gerrit was also asked to pack the sculptures and paintings – which included some by Dutch artists – and to accompany them to London.[34] Accordingly, on 12 November 1660, in the prestigious entertainment space of the Banqueting House in Whitehall, the bed, paintings and other gifts were presented by the Dutch ambassadors (accompanied by Uylenburgh) to Charles II, who professed himself delighted with them, particularly by Titian's *Virgin and Child* and by works by the Dutch artist Gerrit Dou (1613–1675).

While he was in London, Uylenburgh is presumed to have met up with his fellow Dutchman Lely, who had already been given the post of Charles's principal official painter (although he would not be formally appointed until 25 February 1662). They may already have known each other, but certainly from then on they evidently formed a firm friendship, because in 1668 Lely was described as the "trusty and well beloved friend" of the Uylenburgh family. That year Gerrit and his family nominated Lely to represent the interests of their recently deceased brother Abraham Uylenburgh, who had died in Dublin while working there for the Duke and Duchess of Ormonde. The Uylenburghs authorised "mr. Peter Lely" to represent their interests abroad.

Lely was a keen collector of drawings and paintings himself (figs. 15 and 16), and, on occasion, clearly also acted as a dealer and as a business associate of Uylenburgh. In a letter of 1663, Constantijn Huygens the Younger reported that he had visited Lely in London, and that the painter had told him that the nucleus of his Old Master drawing collection had come from the more than 1,100 items owned by Walter van de Voort – a Flemish merchant resident in Venice – a collection which had come on to the market in 1657.[35] Lely apparently told Huygens that "he picked all the best ones out and left the rest for Uylenburgh, who took them with him to Holland". It has been suggested that this transaction took

FIG. 15
Parmigianino (Girolamo Francesco Maria Mazzola) (1503–1540)
Sheet of studies, *c.* 1530
Pen and brown ink on paper, 14.5 × 14 cm
The Courtauld Gallery (Samuel Courtauld Trust), London

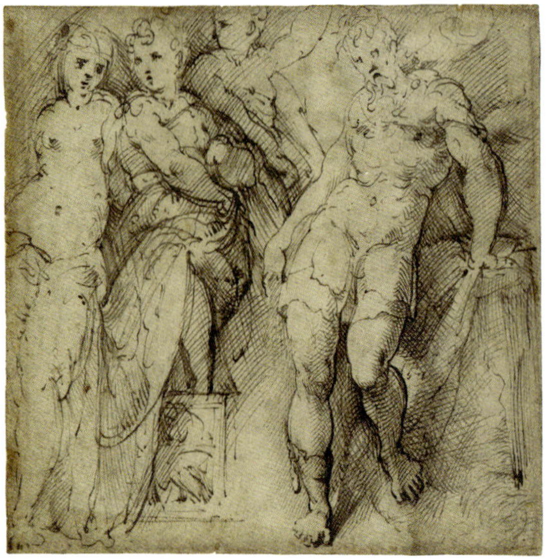

FIG. 16
Attributed to Giovanni Bellini (?)
(active by *c.* 1459; died 1516)
The Nativity, *c.* 1480
Pen and brush and brown ink,
on laid paper, 21.1 × 21.1 cm
The Courtauld Gallery
(Samuel Courtauld Trust), London

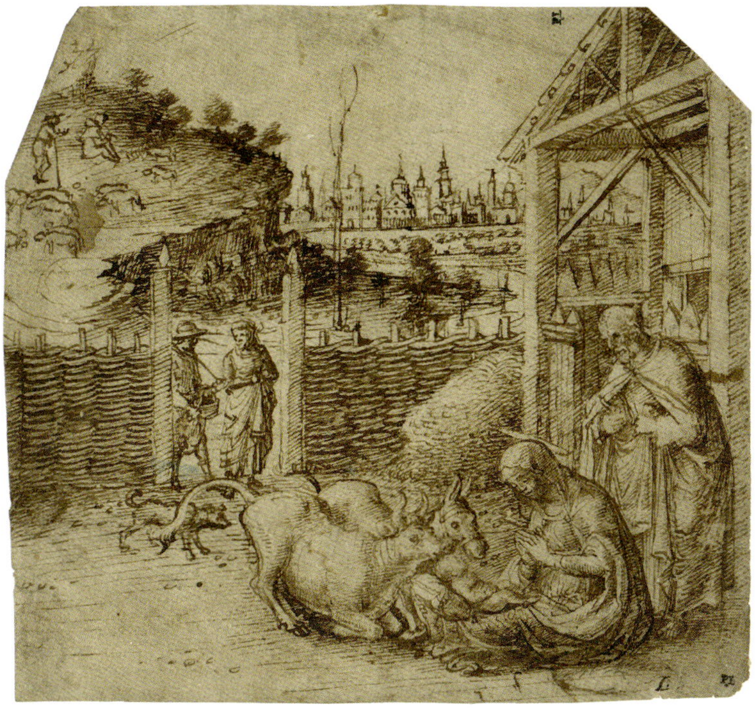

place in Antwerp, while Lely may still have been on the Continent on his trip with Hugh May. Moreover, by December 1659 Lely had sold Sir Ralph Bankes a large landscape painting by Nicholaes Berchem, painted in 1655, as well as a copy after a "night Piece" by Gerrit Dou, the original of which Lely himself owned.[36]

The most significant evidence both of Lely's activity as a dealer and of his business collaboration with his Dutch friend Uylenburgh dates from 1675, when Uylenburgh's paintings were valued on behalf of his creditors. It was noted that a number of his pictures were with Lely in England, presumably for him to sell there. Four were by Caspar Netscher, including an "excellent painting of singers", one was a *Danaë* by Cornelis van Poelenburgh, and others were by Anthonis Mor and Adriaen Brouwer.[37] After his financial collapse, Uylenburgh travelled with his family to England, where, apparently through Lely's influence, he was appointed curator – "Purveyor & Keeper" – of Charles II's collection.[38]

Following the Restoration in 1660, a number of other Dutch artists had settled in London, including Jan Looten, Egbert van Heemskerk, Hendrick and Johan Danckerts, Pieter van Roostraten, Thomas Wijck and Abraham Hondius. After 1672, when the Dutch economy had become depressed, Charles II formally invited Dutch craftspeople with a wide range of skills to migrate to Britain. As a result, further Northern Netherlanders headed for London, among them the marine artists Willem van de Velde – both father and son – Pieter Borsselaer, Adriaen van Dienst, Gerard Edema, Adriaen Hennin, Abraham Begeyn, Adam de Colonia, Jan Griffier and others.[39]

Many of these artists became the subjects of short individual biographies by Bainbrigg Buckeridge, published in 1706 – biographies that carefully noted the national origins of each artist. In these Buckeridge pointed out that a number of the assistants that Lely employed in his studio were Dutch, or had trained in Dutch or Flemish studios. Among them were "John Baptist Gaspars, Commonly called Lely's Baptist"; Joseph Buckshorn; Prosper Henricus Lankrink, Willem Wissing and Jan van der Vaart.[40]

In 1674, the Dutch writer Johannes Vollenhove visited Lely in London, and subsequently penned *Animum pictura pascit*, a poem in appreciation of his fellow countryman, which begins "*Leli, Londens dierbaar pant*" (loosely translated as 'Lely, London's beloved possession').[41]

Lely's Dutch origins, sound artistic training and early professional experience in Haarlem were clearly key to his subsequent success in Britain. Clients in Britain were accustomed to buying and commissioning paintings from artists who had travelled there from overseas, particularly when, as seems to have been the case with Lely, they made an effort to assimilate and to be acceptable in demeanour and behaviour.[42] Simultaneously, although documentary evidence is scant, Lely continued to maintain links with family and professional contacts in the Northern Netherlands. Seventeenth-century London was moreover full of fellow Dutch people, which must have enabled Lely to feel settled among many whose experiences would have parallelled his own.

NOTES

This essay is dedicated, in friendship, to the memory of Professor Kevin Sharpe.

1 J.A.C. Ab. Wittenaar, 'De Geboorteplaats en de naam van Peter Lely: Nieuwe documenten', *Oud Holland*, vol. 67, no. 2, 1952, pp. 122–24, and R.C.C. de Savorin Lohman, 'Heelt des Engelse hofschilder Sir Peter Lely (alias Pieter van der Faes) in zijn jeugd te Deventer bij zijn ouders gewoond?', *De Nederlandsche Leeuw*, vol. 99, 1982, pp. 283–86.

2 See ECARTICO database, http://burckhardt.ic.uva.nl/ecartico/persons/4546 (accessed 1 June 2012); I am grateful to Marten Jan Bok for his advice on this.

3 Arnold Houbraken, *De groote schouburgh der Nederlantsche konstschilders en schilderessen,* 's Gravenhage (J. Swart, C. Boucquet and M. Gaillard) 1753, 3 vols., II, pp. 41–48.

4 *Ibid.*, and discussed by Wittenaar 1952.

5 Wittenaar 1952, pp. 122–24; Friso Lammertse and Jaap van de Veen, eds., *Uylenburgh & Son: Art and Commerce from Rembrandt to De Lairesse*, 1625–1675, exh. cat., Dulwich Picture Gallery, London, and Rembrandthuis, Amsterdam, 2006, p. 263 n. 239.

6 *Ibid.*

7 Pieter Biesboer, 'Judith Leyster: Painter of "Modern Figures"', in Pieter Biesboer and James Welu, eds., *Judith Leyster: A Dutch Master and Her World*, exh. cat., Frans Hals Museum, Haarlem, and Worcester Art Museum, Worcester MA, 1993, pp. 76–77.

8 Houbraken 1718–21 (1753), II, p. 47, actually wrote that Lely was apprenticed to the painter "Piet. Fr. Grebber", presumably muddling the father with his son. R.B. Beckett, in his 1951 monograph on Lely, in turn confused the work of Frans de Grebber with that of his son Pieter (p. 5 and figs. 1 and 2).

9 On Frans de Grebber's oeuvre, see also Haarlem and Worcester 1993, p. 88 n. 6.

10 See Albert Blankert, ed., *Gods, Saints and Heroes: Dutch Painting in the Age of Rembrandt*, exh. cat., National Gallery of Art, Washington DC, Detroit Institute of Arts, and Rijksmuseum, Amsterdam, 1980–81, pp. 192–95; and Albert Blankert, Jeroen Giltaij and Friso Lammertse, eds., *Dutch classicism in seventeenth-century painting*, exh. cat., Museum Boijmans Van Beuningen, Rotterdam, and Städelsches Kunstinstitut, Frankfurt, 1999–2000, pp. 116–43, nos. 13–19.

11 See Haarlem and Worcester 1993, p. 227 n. 1.

12 See Margriet van Eikema Hommes, 'Pieter de Grebber and the Oranjezaal in Huis ten Bosch: Part I: The Regulen (1649)', and Margriet van Eikema Hommes and Lidwien Speleers, 'Pieter de Grebber and the Oranjezaal in Huis ten Bosch: Part II: Variations in Painting Technique', *Netherlands Technical Studies in Art: Art Matters*, III, 2005, pp. 20–36, 37–65.

13 Magda Kyrova, 'Music in Seventeenth-Century Dutch Painting', in *Music and Painting in the Golden Age*, exh. cat., ed. Edwin Buijsen and Louis Peter Grijp, The Hague, and Hessenhuis Museum, Antwerp, 1994, p. 31.

14 Pieter Biesboer, 'The Burghers of Haarlem and Their Portrait Painters', in Seymour Slive, ed., *Frans Hals*, exh. cat., National Gallery of Art, Washington DC, Royal Academy of Arts, London, and Frans Halsmuseum, Haarlem, 1990, pp. 23–25.

15 *Ibid.*

16 Thera Wijsenbeek-Olthuis and Leo Noorderaaf, 'Painting for a Living: The Economic Context of Judith Leyster's Career', in Haarlem and Worcester 1993, pp. 41–42.

17 See Mariët Westermann, *The Art of the Dutch Republic 1585–1718*, London, 1996, p. 61.

18 Christopher White, *The Dutch Pictures in the Collection of Her Majesty The Queen*, Cambridge, 1982, p. 31, no. 33, pl. 22; Lely subsequently returned the painting to Charles II.

19 Seymour Slive, *Dutch Painting 1600–1800*, New Haven and London, 1995, p. 38.

20 Paget Toynbee, 'Horace Walpole's Journals of Visits to Country Seats, &c.', *Walpole Society*, XVI, 1928, pp. 10, 63.

21 Slive 1995, p. 128.

22 Westermann 1996, pp. 118–19.

23 I am grateful to Pieter Biesboer for discussing this question with me in March 2005. It was not until the years 1655–65 that the Dutch economy began to decline as a result of the first two Anglo-Dutch wars and of increasing commercial competition from the textile centres of the Southern Netherlands and Germany.

24 Julia Marciari Alexander, 'A Dutch "stranger ... on the make": Sir Peter Lely and the Critical Fortunes of a Foreign Painter', in Randolph Vigne and Charles Littleton, eds., *From Strangers to Citizens*, Brighton and Portland OR, 2001, pp. 127–28, citing Jacques Foucart, 'Peter Lely, Dutch History Painter, *Hoogsteder-Naumann Mercury*, no. 8, 1989, pp. 17–26.

25 There is, for instance, no relevant mention of Lely in Marion Goosens, *Schilders en de Markt: Haarlem 1605–1635*, Leiden, 2001; I am grateful to Michiel Franken, RKD, for his advice on this.

26 Richard Graham, 'A Short Account' in Du Fresnoy, *De Arte Graphica*, English edition, 1695, pp. 343–44; Graham states that Lely was "committed to the care of one *de Grebber* of *Haarlem*. He came over into *England*. *Anno* 1641." (It should, however, be noted that Graham incorrectly gives Lely's birth year as 1617.)

27 Bainbrigg Buckeridge, 'A Essay Towards an English School', in Roger de Piles, *The Art of Painting, and the Lives of the Painters,* London (1706) 3rd edn, 1754, p. 402.

28 George Vertue, 'Notebooks: I', *The Walpole Society*, XVIII, 1929–30, p. 74.

29 Wittenaar 1952.

30 *Ibid.*

31 TNA, State Papers Domestic 25 /77, 150: permission dated 29 May 1656 for a passport for Holland for "Peter Leley, and his Servt. Hugh May"; see Oliver Millar, *Sir Peter Lely 1618–80*, exh. cat., National Portrait Gallery, London, 1978–79, p. 28 n. 22. Houbraken mentions that Lely returned to the Netherlands during the Commonwealth period (p. 43). It is not clear how long Lely spent there.

32 William Sanderson, *Graphice. The use of the pen and pensil. Or, The most excellent art of painting: in two parts*, London, 1658, p. 20.

33 London and Amsterdam 2006, p. 65.

34 *Ibid.*, pp. 67–70.

35 *Ibid.*, pp. 79, 232, 268.

36 *Ibid.*, pp. 269–70, citing Alastair Laing, 'Sir Peter Lely and Sir Ralph Bankes', in David Howarth (ed.), *Art and Patronage in the Caroline Courts*, Cambridge, 1993.

37 *Ibid.*, pp. 268–69.

38 *Ibid.*, pp. 110–13.

39 *Ibid.*, p. 110. In using the word 'Dutch' Buckeridge does not always differentiate between Northern and Southern (Flemish) Netherlanders.

40 Buckeridge (1706) 1754, pp. 356, 359, 398, 435.

41 Reprinted in Houbraken (1718–21) 1753, pp. 44–46.

42 Graham 1695, p. 344, remarked that Charles II "would often times take great pleasure in his *Conversation*, which he found to be as agreeable as his *Pencil*".

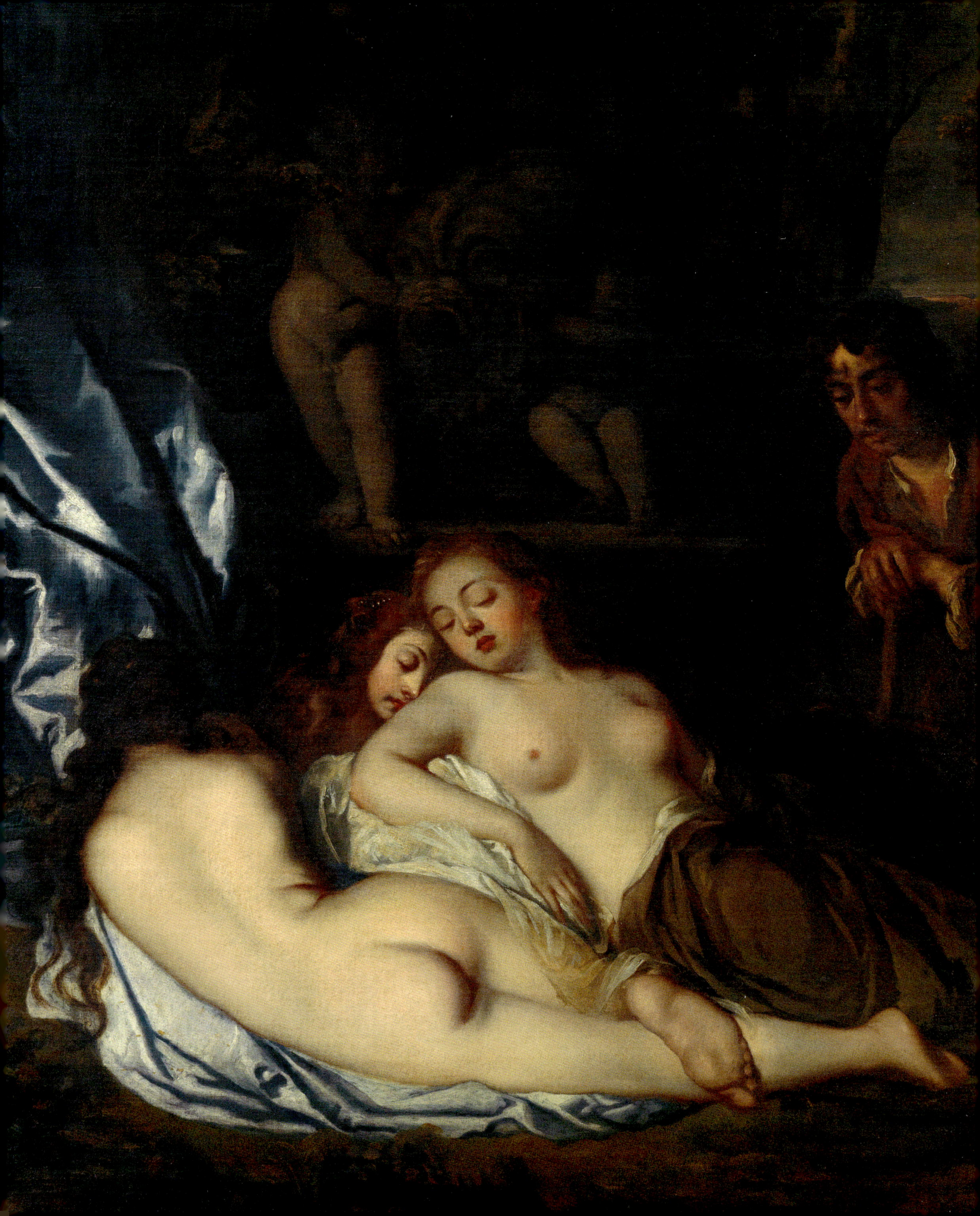

Reception and Rejection: Lely's subject pictures in an "un-understanding land"

DIANA DETHLOFF

IN HIS *Anecdotes of Painting*, the eighteenth-century writer Horace Walpole emphatically declared that "few of [Lely's] historic pieces are known".[1] However, his "Landtscapes with small Figures and Historical Compositions", as these paintings were described by Lely's first biographer, Richard Graham,[2] formed an important part of Lely's output, both in his native Holland and soon after his arrival in England, although, compared to his later work for the court of Charles II, we know very little about these paintings or indeed this period of his life. Trying to establish why and for whom they may have been painted throws interesting light on Lely's early career, and tells us something about the opportunities and problems that existed for a young Dutch artist working in London during the years of civil war and Commonwealth government.

LELY'S EARLY DUTCH CAREER AND THE IMPORTANCE OF FRANS PIETERSZ. DE GREBBER

Before his arrival in England, Lely had worked for Frans Pietersz. de Grebber, a painter of portraits and religious subjects who ran one of the largest and most successful studios in Haarlem.[3] Since the establishment of Karel van Mander's Haarlem 'academy' in the 1580s with its emphasis on the teaching of drawing, including from the live model, Haarlem was recognised as an important artistic centre and its prosperity from the textile and beer industries produced many wealthy art patrons.[4] As well as undertaking major civic commissions to decorate town buildings, the De Grebber studio efficiently produced large numbers of portraits – providing perhaps a useful model which Lely adopted in his own later portrait practice. Like many other Dutch artists, De Grebber was also active as an art dealer, and had been for a number of years before Lely joined his studio. Rubens thought very highly of him and strongly recommended De Grebber to Sir Dudley Carleton, then the

Cat. 11 (detail)

English ambassador at The Hague, as a potential contact and source for supplying pictures to English collectors.[5] On a more local level De Grebber's entrepreneurial enthusiasm had led to his repeated flouting of the Haarlem guild's regulations on public sales and lotteries, which resulted in fines on at least two occasions.[6] By the time Lely entered his studio his art dealing reputation was secure, with contacts both within and outside Holland.

Within a few years, according to the Dutch art writer Arnold Houbraken, Lely had established his own reputation as a portrait painter "of note", and was also producing subject pictures.[7] These small-scale works, with mythological or biblical figures usually in a landscape setting, formed a clearly defined and successful category of painting in seventeenth-century Holland, especially in the work of Cornelis van Poelenburgh, Jacob van Loo, Dirk van der Lisse and Abraham Cuylenburg. Van Mander, writing in his influential *Het Schilder-Boeck* of 1604, stressed how important it was to devote time to painting scenes from mythology or the Bible in landscapes, and advised landscape artists to think very carefully beforehand about which "little story ... from the Bible or classical mythology" they would use.[8] Some of Lely's earliest subject pictures show a strong debt to Van Poelenburgh, and depict similar

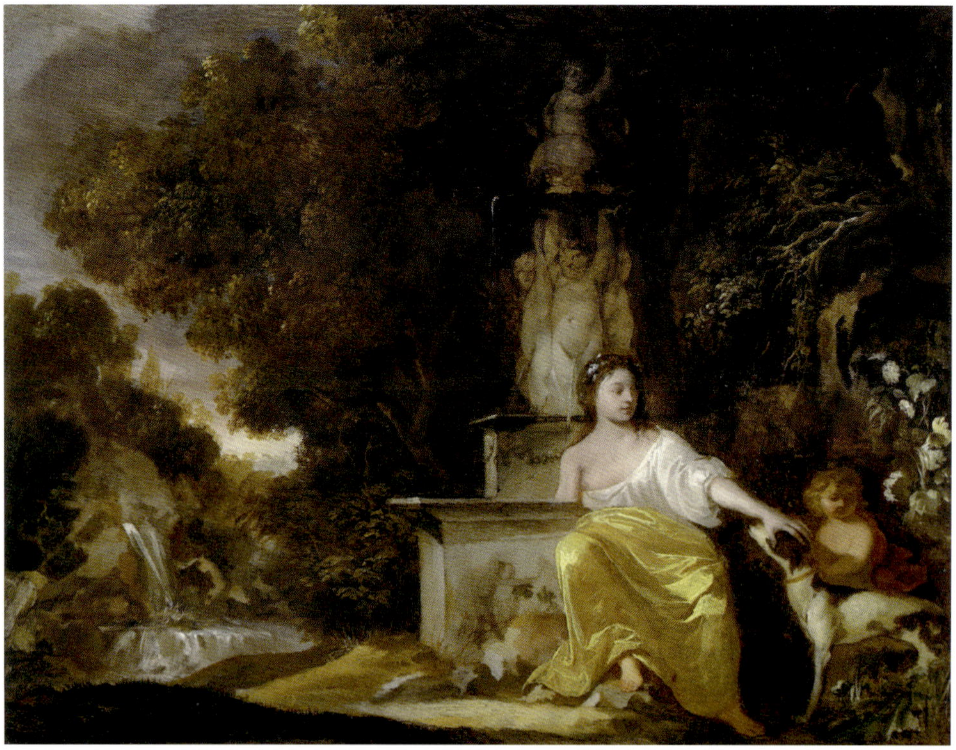

FIG. 17
Peter Lely (1618–1680)
Young Woman (Diana?) seated at a Fountain, early 1640s
Oil on panel, 31 × 39.5 cm
Private collection

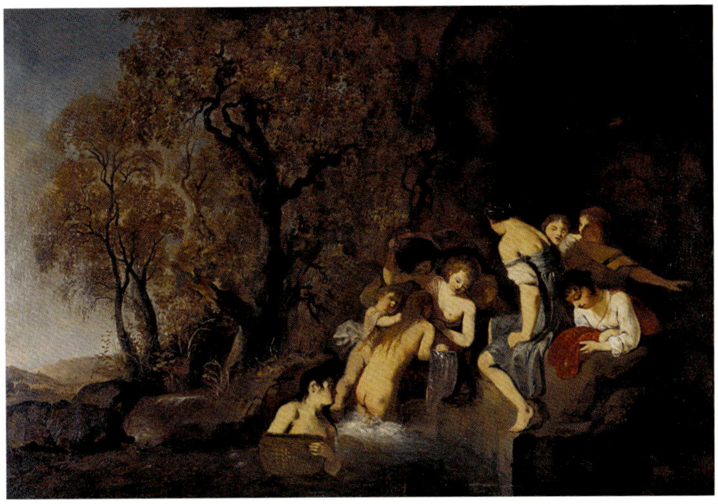

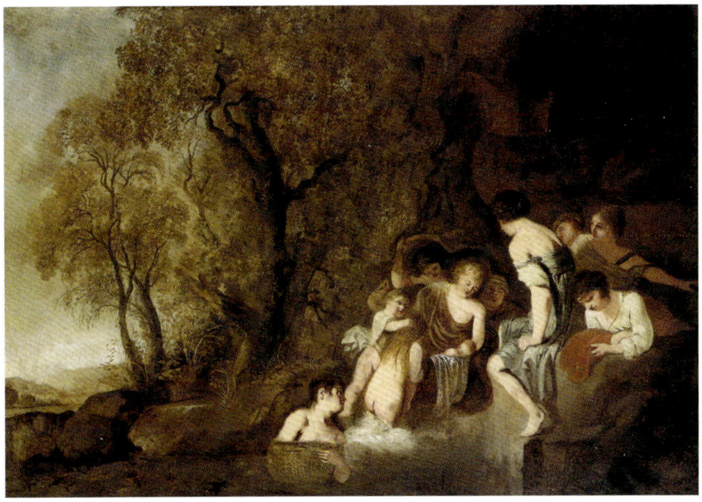

FIG. 18
Peter Lely (1618–1680)
Nymphs bathing (after restoration), early 1640s
Oil on canvas, 94 × 134.5 cm
Private collection

FIG. 19
Peter Lely (1618–1680)
Nymphs bathing, formerly known as *The Finding of Moses* (before restoration)

subject-matter, for example lovers seated in a landscape (cat. 2) or Diana and her nymphs bathing. In some of these early works the small-scale figure groups seem almost secondary to the landscape setting, which Lely depicts in a distinctive way with a careful application of paint of varying thickness to convey tendril-like branches or the different density and texture of foliage. An early work from this period is a small-scale painting on board of a *Young Woman (Diana?) seated at a Fountain* (fig. 17); the girl's right arm, which Lely tries to hide behind the base of the fountain, and her unnaturally long upper left arm show an awkwardness also found in other early pictures. In contrast the delicately painted landscape elements, for example the ivy around the base of the fountain and the trailing branches at upper right, are handled much more confidently and convincingly. Another early work is *Nymphs bathing* (fig. 18), which takes up a theme well established in the work of earlier artists such as Titian and Rubens, intended to give the viewer the pleasure of looking at nude female figures from various angles and in varying stages of dress and undress. This must have been the reason why some time in the later nineteenth century its Victorian owner had the subject changed to *The Finding of Moses* (fig. 19; before restoration) with the baby Moses in his basket added, perhaps to try to elevate the subject. Lely's composition follows a fairly standard pattern, found in other early works, with the figures shown in varying stages of undressing, drying themselves or dressing, arranged in an off-central triangular grouping. The background setting is a characteristically densely foliated landscape, which opens up to reveal the golden light of evening; in other examples it might open into a rocky cavern or gorge.

Unlike the more consistent size of the subject paintings by Van Poelenburgh, Van der Lisse and others, Lely's pictures vary quite considerably, from the cabinet size of *Young Woman at a Fountain* to the large Dulwich *Nymphs by a Fountain* (cat. 9), to the even larger *Finding of Moses* (now generally accepted as by Lely) which appears in the background of two of Vermeer's paintings, *The Woman writing a Letter* (see fig. 32) and *The Astronomer*.[9]

LELY'S EARLY YEARS IN LONDON

Lely left Holland and arrived in London some time between 1641 and 1643. Contemporary accounts put forward different dates: Richard Graham says 1641, whereas Houbraken claims 1643. As yet no other more precise documentary evidence has been found, although 1643 seems more likely. Although Van Dyck, the dominant force in English painting, had recently died, neither date, in terms of the political situation, seems well timed for an apparently rising Dutch artist to establish himself in London. By 1641 relations between the monarch Charles I and his political opponents were fast deteriorating, with some royalist supporters, for example the diarist John Evelyn, fearing unrest and deciding to leave England and travel on the Continent. By 1643 England was at civil war, the king had fled London, which declared for his Parliamentary opponents, and established his court at Oxford. During the mid 1640s, the period historians call 'the First Civil War', London's fashionable population declined and so too the consumption of high-quality goods, with some shops in the New Exchange closing.[10] Many of those with money who supported the king were leaving the capital; many of those who remained would have been uneasy about an uncertain future, so for Lely to try and break into the London painting scene at this point – to find work, establish patrons and a clientele – would have presented challenges and risks even for an artist with a more established reputation, while at Oxford the English painter William Dobson was ably fulfilling commissions for royal and courtly portraiture. It is of course possible that Lely's career in Haarlem was not in fact going that well, despite Houbraken's enthusiastic account. No paintings by him are listed in contemporary Haarlem inventories,[11] although his work could have been confused with that of other artists and misrecorded; for example, Lely's *Young Woman at a Fountain* (fig. 17) was until recently attributed to Dirck van der Lisse. Moreover tighter market restrictions introduced in the early 1640s by the Haarlem guild, aiming to stamp out unauthorised public sales to anyone outside the city, and considerable competition from high numbers of fellow artists, could have constituted a serious block on the career of a young artist such as Lely. It is certainly possible that Lely also worked briefly in The Hague, where his family had property, and a few of his works, including *tronies* (heads) and others of unspecified subject-matter, both originals and copies after them (which, however, suggests his career was secure after all, if other artists were copying his work) were sold by members of The Hague guild of painters in 1647.[12] It has always been assumed that Lely came to England simply as an ambitious painter; but another reason might have been to deal in pictures, especially given De Grebber's reputation as an influential picture dealer and his links with England. Moreover, Lely's first contact in London was the artist-dealer George Geldorp and later in his career he collaborated with the Dutch dealer Gerrit Uylenburgh and became highly regarded in his own right as a collector.[13] Looked at in this light, arriving in London, perhaps at the behest of De Grebber, when political upheavals and sudden changes in circumstances would have resulted in collections being hastily dispersed, and paintings suddenly becoming available, made shrewd business sense, as well as providing Lely with the opportunity of exposing his own work to a new audience.

LELY AND GELDORP AND THE DUTCH COMMUNITY IN LONDON

Following his arrival in London Lely first worked for George Geldorp (fig. 20), the artist-dealer son of the painter Gortsius Geldorp. After a period in Antwerp, where he was a member of the painter's guild, George Geldorp established himself in England in 1623 and by 1626 was working for the 2nd Earl of Salisbury and his wife, painting their portraits[14] and supplying them with fine glasses and embroideries. He also sold a "head of Nero" to Charles, Prince of Wales, shortly before Charles became king in 1625.[15] By the early 1630s he had secured royal patronage and some share in the charge of the royal collection.[16] He clearly became well connected "with people of Quality", allegedly entertaining "Ladies and Gentlemen with wine and hams and other curious eatables",[17] and offering hospitality to visiting Netherlandish artists; Van Dyck stayed with him during his first visit to London in late 1620,[18] as did the Dutch artist Jan Lievens in 1632. Between 1637 and 1638 he acted as agent and intermediary for the wealthy Cologne banker and collector Edvard Jabach in the commission of an altarpiece from Rubens for St Peter's in Cologne. From the mid 1630s he supplied paintings, including a number of Van Dycks, and picture frames to the 10th Earl of Northumberland, son-in-law to Salisbury and himself an important collector and patron.[19] He also supplied frames and pictures to the Earl of Middlesex, the Earl of Huntingdon and the Earl of Lothian.[20] His big break as a dealer came during the late 1640s and early 1650s, when he played a key role in the dispersal of the royal collection following Charles I's execution. The king had left substantial debts and the sale of his art collection, one of the most important in Europe, was intended to pay off his creditors.[21] Both Geldorp and Lely made a number of purchases.[22] With the restoration of the monarchy in 1660, serious attempts were made to recover those of "the late king's goods" which remained in Britain and Geldorp was a member of the commission set up to retrieve them.[23] In 1662 he was appointed Charles II's picture cleaner and mender.

From 1642 Geldorp lived in Chapel Street by the New Chapel near Tothill's Fields, which seems to have had a number of previous Dutch tenants including Van Poelenburgh, who was in London from 1637 to 1641, and the silversmith Christian van Vianen, and it is likely Lely lodged there when he first arrived.[24] Lely would have found himself amongst a large and well-established Dutch community, since from the early 1530s Netherlandish artists and craftsmen had settled in London in large numbers. Many of these earlier artists had left the Continent to escape religious persecution and enjoy freedom of worship, but many also came in search of work, to "get a living", according to many parish returns of the period, intensifying the competition for employment within London's growing population. These pressures, together with their different languages and customs, caused resentment among many Londoners, who regarded these émigré artists as 'aliens' or 'strangers', the name 'foreigner' being reserved for itinerant Englishmen from outside London who came to look for work.[25] Lely's early contacts would have been within this 'stranger' community but he also met and befriended a number of English writers and artists, so must have learnt some English reasonably quickly. His admission in 1663 in a letter (written in another's hand) that he was "a stranger to the English tongue"[26] probably meant he did not speak it very well rather than not at all.[27] His early work for Geldorp may have included copying pictures from Geldorp's dealing stock. He also continued to produce a number of subject paintings, pursuing what Richard Graham called his "natural genius" – but for whom?

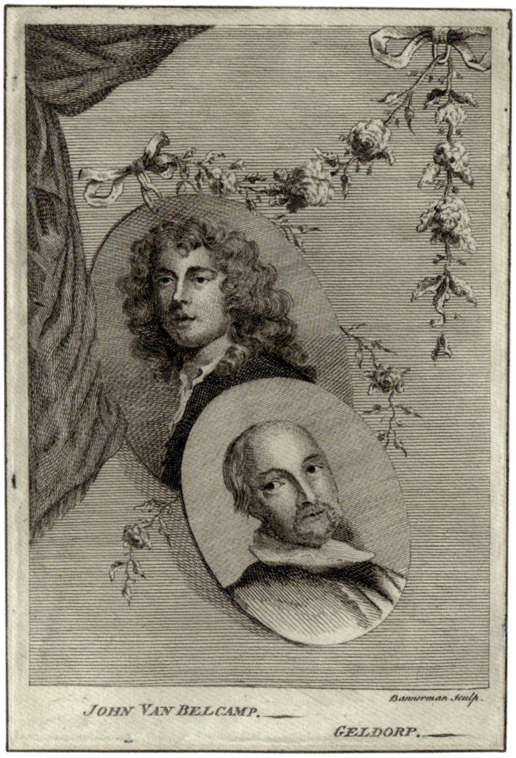

FIG. 20
Alexander Bannerman
(*c.* 1730– after 1774)
Jan van Belcamp and George Geldorp, *c.* 1750
Engraving, 18.1 × 12 cm
National Portrait Gallery, London

SELLING PAINTINGS AND PROMOTING THE ARTIST

There is very little known about the early ownership of Lely's subject pictures, and in many cases we can only start tracing their provenance from the late eighteenth century, some much later. Those produced in Holland, like much of the work produced by Dutch artists at the time, were almost certainly not painted for a specific patron but for a general market and distributed through De Grebber's studio or local sales. The Dutch art market was extremely well developed and operated on several levels, from that of sixteenth-century Old Masters sold through specialist dealers to wealthier clients to more affordable paintings sold through artists' studios, guild and estate auctions, right down to cheap pictures sold at local markets and fairs, on which contemporary visitors commented.[28] Despite local guild restrictions as to where and to whom works could be sold, many affordable and cheap pictures were clearly passing between the local towns and dealers, perhaps through the few open fairs each town was allowed each year, or more covertly and unofficially. The presence of Lely's *Finding of Moses* in the background of two of Vermeer's paintings suggests that De Grebber (or perhaps Lely himself) was using sources outside Haarlem to market his pupils' work, and that Vermeer, who also dealt in pictures, included Lely's work in his own paintings in order to market it.

Our knowledge of the English art market during this period is more limited, although the research that has been carried out so far suggests it was more active and developed than previously thought.[29] The Outroper's Office in the City of London, officially established in 1638 but in existence since 1612, provided opportunities for selling various goods by public 'outcry', although these were mostly household items. Art auctions for high-quality specialist works began only in the 1670s, and those for cheaper works in the 1690s, in London's many coffee houses.[30] The English artists' guild, the Painter-Stainers Company, does not seem to have been particularly active in helping artists sell their work, allowing on just one occasion their hall to be used for the sale of pictures – when, on 15 August 1654, "Mr Joshua Carpenter at this point made a notion [to the Painter-Stainers] that he might have leave to sell his pictures in the court roome".[31]

However, a well-established system for artists to sell their work at their studios certainly existed and it is very likely that, in the few years following his arrival in London, Lely's subject pictures were painted speculatively for and sold through Geldorp. Geldorp would have known, from the success of Van Poelenburgh's work

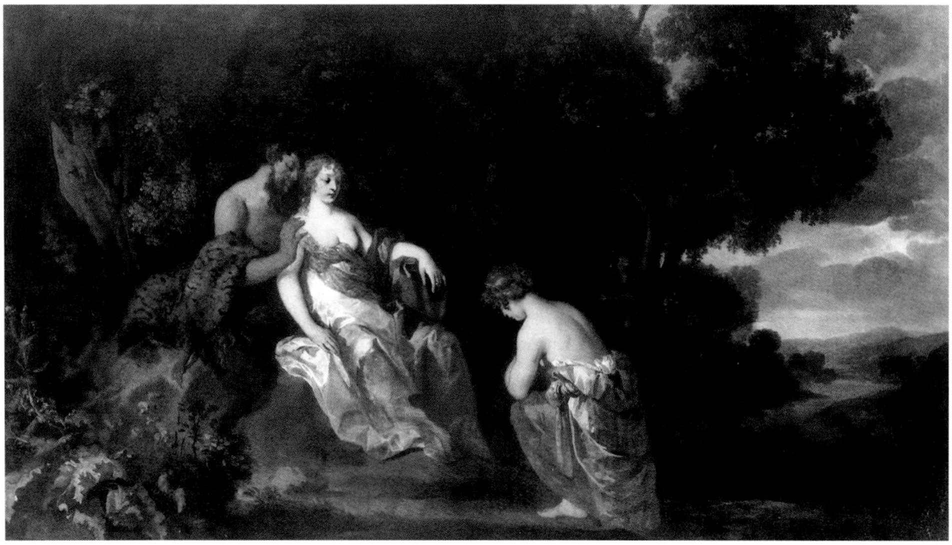

FIG. 21
Peter Lely (1618–1680)
An Idyll, *c.* 1650
Oil on canvas, 113 × 199.4 cm
Formerly collection of
Sir Edmund Davis
(destroyed during
World War II)

while he was in London, of the interest among aristocratic collectors for mythological landscapes and he may also have been aiming for a new and more socially diverse market through the sale of Lely's work. But Lely may also have produced these pictures in order to establish his own clientele, as works to be seen when potential patrons and sitters came to the studio. They would have helped to dress the studio appropriately, in the way that he did later, when he was wealthier and more established, using works from his collection – paintings by sixteenth-century Venetian artists as well as his Dutch and Flemish contemporaries, which may of course have also been available for purchase – to decorate the walls of his Covent Garden house.[32] This fits in very well with an existing Netherlandish tradition for which Rubens,[33] Frans Floris and Rembrandt all provide important reference points.

The Concert (cat. 7) is perhaps a perfect example of a 'show piece' that remained in the studio, with Lely working on it and returning to it over time and never in fact finishing it.[34] It shows a world of Giorgionesque leisure, a world of the senses, with Lely represented in a self-portrait in his artist's red cap appearing as the bass viol (five-stringed cello) player. Now generally accepted as an allegory of love and music,[35] it can also in retrospect stand for Lely's changing experiences as an artist during these early years in London. The left-hand side of the composition, with the theme of music, often depicted in Dutch painting, and its golden landscape, represents his career in Holland. In contrast, the right-hand side suggests a world of courtly sophistication and feminine beauty he was discovering at first hand in London in the work of Titian and Van Dyck. By the time this painting was at least started Lely had

FIG. 22
Peter Lely (1618–1680)
Arcadian scene with a nymph advancing towards a couple seated, c. 1650
Brush drawing in brown ink,
over red chalk on paper, 15.1 × 19 cm
The British Museum, London

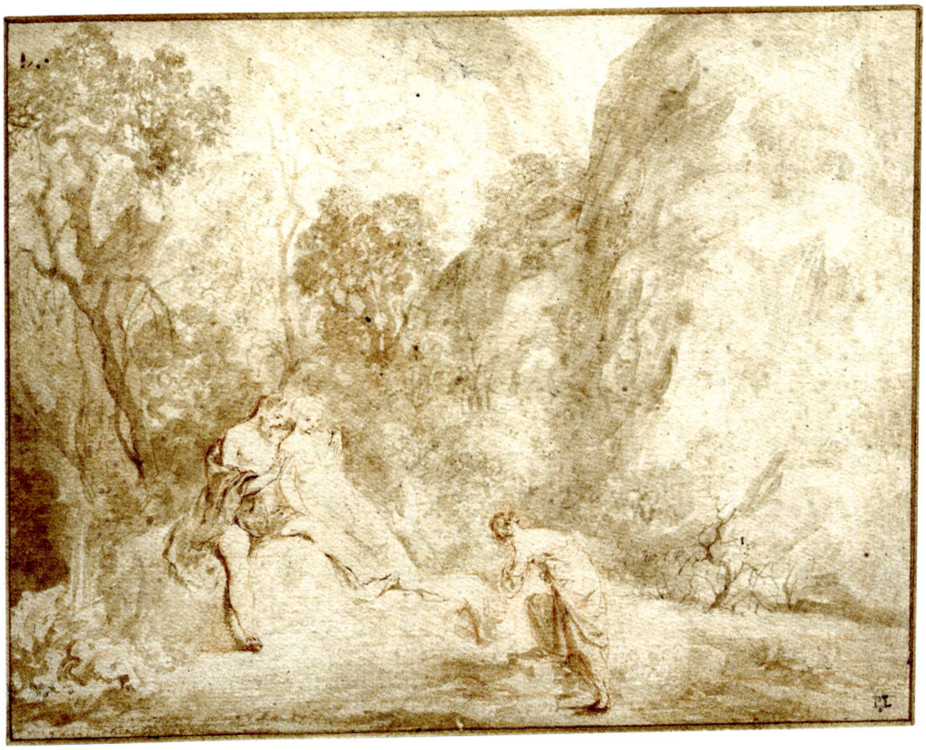

FIG. 23
Peter Lely (1618–1680)
The Finding of Moses, c. 1641
Brush drawing in brown ink,
over red chalk on paper, 15 × 18.2 cm
The British Museum, London

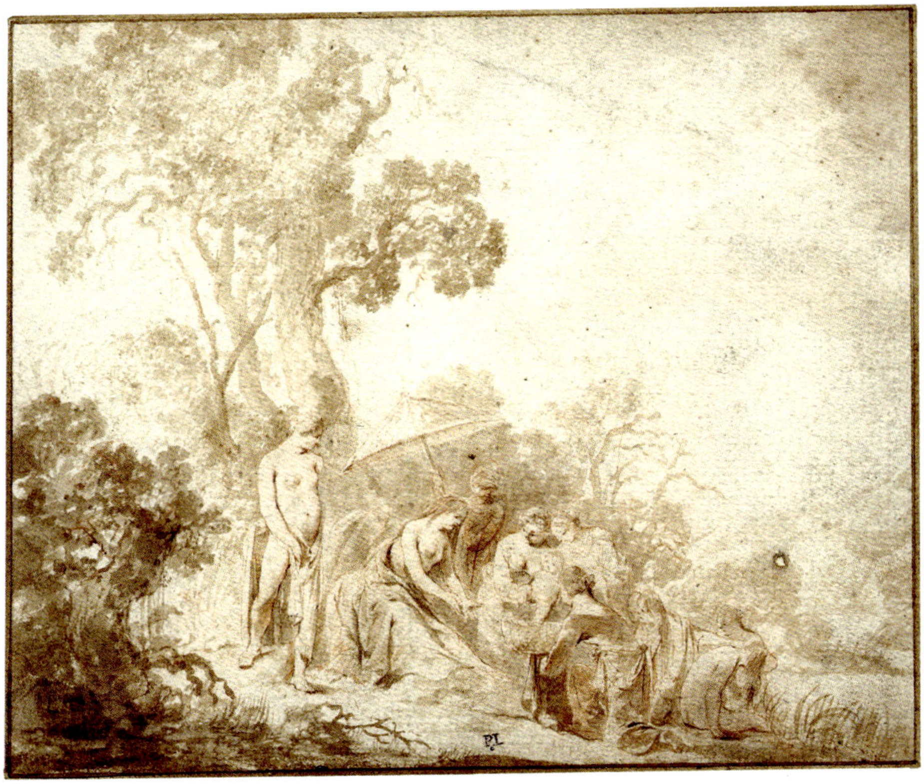

been introduced to the 10th Earl of Northumberland, an extremely important early patron, and would have been given access to his remarkable collection of works by Titian, Correggio, Rubens and most particularly Van Dyck, who was to have an important influence subsequently on his work as a portrait painter.[36]

A few of Lely's subject pictures, however, must have been special commissions, for example *Reuben presenting Mandrakes to Leah* (cat. 4), which depicts an unusual episode of the biblical story of Rachel and Leah. Perhaps it was intended to celebrate the birth of a long awaited child, a theme of personal relevance to the unknown patron. The musician pictures (including cat. 5 and 6) may have been painted as a set with a specific location in mind, for example a music room, but their provenance can only be established from the early eighteenth century, so again we can only speculate.[37]

There are at least two paintings, *The Finding of Moses* (cat. 1) and the now destroyed *Idyll* (fig. 21) that Lely appears to have painted after showing presentation drawings to potential buyers or patrons (figs. 22 and 23).[38] Although these carefully worked-up and finished drawings have previously been linked to the work of Van Poelenburgh and his circle, they share stylistic characteristics and similarities with other wash landscape drawings by Lely, for example one in the British Museum (fig. 13), particularly in the way the tree branches and river weeds are carefully and precisely rendered and the specific treatment of foliage. In the far left bottom corner of *The Finding of Moses* drawing, discernible only under strong light, is Lely's *PL* monogram in ligature; there is no monogram in the other drawing, though they are clearly by the same hand. On both sheets is a distinct *PL* mark, which was stamped posthumously on his drawings collection with almost obsessive care by Lely's executor, Roger North, so these drawings must have remained in Lely's possession throughout his career. North's stamping, a clever and successful marketing ploy, was more usually applied to individual drawings or prints by other artists, particularly sixteenth-century Italian ones, in Lely's extensive graphic collection, in readiness for their sale (the collection had to be sold to cover Lely's debts). Occasionally, however, as in this case, and perhaps by accident during the repetitive task of stamping over 10,000 sheets, North, who by his own admission was no drawings specialist, stamped Lely's own work.[39] Lely made some additions and changes between the drawings and the finished paintings: a classical building was added to the background in the *Finding of Moses*, the bearded man supporting the young woman in the *Idyll* became a satyr with the hairy left leg of a goat, and the parasol over the central group was removed. The drawings are

Detail of fig. 43

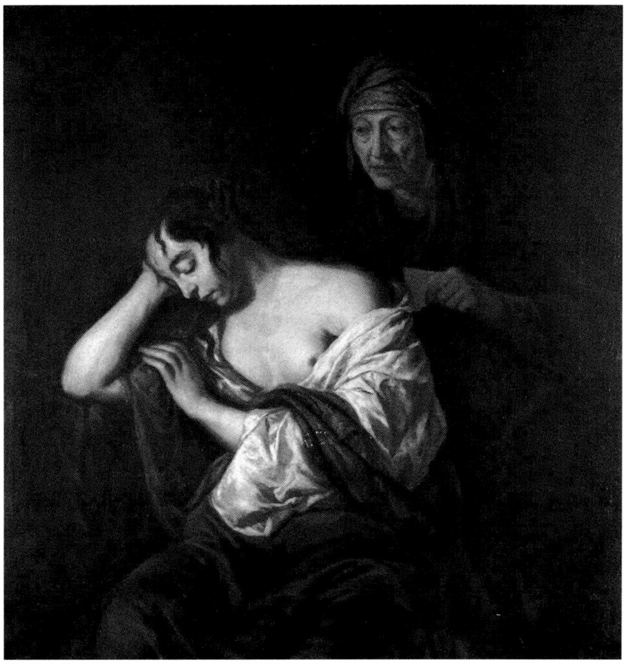

FIG. 24
Peter Lely (1618–1680)
Vertumnus and Pomona
(*A Lady and her Duenna*), *c.* 1650
Oil on canvas, 103.5 × 99 cm
Hatfield House, Hertfordshire

clearly the source for rather than a record of the paintings, and might have been intended as companion purchases for the same buyer,[40] although their different sizes make this rather unlikely.

By the later 1640s Lely was establishing his reputation as a portrait painter but, as in Holland, continued to produce subject pictures. Many of his potential 'competitors', such as Cornelius Johnson and William Dobson, had left London at the beginning of the Civil Wars (Johnson for Holland, Dobson for Oxford), which must have made it easier for Lely to make his mark during this period, and by the end of the 'first' Civil War in 1646 the economic situation in London had begun to improve.[41] Lely's early patrons included gentry and aristocrats of opposing political allegiances, from in and outside London, as well as unidentified sitters some of whom were probably friends and professional acquaintances. A number of these patrons, such as Elizabeth Dysart, then Lady Tollemache (fig. 43), maintained their patronage right throughout Lely's career. Others came through Geldorp's connections, for example the collector Edvard Jabach, whom he painted probably while he was in London for the sale of Charles I's pictures,[42] and the 10th Earl of Northumberland, who was responsible for two specific commissions which clearly signalled Lely's growing reputation – one indirectly in 1647 when Lely was commissioned by the now captive Charles I to paint a group portrait of three of the royal children, the Dukes of York, Gloucester and Princess Elizabeth (fig. 52), who were in Northumberland's care, and the second the

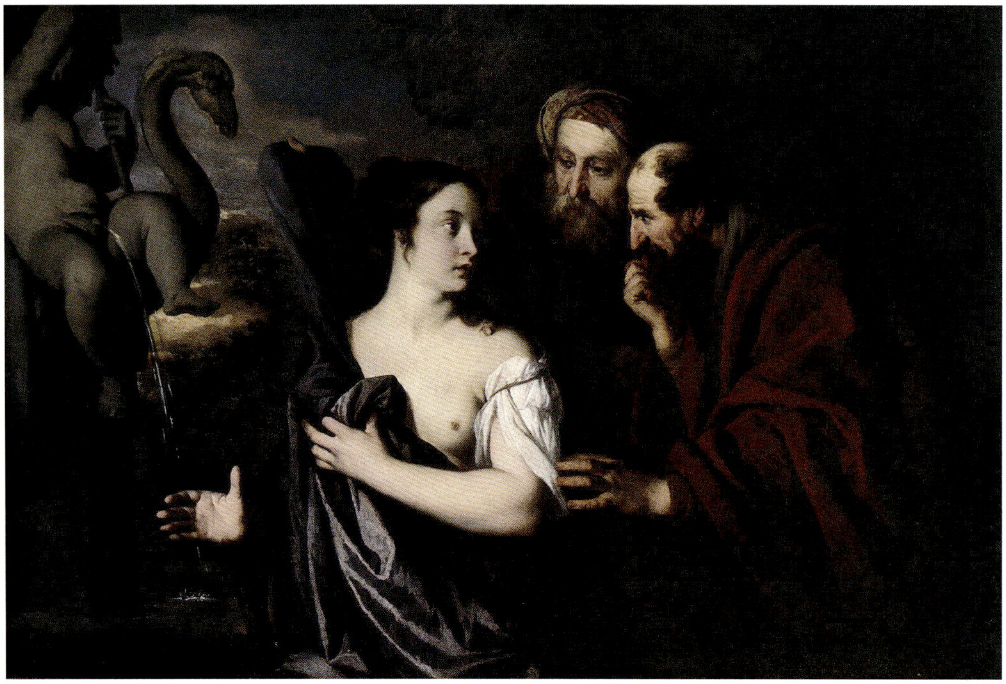

FIG. 25
Peter Lely (1618–1680)
Susanna and the Elders, *c.* 1648
Oil on canvas, 104.1 × 152.4 cm
Burghley House Collection, Lincolnshire

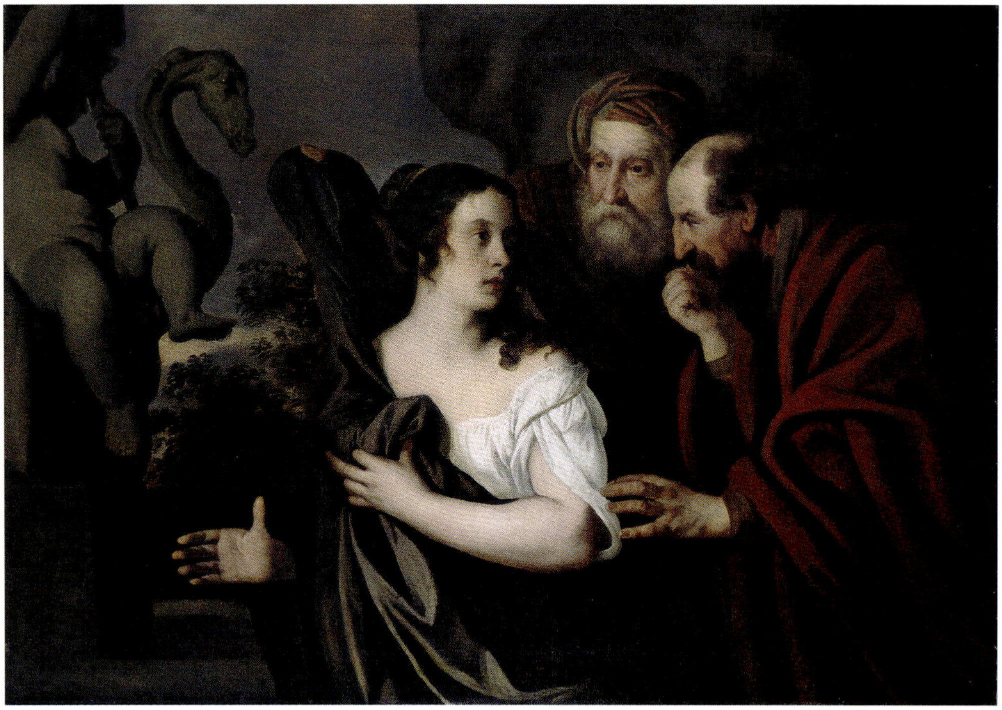

FIG. 26
Peter Lely (1618–1680)
Susanna and the Elders, *c.* 1650
Oil on canvas, 117 × 157.5 cm
Birmingham Museums and Art Gallery, Birmingham

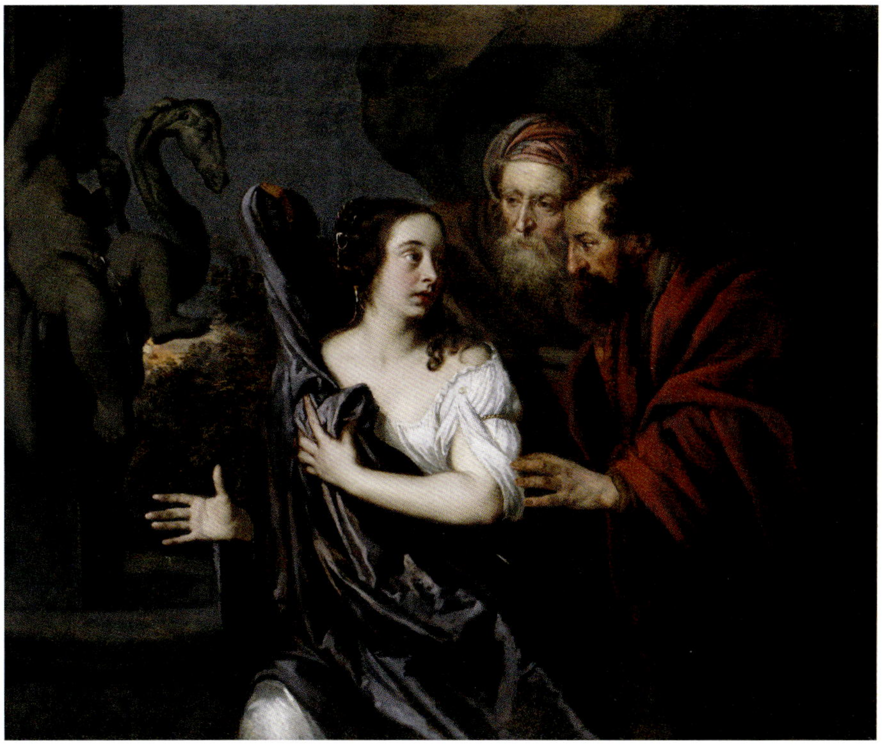

FIG. 27
Peter Lely (1618–1680)
Susanna and the Elders, *c.* 1650–55
Oil on canvas, 127 × 149.2 cm
Tate, London

following year, when Northumberland himself commissioned a double portrait of Charles I and James, Duke of York.[43] Other patrons came about when relatives recommended Lely to other members of their family or friends, for example the young Edward Montagu and his wife's family the Crewes. Within a few years Northumberland's brother-in-law Salisbury was to become a patron, commissioning from Lely portraits of himself and his wife.

Although a number of subject pictures are in the family collections of many of these early patrons, few were acquired at the time of their painting. For example Lely's *Vertumnus and Pomona*, also known as *A Lady and her Duenna* (fig. 24), still in the Salisbury collection, does not appear in the family inventories until the early nineteenth century,[44] and the *Infant Bacchus* (cat. 3) was seen by the antiquarian George Vertue at a sale of a Mr Collivoe's pictures in 1727, before it entered the Tollemache collection.[45] The earliest secure link we have between an early patron and one of Lely's subject pictures is in the late seventeenth century, when a *Susanna and the Elders* (fig. 25, one of three versions of this subject; the others are figs. 26 and 27) came to Burghley as part of the 1690 deed of gift from Elizabeth Cavendish, née Cecil, daughter of the 2nd Earl of Salisbury, to her own daughter, the 5th Countess of Exeter.[46]

LELY, THE PAINTER-STAINERS AND THE POET RICHARD LOVELACE

On 26 October 1647, Lely was admitted to the Painter-Stainers Company, which allowed him to work freely without the restrictions imposed on earlier Netherlandish artists and to take on apprentices.[47] The Painter-Stainers have often been portrayed as a reactive and xenophobic guild of painters, obsessed with exacting fines if members broke rules or forgot to pay their dues. They were certainly very conservative and made few if any attempts to provide training or professional encouragement to their members, unlike their counterparts in Holland. But like their Dutch counterparts they were anxious about out-of-towners and strangers taking work and opportunities from their members and took measures to prevent it. Geldorp had been one of a number of Netherlandish artists who had earlier fallen foul of the Company and been accused of threatening the livelihood of many of its members, and the Company's Court Minute Book records several complaints made against Geldorp and others in 1626 for this behaviour: "Certayne picture makers some freeman of our own Compayne and some free of other Compaynes desiring the Company to assist them in subpressing of certain strangers".[48] Lely's admittance over twenty years later suggests that the Painter-Stainers had become much more welcoming to 'stranger' artists, especially if it was felt these artists were settled in London and working with local painters. Lely either had sympathetic supporters or had sufficiently established himself within the artist community in London to be seen as an asset rather than a threat. He is rarely recorded in the Company's Minutes, so clearly was not very active within it, although he seems on the whole to have paid his dues regularly and remained a member all his life.

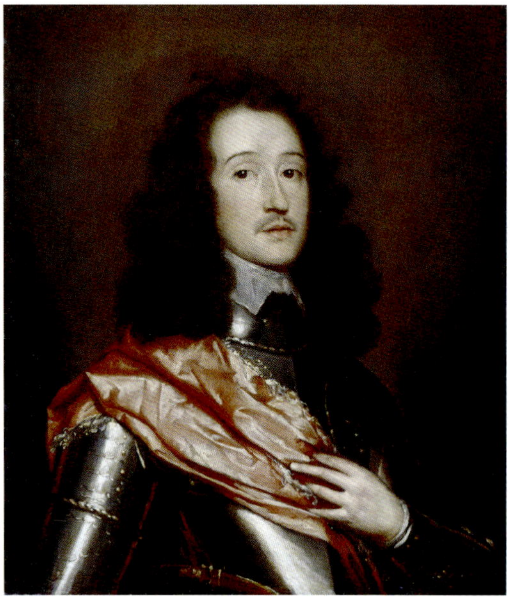

FIG. 28
William Dobson (1611–1646)
Richard Lovelace, c. 1645–6
Oil on canvas, 74.9 × 63.5 cm
Dulwich Picture Gallery, London

The poet Richard Lovelace (fig. 28) was admitted at the same time and he and Lely became good friends. Born in the same year, it is possible that the two met in Holland, where, according to John Tatham's poem 'Upon my Noble Friend Richard Lovelace', Lovelace travelled some time before 1645.[49] Lovelace's admittance to the Painter-Stainers does not necessarily mean he himself painted, as many guilds admitted members who were not specialists in their particular area – for example, some painters were members of the Goldsmith's Company – but, whether or not he had practical experience, he could certainly judge and discuss pictures eloquently, 'painting' with the words of the poet.[50] His poem 'To my Worthy Friend Peter Lely' (transcribed in full in an appendix in this volume), written in response to Northunberland's double portrait of Charles I and the Duke of York, praises Lely's skill as a painter.

It is a very astute and sympathetic reading of the picture, which Lovelace had clearly seen at first hand, indicating an understanding not just of painting itself but also of various art historical writings such as the works of Van Mander and Vasari.[51] In a later poem, 'Peinture. A Panegyrick to the best Picture of friendship. Mr Pet. Lilly', published posthumously in 1659 in the Lucasta series of poems, Lovelace recalls and admires other paintings by Lely, not portraits this time but pictures of Venus, Neptune, Echo and Cupid in landscapes:

> .... That pow'rful *Lilly*, now awakened, we
> This new Creation may behold by thee.
> To thy victorious pencil, all that Eyes
> And minds can reach, do bow; the Deities
> Bold *Poets* first but feign'd, you do, and make
> And from your awe they our Devotion take.
> Your beauteous Pallet first defin'd Loves Queen
> And made her in her heav'nly colours seen;
> You strung the Bow of the Bandite her Son,
> And tipp'd his Arrowes with religion.
> *Neptune*, as unknown as his Fish might dwell,
> But that you seat him in his throne of Shell.

And later:

> Who ere yet view'd Airs child invisible,
> A hollow Voice, but in thy subtile skill?
> Faint stamm'ring *Eccho*, you so draw, that we
> The very repercussion do see.[52]

This could of course be Lovelace's metaphorical response and reference to works he wants Lely and other artists to paint; the lack of interest and understanding, or what he refers to as "our transalpine barbarous Neglect" in the "un-understanding land" of England, becoming a metaphor for the threat of censorship of his own work by the Parliamentary authorities. But equally, as others have argued, these could be references to existing paintings by Lely, seen by Lovelace in his studio, which no longer survive or have yet to be traced.[53] We certainly have other references to similar paintings now lost: for example, a *Hero and Leander* by Lely was sold in the various sales after his death and his *Judgement of Paris* was reproduced as a mezzotint later in the seventeenth century by Bernard Lens senior, who, as Vertue recorded, "did a multitude of Plate Mezzotint . . . mostly small figures Landskips histories".[54]

SLEEPING NYMPHS AND DRAWING FROM LIFE

The 1650s, the decade of Commonwealth government, saw Lely become increasingly busy, producing what are arguably his most sympathetic and psychologically interesting portraits. In November 1652 he was granted permission by the Painter-Stainers to take on an apprentice,[55] although he had, for a number of years previously, employed an assistant, for example Robert Hooke, the future architect, who worked briefly for him in 1648. By 1650 he was living in the house in the Great Piazza in Covent Garden in which he would continue to live until his death in 1680 and which he shared with fellow Dutch artist Tobias Flushier and the English architect Hugh May.[56] His association with Geldorp continued probably until Geldorp's death in 1665, and in 1653 he, Geldorp and fellow Dutch artist Balthasar Gerbier ambitiously, but unsuccessfully, petitioned Parliament to commission them to produce for Whitehall a series of wall paintings and portraits celebrating Parliamentary victories in the Civil War – "the most remarkablest Battails and the most considerablest Sieges of Towns . . . beset with the Portraitures of . . . Generals and Commanders".[57]

During this period Lely continued to produce subject pictures. He revisited the theme of Susanna and the Elders that he had first depicted in 1648, producing two further, slightly different versions (figs. 26 and 27), and he painted a number of other biblical subjects, for example *Judith with the Head of Holofernes* (Baroda collection) and *Mary Magdalen* (fig. 56); in all these the figures, rather than the landscape, now become the focal point. He also returned to the theme of nymphs, first in *Cimon and Efigenia* (cat. 11) – he had produced an earlier painting of this same subject, which is at Knole (fig. 58) – and finally in his last known subject picture, undeniably the most sensuous painting produced in seventeenth-century England, *Nymphs by a Fountain* (cat. 9). Sleeping women or sleeping nymphs, with their association of vulnerability, death and dreams, had been a recurring visual theme since antiquity,[58] and became particularly popular in the sixteenth century in Venetian painting and in the seventeenth century in the work for example of Rubens and Van Dyck, whose *Cupid and Psyche*, formerly in the royal collection, was still in Lely's possession at this point (fig. 5).

In *Cimon and Efigenia*, the simpleton shepherd in Boccaccio's tale, enraptured by Efigenia's beauty, becomes the viewer's intermediary as he gazes on the sleeping women, while in the *Nymphs by a Fountain* the voyeur becomes the artist himself, with the

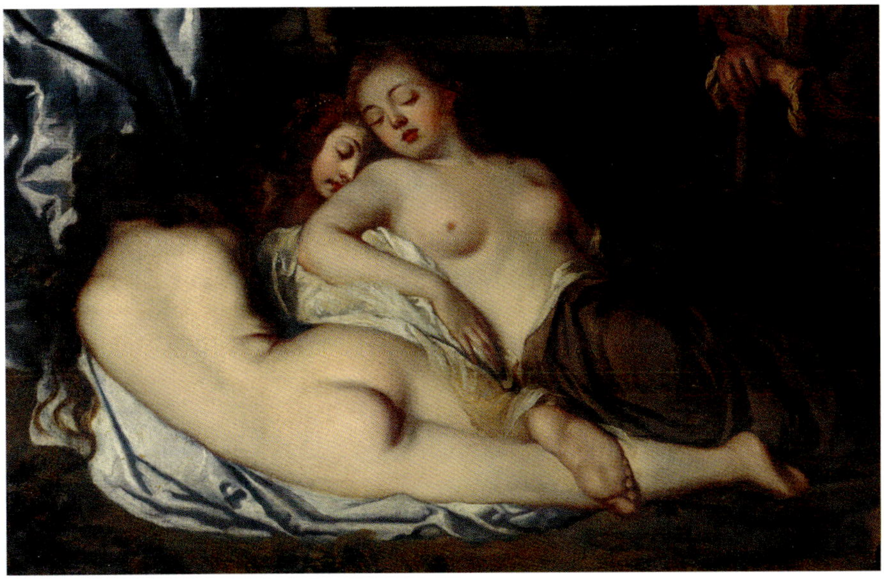

Detail of cat. 11

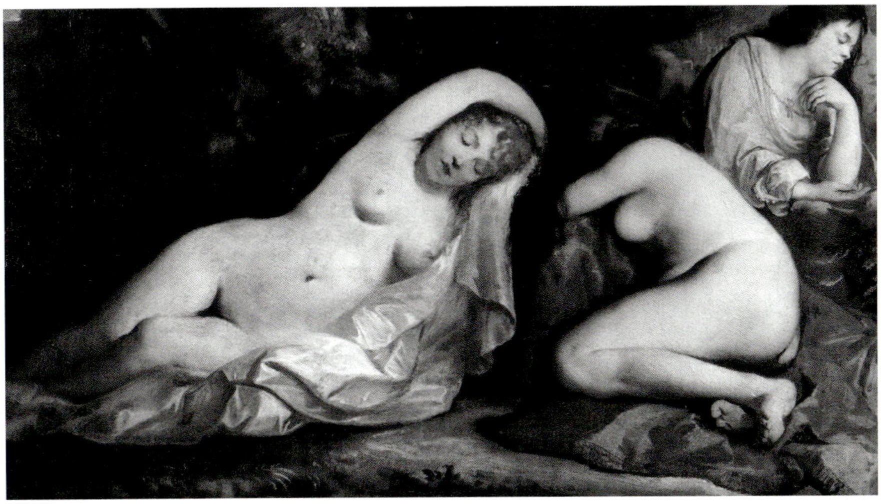

Detail of fig. 58

traditional exchange of male viewer and female viewed confused by the ambiguous gender of the right-hand sleeping figure. Compositionally there are strong similarities with other Dutch works, for example a *Nymphs sleeping* by Van Loo (fig. 54), but the forms of Lely's nymphs, so unlike the meagre, almost undeveloped bodies of his earlier bathing figures, owe a great deal to the study of the live model. Later in his career Lely seems to have organised an informal drawing school at his Covent Garden studio, encouraging his assistants and other young artists – in true Continental art academy style – to draw from casts and Old Master drawings and prints and from the live model. A drawing of a nude sleeping figure seen from the back (fig. 57), which relates to the second and later

Cimon and Efigenia, suggests that he was already making studies from life in the 1650s. On the evidence of this, of his later practical encouragement of life drawing and his strong conviction that "painting is nought but draught", it is very probable that Lely was one of the artists behind the application to the Painter-Stainers in early 1657 to initiate a life-drawing class. On 24 January 1656 (OS) a request was made to the Court of the Painter-Stainers to use the "Lower Parlour of the Guildhall for an attendance to make use of drawing by the life". Three weeks later the court ruled "that there shall be noe meetinge of any members of the Company or applying to the Guildhall whereby to keepe an Academie in any parte thereof for drawing to the life".[59] Putting aside the Painter-Stainers' default conservatism, there were strict rules even within the various official European academies about life drawing, and female nude models were not permitted in them until the nineteenth century. Within the more private studio environment, however, female models were used much earlier. Lely was certainly using a number of different female models during this time: for example, the model used for *Mary Magdalen* also posed for the sleeping girl in *Vertumnus and Pomona* (fig. 24) and the far right-hand figure in *The Rape of Europa* (cat. 10). Europa herself is the same model as that in the finished pastel head-and-shoulders drawing of a *Young Girl* (private collection), and the *Portrait of a Lady* (fig. 50), it has been pointed out, is very similar to Susanna in the *Susanna and the Elders* paintings.[60] It has also been suggested, very plausibly, that the models for his musician paintings were from Lely's circle of personal friends.[61]

In 1657, when William Sanderson published his *Graphice: Or the Art of Pen and Pensil*, he referred to Lely solely as a portrait painter, and no known subject pictures seem to have been produced after that date. Lovelace had railed against the ignorance of "an un-understanding land", but Richard Graham was much more calmly matter-of-fact, noting that Lely "finding the Practice of Painting after the Life generally more encourag'd he apply'd himself to Portraits". Clearly, there was only a limited interest in subject pictures, the earlier positive reception of Van Poelenburgh's cabinet-size paintings seemingly reserved for aristocratic circles. During the early 1640s William Dobson produced two paintings depicting biblical themes, a *Woman taken in Adultery* and a *Beheading of Saint John the Baptist*[62] (in fact a copy after Stomer),[63] which Lely allegedly particularly admired,[64] as well as an allegory of *The Civil Wars of France* (private collection, England), engraved as the frontispiece to the translation of D'Avila's *Istoria delle Guerre Civili di Francia*;[65] but the majority of Dobson's works were portraits. In the 1650s and 1660s Isaac Fuller painted a number of pictures of satyrs and Venus, Mercury, Pallas, Diana, Apollo and Bacchus for the Mitre Tavern in Fenchurch Street, as well as *The Resurrection* for All Souls' Chapel in Oxford.[66] But these were decorative *in situ* pieces, not portable works to hang in a domestic setting, as were the paintings by Emmanuel de Critz and Edward Pierce produced for Wilton House during the 1650s illustrating scenes from Sidney's *Arcadia* or after prints by Tempesta and Polidoro da Caravaggio.

In his 1951 monograph on Lely, R.B Beckett wrote that "Lely may, of course, have filled in his time for a while with his 'land-scapes with figures'; but even of these there is no great number, and none which can be assigned to a particular year".[67] We now know of about thirty-five subject pictures (including the musician paintings), a few of which are inscribed with dates. The fact that a number of versions were produced of particular subjects, for example *Susanna and the Elders* and *Vertumnus and Pomona*, prove there was certainly interest in some of these works. Others remained in the studio but must eventually have found buyers as they were not included in the 1682 posthumous sale. In contrast, *The Rape of Europa* (cat. 10) never seems to have been sold during Lely's lifetime, remaining as part of his stock of paintings before being purchased by his executor Roger North, who then sold it on to Lely's son – "Bought and parted with againe The Europa of Sr P.Lely to his son".[68]

Rather than simply "filling in his time", it seems Lely continued to work very much as a Dutch painter when he first arrived in England, combining art dealing with painting and using his subject pictures to help generate income, provide an appropriate studio environment and build up his clientele during the difficult and unpredictable years of the Civil Wars. He adroitly integrated himself within the wider London community and made contacts with influential supporters and potential patrons. All artists during this period had to respond to the interests of patrons and the market and focus on what would sell. For Lely his landscapes with figures and histories were, for the most part, though not entirely, a means to a further end. By 1654 he was described as "the best artist in England";[69] however, as far as many English contemporaries were concerned, this reputation had relatively little to do with his subject pictures.

NOTES

Acknowledgments: I would like to thank Charles Ford, Catharine MacLeod and Jeremy Wood for their helpful comments and advice during the preparation of this essay.

1 Horace Walpole, *Anecdotes of Painting*, Twickenham, 1761–71, vol. III, p. 18.

2 Richard Graham, 'A Short Account of Ancient and Modern Painters', in Charles-Alphonse Du Fresnoy, *The Art of Painting /De Arte Graphica*, London, 1695, pp. 343–44.

3 In the October–November 1637 minutes of the Haarlem guild Lely was listed as a pupil of De Grebber.

4 For a discussion of the social and economic as well as artistic situation in Haarlem see Frima Fox Hofrichter, ed., *Haarlem: The Seventeenth Century*, exh. cat., Jane Voorhees Zimmerli Art Museum, Rutgers University, Newark NJ, 1983.

5 Letter dated 17 March 1618, Rubens to Dudley Carleton, in Max Roose and Charles Ruelens, *Correspondance de Rubens*, Antwerp, 1898, vol. II (1609–25 July 1622), p. 131.

6 Neil B. De Marchi and Hans van Miegroet, 'Art, Value and Market Practices in the Netherlands in the Seventeenth Century', *The Art Bulletin*, vol. 76, no. 3, September 1994, p. 458 n. 55.

7 Arnold Houbraken, *De groote schouburgh der Nederlantsche konstschilders en schilderessen*, 's Gravenhage (J. Swart, C. Boucquet and M. Galliard) 1753, vol. II, pp. 41–48.

8 Albert Blankert, in *Gods, Saints and Heroes. Dutch Painting in the Age of Rembrandt*, exh. cat., National Gallery of Art, Washington DC, the Detroit Institute of Arts and Rijksmuseum, Amsterdam 1981, p. 17, citing Karel Van Mander, *Het Schilder-Boeck*, Haarlem, 1604, chapter 8, 'Grondt'.

9 Willem van de Watering, in Gilles Aillaud, Albert Blankert and John Michael Montias, *Vermeer*, Amsterdam, 1992, p. 193.

10 See Linda Levy Peck, 'Luxury and War, 1640–1660', in *Consuming Splendour. Society and Culture in Seventeenth-Century England*, Cambridge, 2005, pp. 230–76.

11 Pieter Biesboer, 'Collections of paintings in Haarlem 1572–1745' (Documents for the History of Collecting: Netherlandish Inventories, I, ed. Carol Togneri), Los Angeles, 2001; also its review by Jaap van der Veen in *Simiolus*, vol. 31, no. 1 / 2, 2004–05, pp. 111–15.

12 Abraham Bredius, *Kunstler-Inventaire. Urkunden zur Geschichte der Hollandischen Kunst des XVI, XVII and XVIII Jahrhunderts*, The Hague, 1915–22, vol. II, pp. 493, 504, 516, 520, which contains references, in the 1647 register of The Hague Guild of Painters, of sales of paintings. I am grateful to An van Camp, Curator of Dutch and Flemish Drawings in the Print Room at the British Museum, for help with translation.

13 For Lely as a collector see 'Editorial: Sir Peter Lely's Collection', *Burlington Magazine*, LXXXIII, 1943, pp. 185–91, and Diana Dethloff, 'The Executors' Account Book and the Dispersal of Sir Peter Lely's Collection', *Journal of the History of Collections*, vol. 8, no. 1, 1996, pp. 15–51; as a dealer see Friso Lammertse and Jaap van der Veen, *Uylenburgh & Son. Art and Commerce from Rembrandt to De Lairesse 1625–1675*, exh. cat., Dulwich Picture Gallery, London, and Rembrandthuis, Amsterdam, 2006, pp. 263–72, and Alastair Laing, 'Sir Peter Lely and Ralph Bankes', in *Art and Patronage in the Caroline Court: Essays in Honour of Sir Oliver Millar*, ed. David Howarth, Cambridge, 1993, pp. 107–33.

14 George Vertue, 'Notebooks: I', *The Walpole Society*, XVIII, 1929–30, p. 74; also Oliver Millar, 'Geldorp' in *Grove Art Online*.

15 BM Add. MS 10112, f. 17, published in 'Abraham van der Doort's Catalogue of the Collections of Charles I', introduction by Oliver Millar, *The Walpole Society*, XXXVII, 1958–60.

16 Vertue 1929–50, XVIII (1929–30), p. 74.

17 *Ibid.*, p. 116.

18 Vertue 1929–50, XX (1931–32) p. 97.

19 Jeremy Wood, 'Van Dyck and the Earl of Northumberland: Taste and Collecting in Stuart England', in Susan Barnes and Arthur Wheelock, eds., *Van Dyck 350* (Studies in the History of Art 46. Center for the Advanced Study in the Visual Arts. Symposium Papers XXVI), Washington DC, 1994, pp. 281–324.

20 See Jacob Simon's online directory of seventeenth-century artists, restorers, suppliers and framemakers on the National Portrait Gallery website, http://www.npg.org.uk/research/conservation/directory-of-british-framemakers/g.php.

21 See Francis Haskell, 'Charles I's Collection of Pictures', in Arthur MacGregor, ed., *The Late King's Goods*, Oxford, 1989, pp. 203–31.

22 In total eight pictures, including Van Dyck's *Cupid and Psyche* and *Three Eldest Children of Charles I* and Ter Bruggen's *Musician*, plus a number of pieces of sculpture and frames. It is interesting that Lely did not sell on any of these purchases, suggesting that in this instance his artist-collector interests prevailed over those of the dealer and that financially he could afford to retain these prestigious works.

23 See Stephen Gleissner, 'Reassembling a Royal Art Collection for the Restored King of Great Britain', *Journal of the History of Collections*, vol. 6, no. 1, 1994, pp. 103–15.

24 Johannes Rein ter Molen, *Van Vianen: een Utrechtse familie van zilversmeden met een internationale faam*, PhD thesis, Leiden University, 1983, cited in Ronald Lightbown, 'Charles I and the Art of the Goldsmith', in MacGregor 1989, p. 255 n. 7.

25 David Ormrod, *The Dutch in London. The Influence of an Immigrant Community 1550–1800*, London, Her Majesty's Stationery Office, 1973, unpaginated.

26 British Library, Egerton 2713, vol. 1, f. 5.

27 Lodewijck Huygens, a member of the Ambassadors' entourage during a special mission of Dutch diplomats to England in 1651, was advised by his father Constantijn Huygens that to learn English "promptly and well, conversations with ladies" would be very good for him as "ladies will inform him about all kinds of minutiae of which the dictionaries make no mention": Koninklijke Bibliotheek, The Hague, K.A.XLVI, pp. 390–91, cited in *Lodewijck Huygens. The English Journal 1651–1652*, ed. and trans. Alfred G.H. Bachrach and R.G. Collmer, Leiden University Press, 1982, p. 5. See also Jeremy Wood, 'Orazio Gentileschi and Some Netherlandish Artists in London: the Patronage of the Duke of Buckingham, Charles I and Henrietta Maria', *Simiolus*, vol. 28, no. 3, 2000–01, pp. 103–28, for a discussion of the problems of language and integration amongst artists in 1620s and 1630s London.

28 There is an extensive and excellent literature on the Dutch art market; the following were particularly relevant: Neil B. De Marchi and Hans Van Miegroet, 'Art, Value, and Market Practises in the Seventeeth Century Netherlands', *Art Bulletin*, XXVI, 1994, pp. 451–64, note 6; M. Prak, 'Guilds and the Development of the Art Market during the Dutch Golden Age', *Simiolus*, XXX, nos. 3/4, 2003, pp. 236–51, and John Michael Montias, 'Art Dealers in the Seventeenth-Century Netherlands', *Simiolus*, XVIII, no. 4, 1988, pp. 244–56.

29 For example, ongoing work by Edward Towne as part of the Making Art in Tudor Britain project.

30 Brian Cowan, 'Arenas of Connoisseurship: Auctioning Art in Later Stuart England', in *Art Markets in Europe 1400–1800*, ed. Michael North and David Ormrod, Basingstoke 1998, Chapter 12.

31 Painter-Stainers Court Minute Book 1649–1723, MS 5667/2, Guildhall Library.

32 *The Diary of Samuel Pepys*, ed. Robert C. Latham and William Matthews, London, 1995, vol. VII, p. 102 (18 April 1666).

33 Elizabeth McGrath, 'The Painted Decoration of Rubens's House', *Journal of the Warburg and Courtauld Institutes*, XLI, 1978, pp. 245–77.

34 I am grateful to Charles Ford for a very helpful conversation about this.

35 See Oliver Millar, *Sir Peter Lely*, exh. cat., National Portrait Gallery, London 1978–79, p. 40, no. 11.

36 See Wood 1994, note 19.

37 See London 1978–79, p. 41, no. 12. Although these pictures were in the Craven collection in 1739, there is no evidence, as Millar points out, to link these paintings with the 1st Earl Craven, who is also sometimes identified as the central figure in Lely's now much damaged *An Allegory of Love* (here fig. 35).

38 I am grateful to An van Camp, Stephen Coppel and Jeremy Wood for confirming my opinion and for a very helpful discussion when we looked at these drawings together.

39 See Diana Dethloff, 'Sir Peter Lely's collection of prints and drawings', in *Collecting Prints & Drawings in Europe c. 1500–1750*, ed. C. Baker, C. Elam and G. Warwick, Aldershot, 2003, pp. 123–39.

40 As suggested by Jeremy Wood in a conversation with the author.

41 Levy Peck 2005, note 19.

42 Lely painted two portraits of Jabach, both now in the Wallraf-Richartz Museum, Cologne (WRM 1041 and 1042).

43 Wood 1994, note 19.

44 Erna Auerbach and Charles Kingsley Adams, *Paintings & Sculpture at Hatfield House*, London, 1971, no. 359, p. 237.

45 Vertue 1929–50, XX (1931–32), p. 23.

46 Information kindly supplied by John Culverhouse, curator at Burghley, who suggests that the picture may have been part of Elizabeth Cavendish, neé Cecil's dowry or left to her by her father, 2nd Earl of Salisbury.

47 Painter-Stainers Court Minute Book (see note 31), f. 221.

48 *Ibid.*, ff. 28–29.

49 John Tatham, *Ostella*, 1650, pp. 82–83, cited in Raymond A. Anselment, 'Lovelace, Richard (1617–1657), in *Oxford Dictionary of National Biography*, Oxford University Press, Oxford, 2004.

50 See 'Richard Lovelace, Edmund Waller and the Flowering of English Art', in Norman K. Farmer Jnr, *Poets and the Visual Arts in Renaissance England*, Austin TX, 1984, p. 54.

51 For two excellent discussions of this picture see Raymond A. Anselment, '"Clouded Majesty": Richard Lovelace, Sir Peter Lely, and the Royalist Spirit', *Studies in Philology*, LXXXVI, no. 3, Summer 1999, pp. 367–87; and Frances Harris, 'An ambivalent image: Lely's double-portrait of Charles I and the Duke of York', *Burlington Magazine*, CXLIX, March 2007, pp. 180–82.

52 Transcribed in Farmer 1984, pp. 58–59 n. 50.

53 *Ibid.*

54 Vertue 1929–50, XXIV (1935–36), p. 184.

55 *Painter-Stainers*, *op. cit.*, note 31, f. 22r, 18 November 1652.

56 Rate Books for the Westminster area, cited by Millar in London 1978–79, note 21, p. 28.

57 BL, Miscellaneous Historical Papers, Stowe MS 184, f. 283.

58 See Udo Kultermann, 'Women Asleep and the Artist', *Artibus et Historiae*, II, no. 22 (1990), pp. 129–61.

59 Painter-Stainers Court Minute Book (see note 31), f. 46r, 18 February 1656.

60 London 1978–79, p. 34, no. 3.

61 *Ibid.*, p. 42, no. 14.

62 Vertue 1929–50, XXIV (1935–36), pp. 19 and 53.

63 Malcolm Rogers, *William Dobson 1611–46*, exh. cat., National Portrait Gallery, London, 1984, p. 27, no. 4.

64 Vertue 1929–50, XXIV (1935–36), p. 19 n. 52.

65 London 1984, p. 73, no. 34.

66 Vertue 1929–50, XVIII (1929–30), pp. 101, 135.

67 R.B. Beckett, *Lely*, London, 1951, p. 8.

68 BL, Add MS 32, 504, f. 49.

69 James Waynwright writing to Mr Bradshaw, 6 October 1654, M.M.C. Sixth report, I (1887), 437b–38a.

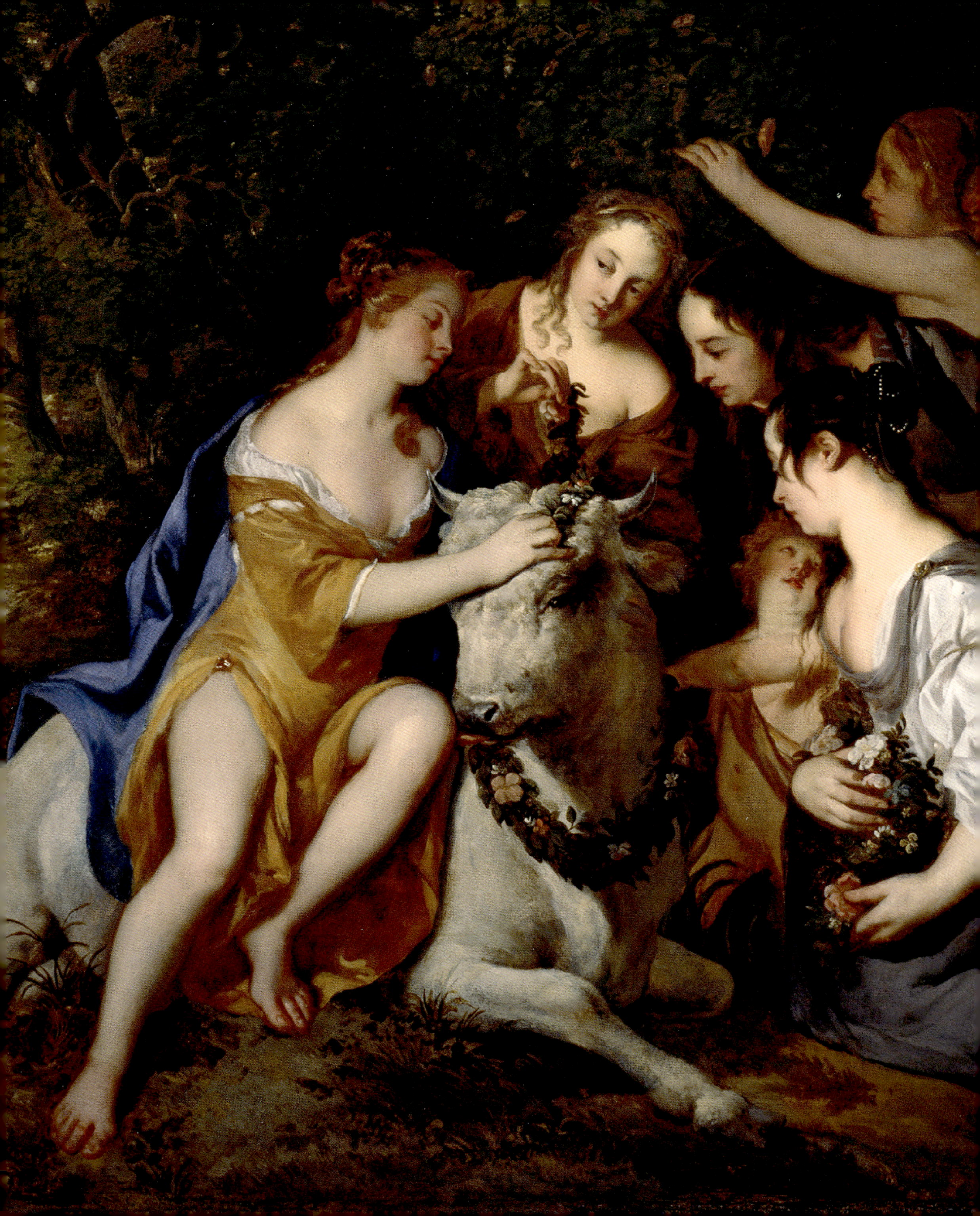

Lely in Arcadia: Religious, pastoral, musical and mythological themes in Peter Lely's subject pictures

DAVID A.H.B. TAYLOR

Ye goat-herd gods, that love the grassy mountains
Ye nymphs that haunt the springs in pleasant valleys
Ye satyrs joy'd with free and quiet forests ...
Sir Philip Sidney, *The Countess of Pembroke's Arcadia* (1593)

THE SUBJECTS OF THE SUBJECT PICTURES

According to Richard Graham's 1695 account Peter Lely was a painter of "*Landtschapes* with *small Figures*, and Historical *Compositions*" when he arrived in England in the early 1640s, but "finding the practice of *Painting after the Life* generally more encourag'd, he apply'd himself to *Portraits*".[1] This account, emphasising Lely's training and experience in Holland before he discovered that the taste of those who commissioned and collected new pictures in his adopted country was predominantly for portraiture, has often been repeated, perpetuating the idea that the English were somehow against purchasing and displaying subject pictures, which was certainly not the case. Charles I and his courtiers bought plenty of pictures with 'landscapes with small figures' and English collectors appear to have appreciated the Flemish and, in particular, Dutch *kabinetstukken* or 'cabinet pieces' which they displayed in rooms of their houses devoted to that purpose, as well as larger versions of these subject pictures. Moreover, even if the English especially liked portraiture, and Lely would go on to become one of the most celebrated of 'English' portrait painters, he also produced a number of subject pictures, most of which, it would appear, were painted in England, though before he began his portrait painting career in earnest.[2] Evidently the ever business-minded and realistic Lely saw a lucrative opportunity in satisfying a ready English demand for portraits, but R.B. Beckett, in his 1951 monograph on

Detail of cat. 10

Lely, believed that the subject pictures were "of importance as suggesting that Lely's natural bent may have been towards a decorative story-telling type of picture, in an outdoor setting, and that portraiture may have been forced upon him by circumstance as his main occupation".[3]

There are around thirty subject pictures by Lely that are currently known, constituting a largely forgotten and neglected section of his oeuvre. These paintings, despite their differing dimensions and compositional formats, can be subdivided into identifiable subject groups, ranging from religious to pastoral, musical and mythological works. Indeed they are not easy to read as a visually coherent group, and they leave us with more questions than answers regarding the beginnings of Lely's English career. For example, we know little about the early provenances of the subject pictures, or indeed whether they were painted as specific commissions or for the art market. Were they part of an exercise Lely undertook in order to establish himself in England in the first place as a dealer (producing stock for potential clients) – an occupation he was certainly also involved in?[4] The production of these pictures seems to peter out before the Restoration of 1660 and Lely's speedy appointment as Charles II's Principal Painter soon after. Did Lely himself lose interest in producing subject pictures, or did he, as his friend the poet Richard Lovelace wrote in '*Peinture. A Panegyrick to the best Picture of Friendship, Mr.* Pet. Lilly', find that in England, an "un-understanding land", rich patrons would only "their own dull counterfeits adore"?[5]

Among the subject pictures that Lely did produce there are two common themes. The majority are set in a timeless Arcadian landscape, with figures positioned in dark glades around rocky outcrops, next to fountains or bodies of natural water, and usually posed in or at the edge of a forest, a wild, natural setting seemingly far from a corrupt society. There is also a clear sexual element to most of the pictures, notably the erotically charged, gendered pastoral scenes, and including canvases littered with naked or near-naked women, as well as men, satyrs, nymphs and classical and religious figures.

Of the currently identifiable twenty-nine subject pictures by Lely (individual compositions, not counting versions and copies) eight are religious, another eight are pastoral, seven are musical, and the remaining six are mythological. Lely would sometimes paint more than one composition of the same story or theme; of the eight religious pictures, there are two different compositions depicting the Finding of Moses and two different Mary Magdalen types; five of the six pastoral paintings are of nymphs (and four of these pictures show the nymphs next to a fountain or bathing); and two of the six mythological pictures show the story of Cimon and Efigenia. The religious, pastoral and mythological pictures mostly conform to the 'landscape with small figures' format, while the images of musicians generally depict a single figure, at three-quarter or half-length, predominating in an otherwise plain and dark canvas.

PAINTERLY AND LITERARY INFLUENCES

The main influences on Lely's subject pictures were Dutch and Flemish paintings, both antecedents and contemporary works, as might be expected. These included works by the celebrated Anthony van Dyck, whose pastoral masterpiece, *Cupid and Psyche* (fig. 5), was bought by Lely at the dispersal of the royal collection following Charles I's downfall, and he was probably familiar with the painting beforehand. Among Lely's various images of sleeping women in the subject pictures, the central character in *Nymphs by a Fountain* (cat. 9) is clearly reminiscent of Van Dyck's Psyche. But Lely also took inspiration from Italian paintings. He built up one of the finest collections of paintings, prints and drawings in England and it included many Italian works, including pictures by the great Venetian artists Titian and Veronese. Both these painters influenced aspects of Lely's subject pictures, especially their compositions and colour schemes. Lely's knowledge of Titian can be seen again in his *Nymphs by a Fountain*, where the figure of the sleeping nymph in the background recalls the naked nymph at the front of *The Andrians* (fig. 29). Veronese's *Rape of Europa* (fig. 30) prefigures Lely's *Rape of Europa* (cat. 10), with its recumbent and garlanded bull licking the seduced Europa and figures and trees predominating on one side of the canvas, creating a stage-like scene with a seascape in the left background.

Among the Northern Netherlandish influences were works by artists who, like Lely, had travelled to England and produced pictures there. The most notable of these was the Utrecht painter Cornelis van Poelenburgh, who painted Italianate 'landscapes with figures' cabinet pictures, mostly on copper.[6] Van Poelenburgh, like Lely after him, would paint images of nymphs and satyrs "not illustrating a specific subject but rather providing a scene for the pleasure of the spectator".[7] Bartholomeus Breenburgh, an associate of Van Poelenburgh, was another artist whose work Lely would have known, for example the pictures in the Dysart collection at Ham House. Lely certainly acquired an intimate knowledge of the pastoral works of many Netherlandish artists after he moved to England, among them Nicolaes Berchem, the sale of whose

Landscape with Herdsmen to Sir Ralph Bankes (National Trust, Kingston Lacy) was negotiated by Lely.

The majority of Lely's subject pictures show figures from literary sources. Biblical stories are the most frequent, with depictions of Moses, Reuben, Susanna and Jacob from the Old Testament and Mary Magdalen from the New. After the Bible, Ovid's *Metamorphoses*, of which there were many translations and editions, often illustrated, in the seventeenth century, provided the largest group of figures. Lely depicted scenes from the tales of Vertumnus and Pomona and Europa and the Bull, both popular and well-known stories. Giovanni Boccaccio's fourteenth-century masterpiece, *The Decameron*, provided the source for Lely's two versions of the story of Cimon and Efigenia. The story had been

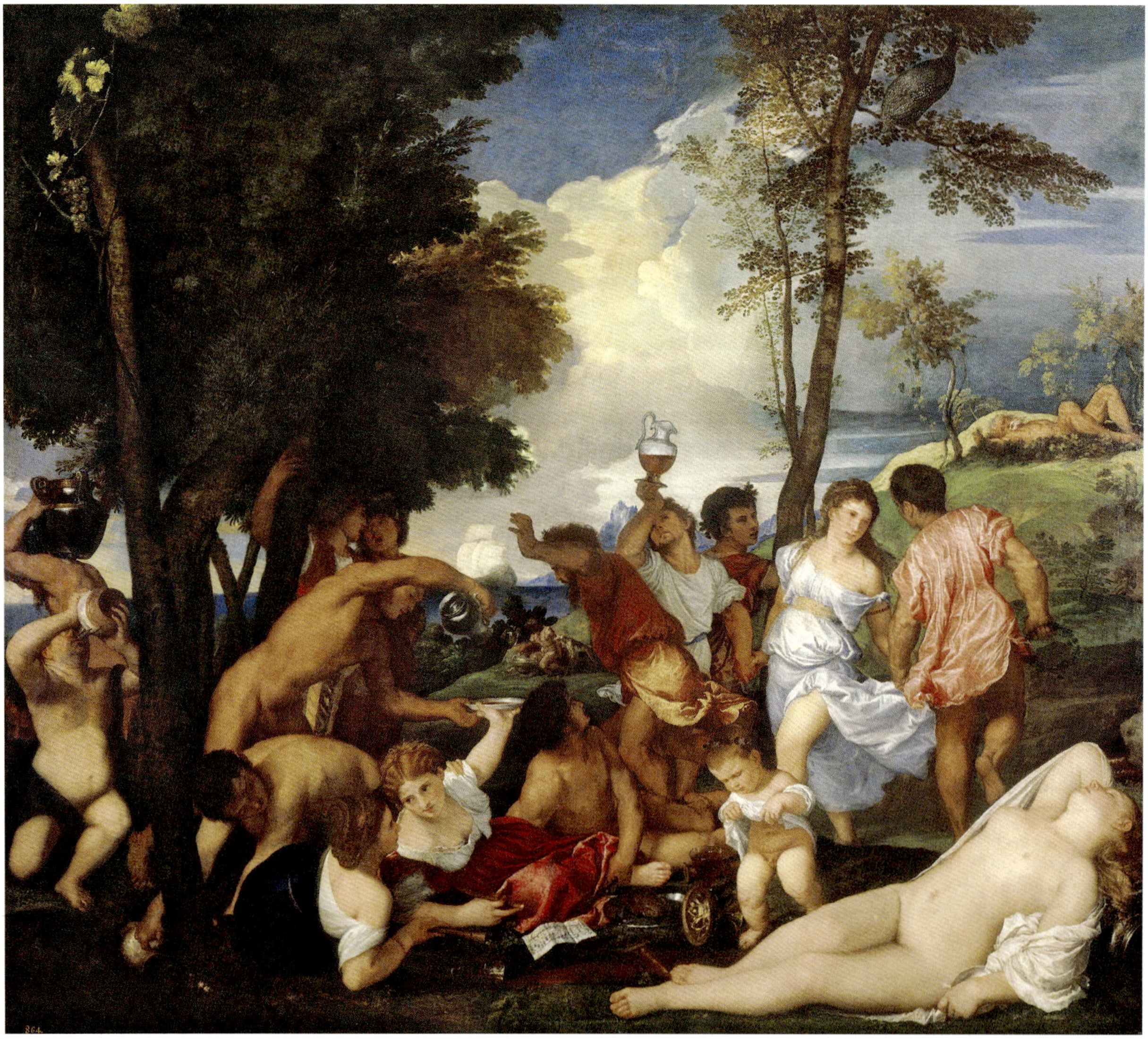

FIG. 29
Titian (Tiziano Vecellio; active *c.* 1506–1576)
The Andrians, *c.* 1523–26
Oil on canvas, 175 × 193 cm
Museo del Prado, Madrid

FIG. 30
Paolo Veronese (1528–1588)
The Rape of Europa, *c.* 1570
Oil on canvas glued to oak panel,
59.5 × 70 cm
The National Gallery, London.
Holwell Carr Bequest, 1831

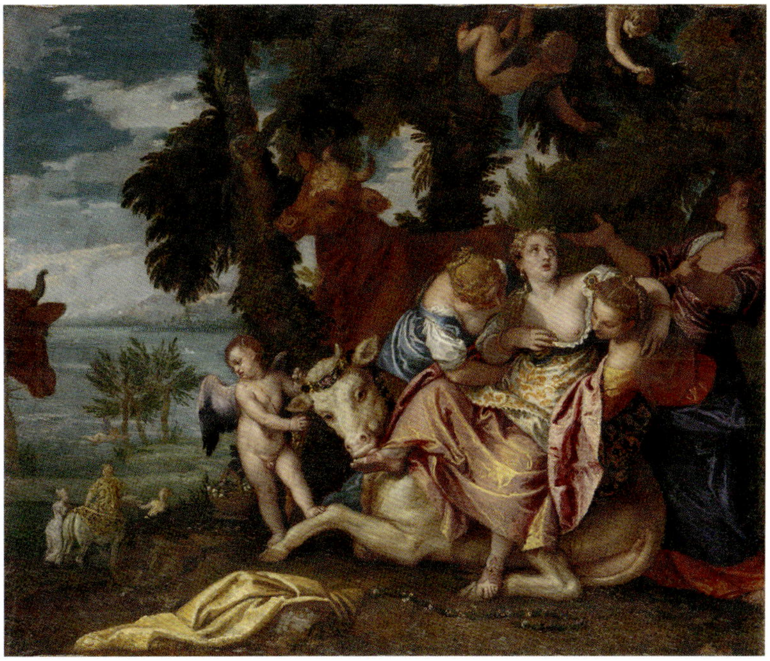

made popular in the Netherlands by an abridged translation of the *Decameron* into Dutch by Dirck Volckerstsz. Coornhert of 1564 and in England by John Florio's translation, first published in 1620.

Lely's pastoral subject pictures, by contrast, were not based on any specific literary works, although one might be able to find similar themes occurring in the very large number of published and performed works adopting pastoral conventions. Besides his large collection of paintings and works on paper (which he described as "the best in Europe"), Lely was the owner of a sizeable library. He certainly owned a copy of Torquato Tasso's epic poem *Gerusalemme Liberata* (1581), which became a significant source of amorous stories in England after its translation by Edward Fairfax in 1600 (*The Recoverie of Jerusalem*), above all the central tale of Rinaldo and Armida and the interruption of war by love. This epic also included the pastoral interlude of Erminia among the Shepherds, frequently painted by Italian artists.

Karel van Mander's *Het Schilder-Boeck* (1604), which included a discussion of Ovid's *Metamorphoses*, was a huge influence on Netherlandish artists, and its section on the lives of various artists encouraged many painters from the Low Countries to travel to Italy. Van Mander also articulated the desire that Dutch artists should no longer concentrate on portraits (including group militia portraits) but should turn to subject painting, claiming that "the majority of artists, by the temptation of gain or to make a living strike off on this side road of art ... and thus proceed without having time or inclination to seek the path or trace the road of history and figures, which leads to the highest perfection".[8] Another pastoral work that was popular in the Netherlands, and Lely would have known, was Jacob Cats's 1637 *Het Spaens Heydinnetje* (The Spanish heathen), based on Cervantes's *La Gitanella*, which was also produced as a play and provided material for engravers and painters, including Lely's contemporary Philip Wouwermans.

Throughout the seventeenth century, the best-known pastoral book by an English writer was Sir Philip Sidney's *Arcadia* (in the revised version first printed in 1593 known as *The Countess of Pembroke's Arcadia*). Another work likely to have been influential for Lely was the Dutch writer Pieter Cornelisz. Hooft's *Granida*

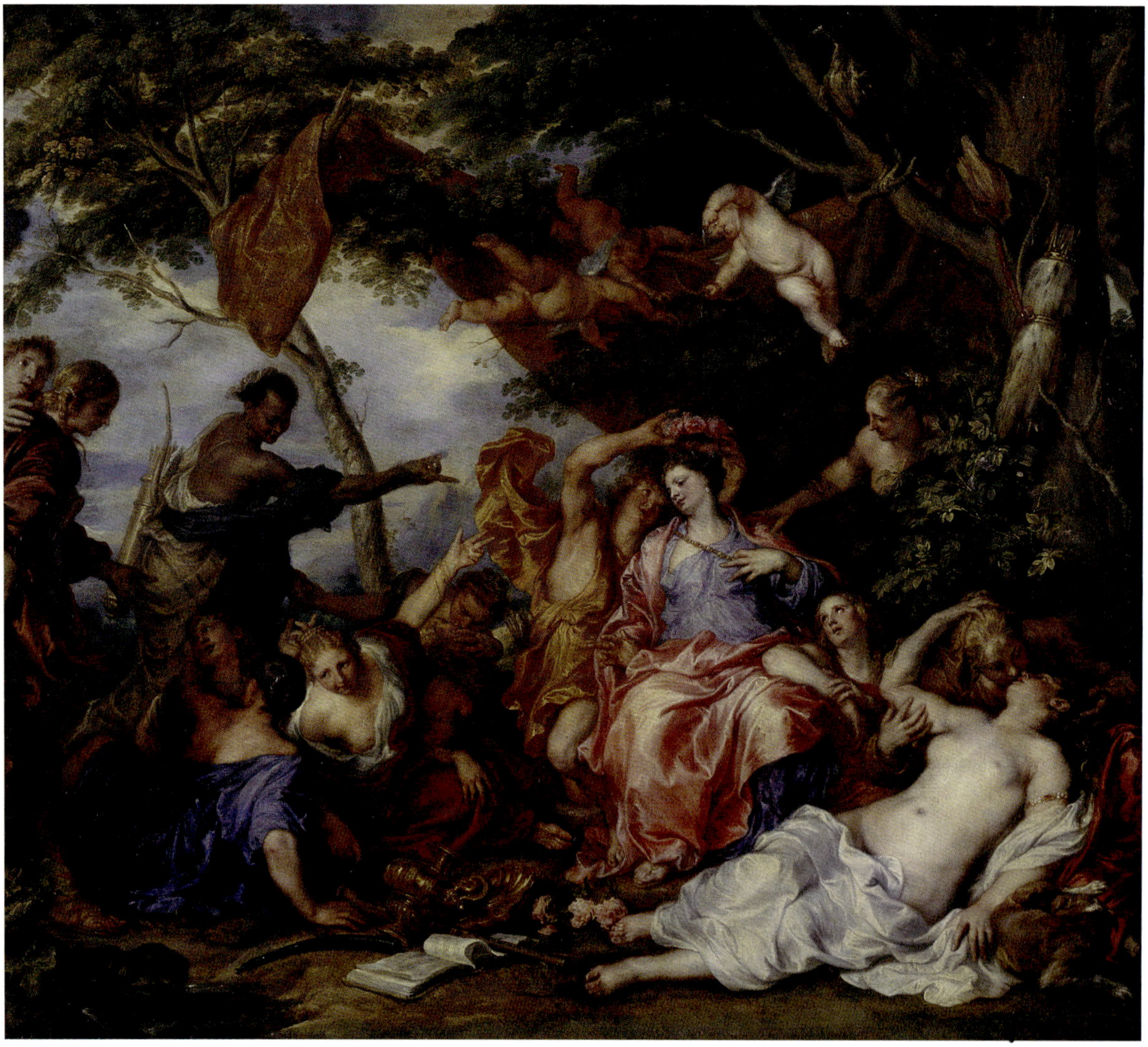

FIG. 31
Anthony van Dyck (1599–1641)
Amaryllis and Mirtillo, *c.* 1630–32
Oil on canvas, 123 × 137 cm
Kunstammlungen Graf von Schonborn, Schloss Weissenstein, Pommersfelden

(1605). A play set in a world that created an Arcadia as a romantic playground, far from the city and the intrigues of court,[9] it encouraged the use of pastoral imagery as a vehicle for more or less veiled political comment during a complex and turbulent period in England. It was very popular in the Northern Netherlands, and the central characters, the shepherd Daifilo and Granida, a princess, who become lovers, featured in a large number of Dutch paintings in the seventeenth century. *Granida* itself drew upon Giovanni Battista Guarini's hugely influential tragicomedy *Il Pastor Fido*, translated by Richard Fanshawe as *The Faithful Shepherd* in 1647, around the same time that Lely painted *The Concert* (cat. 7). Particular stories from *Il Pastor Fido* were popular with artists and collectors, such as the kissing scene between the shepherd Mirtillo, disguised as a woman, and Amaryllis, that followed the female "kissing warre" between her nymph attendants that she orders and judges. This unmistakably erotic subject was painted a number of times, not least by Van Dyck (fig. 31).[10]

RELIGIOUS SUBJECT PICTURES

The penitent Mary Magdalen was a popular figure for painters to depict, both as a moralising tale of the sinner who removes herself from a life of prostitution through her love of Christ and (sometimes) as an excuse to paint a beautiful woman in a state of undress. Lely painted two pictures of the Magdalen. His first (fig. 56) shows a woman in a plain, dark interior, staring into the distance. Although there is little to indicate who the figure is meant to represent, her loose hair on one side (as the Magdalen was commonly portrayed), her intense gaze that suggests her new life of contemplation, and her plain clothes indicative of the saint's time in the wilderness all hint at the identity of the role the sitter is playing. By painting the sitter modestly attempting to cover her exposed breast, Lely symbolises the Magdalen's repentance at the same time as recalling her previous life. The model for this picture was painted several times by Lely, in *Susanna and the Elders* (figs. 25–27), in *Vertumnus and Pomona*, also known as *A Lady and her Duenna* (fig. 38) and as the dark-haired nymph in *Nymphs by a Fountain* (cat. 9).

A second *Mary Magdalen* (fig. 55) is one of Lely's subject pictures that remind us of his later portraits, both in scale and mood.[11] It shows the saint alone and at full length, with one hand on a crucifix next to a skull at the mouth of a dark cave. Lost in contemplation, she only half-heartedly manages to hold her robe together, and one breast remains exposed. The picture was painted around 1650–55, and was in the collection of Ralph Bankes from 1656, where it was listed in his *Pictures in my Chamber att Grayes Inne* as "Magdalen by m^r^ Lilly".[12] This sitter, presumably one of Lely's circle, appears again as the woman playing a guitar in *The Music Lesson* of 1654 (formerly in the collection of Lord Dulverton) and as the eponymous heroine in *The Rape of Europa* (cat. 10), which uses the same pose for the head. A surviving drawing by Lely shows the same model at head and shoulder length, in a similar pose. (There is another that shows her in a different pose.)[13]

Another religious subject to which Lely appears to have returned was the story of the finding of Moses (Exodus 2: 1–10), in which Pharaoh's daughter and her handmaids discover the baby Moses in a basket made of bulrushes on the banks of the Nile. Because the women were bathing in the river when they found the baby, the subject gave painters the opportunity to depict female nudity, securing its popularity with artists and collectors. However, this was also a moralising tale, in which Pharaoh's daughter, in seeking a Hebrew nurse for the foundling, puts the needs of the baby before her own. Moreover the Dutch had particular respect for this biblical story, as the baby Moses being discovered by Pharaoh's daughter was understood "as evidence of divine providence and as an indication of God's ability to bring together opposing factions".[14] As such, the scene was painted by many of Lely's contemporaries, including Pieter de Grebber, the son of Lely's master in Haarlem, Frans Pietersz. de Grebber, whose multi-figure composition and forest-side setting of the subject (fig. 11) is close in mood to many of Lely's subject pictures. It is not entirely clear how many different compositions of the subject Lely painted. There is one known extant picture (cat. 1) showing a group of women by the banks of a river, including Pharaoh's daughter being presented with the baby Moses, with the stone balustrade of a grand building among the trees behind them. There is also what seems to be a second composition by Lely of the subject, tantalisingly shown in the background of Johannes Vermeer's *Lady writing a Letter, with her Maid* (fig. 32), and again, in reduced form, in Vermeer's *Astronomer* (Musée du Louvre, Paris).

Lely painted at least three versions of his composition of *Susanna and the Elders* (figs. 25–27), which differ slightly in their dimensions and in the degree of nudity in which Susanna appears. The composition depicts the section of the biblical story (Apocrypha) in which two lustful elders have emerged from their hiding place to approach the terrified Susanna in her garden. They interrupt her as she dresses after bathing at one of Lely's fanciful fountains,

FIG. 32
Johannes Vermeer (1632–1675)
Woman writing a Letter, with her Maid, c. 1670
Oil on canvas, 71.1 × 60.5 cm
National Gallery of Ireland, Dublin. Presented by Sir Alfred and Lady Beit, 1987

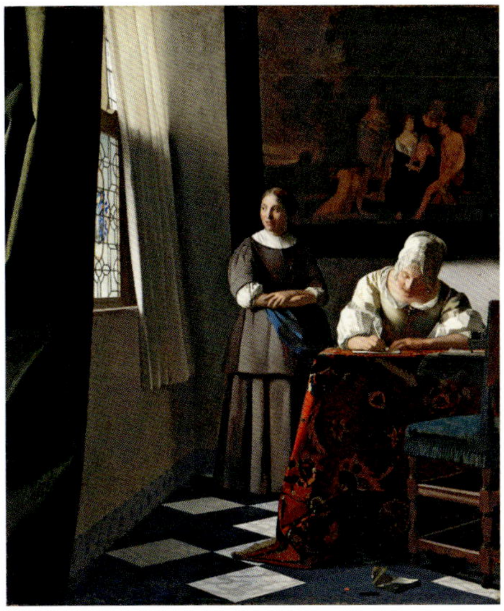

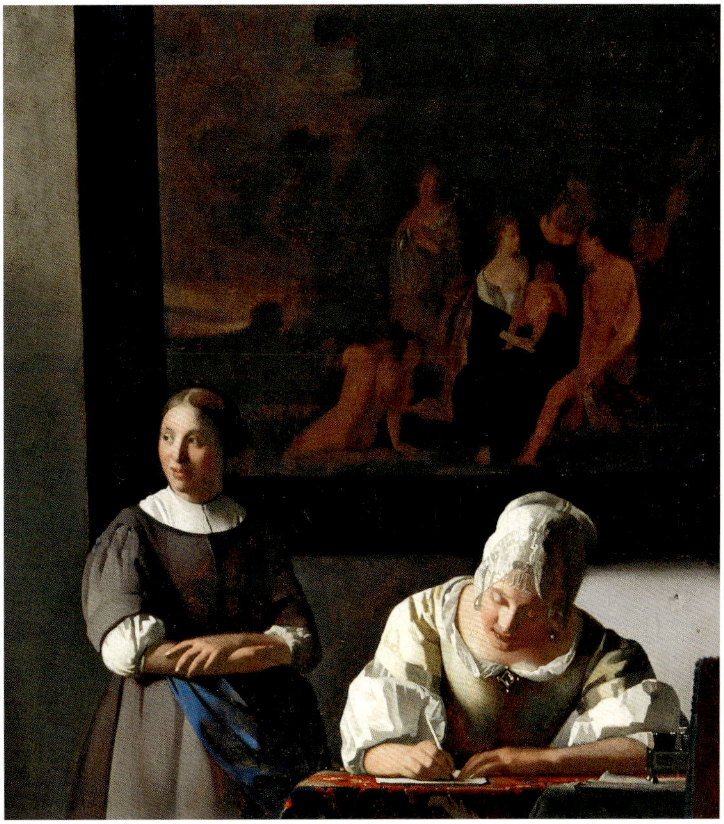

which features a rather Rubensian infant urinating and leaning on the neck of a camel. In the biblical story the elders, when she refused to yield to their sexual demands, accused Susanna of adultery, but her virtue was proven when the elders were shown to have concocted their evidence. The rehabilitation of her reputation could become an allegorical vehicle for the triumph of good over evil but, again, it also enabled painters to portray the naked or near-naked female body, and this is presumably the main reason why Susanna was "the most popular biblical theme among Dutch painters of the seventeenth century". Curiously, however, Lely painted her with an exposed breast in only one of his three versions (fig. 25).[15]

An oddity among Lely's religious subject pictures is *Reuben presenting Mandrakes to Leah* (cat. 4). This story from Genesis 30: 14, which concerns the rivalry between Jacob's wives, the sisters Leah and Rachel, was a rare theme for artists to paint. Lely shows the young Reuben presenting his mother Leah with some mandrakes he has found, while her younger sister Rachel bargains for the plants, offering in exchange a night with Jacob. The unusually large dimensions of the canvas suggest it was painted for a specific site, and therefore was specially commissioned, and the biblical story may have had particular meaning for the unknown patron. Certainly Lely indicated the sexual element of the story by depicting Rachel with an exposed breast, a somewhat incongruous inclusion but one that might have been included to order. The dog is a copy by Lely of the huge mastiff from Van Dyck's *Five Eldest Children of Charles I* (Royal Collection), reduced to miniature form.

The subject of Judith with the head of Holofernes was more commonly painted. The apocryphal Book of Judith (13: 1–10) describes how the beautiful widow Judith ingratiated herself with Holofernes, one of Nebuchadnezzar's generals, who was besieging her hometown of Bethulia, and how, in his tent, she intoxicated him and cut off his head with his own sword. Lely's *Judith and Holofernes* (Vadodara Museum and Picture Gallery, India) shows Judith holding both Holofernes's head and the sword with which she has just decapitated him. She appears to be lost in a state of pensive reflection, staring towards the heavens, despite the horrible act she has just committed, consequently ignoring the maid who carries a sack in which she waits for her to deposit the severed head. This subject gave artists the opportunity to portray the beautiful and the grotesque together on one canvas, to depict a highly sexualised murder, committed by a heroic and powerful woman taking over a traditionally male role. Through the translation of the story of the Israelites overcoming the might of the Assyrians into a more straightforward triumph of good over evil, the story could also be utilised to refer to contemporary political issues.

PASTORAL SUBJECT PICTURES

Lely's pastoral scenes are the best known of his subject pictures, embodying the modish bucolic world of shepherds and maidens, where "his nymphs trail fringes and embroidery through meadows and purling streams" (Horace Walpole).[16] Such pastoral landscapes could also be interpreted as the setting for ideas of political or social commentary, being conventionally contrasted to the city and its inevitably corrupt court and society. The scenes are often played out at the edge of a forest, or in the moody shadows of large rocky outcrops, providing a dramatic setting familiar to patrons from their experiences of the theatre or the court masque. A potent symbol, often repeated in the subject pictures, is water. The sea, lakes, streams and fountains, redolent of rebirth and purity or simply of the overriding power of the natural world in comparison to that of man, are motifs in Lely's subject pictures to which he frequently returned also in his later portraiture.

FIG. 33
Dirck van der Lisse
(active from *c.* 1630, died 1669)
Nymphs sleeping, *c.* 1650
Oil on panel, 24.5 × 41 cm
Private collection

The most sensuous and best known of Lely's subject pictures is his *Nymphs by a Fountain* (cat. 9), in which a group of women, mostly naked, sleep off their exertions at the base of a fountain. The Titianesque appearance of this picture (beyond the citation of the nymph in the background from Titian's *Andrians*), especially in its colour scheme, reflects Lely's first-hand knowledge of the Venetian painter, pictures by whom (or at least attributed to whom) were in his own collection.[17] The fountain features putti and a dolphin, often associated with Bacchus (relating to the story of his turning sailors who had attempted to abduct him into dolphins). This could lead to an interpretation of the human subjects as maenads, or some other Bacchic associates, sleeping off their drunken and sexual revelling, or to an even more erotic reading if the scene were to depict the aftermath of an orgiastic ritual. Whatever the understanding is of the story shown in the picture, the depiction of naked, sleeping women in the outdoors was common enough in contemporary Flemish and Dutch as well as sixteenth-century Italian art, pandering to the viewer's voyeurism. Examples by artists whose work Lely knew well are Van Dyck's *Cupid and Psyche* (fig. 5), Dirck van der Lisse's *Nymphs sleeping* (fig. 33) and Van Poelenburgh's *Cimon and Efigenia*

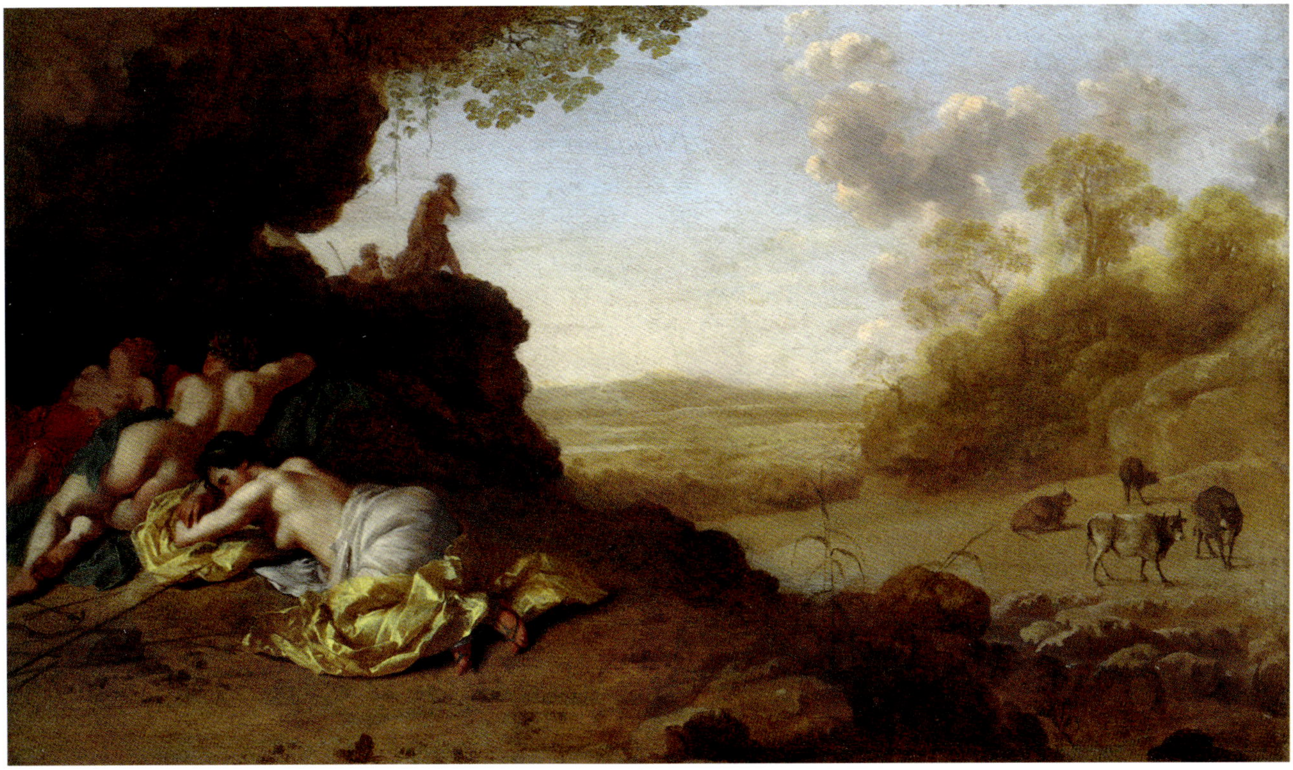

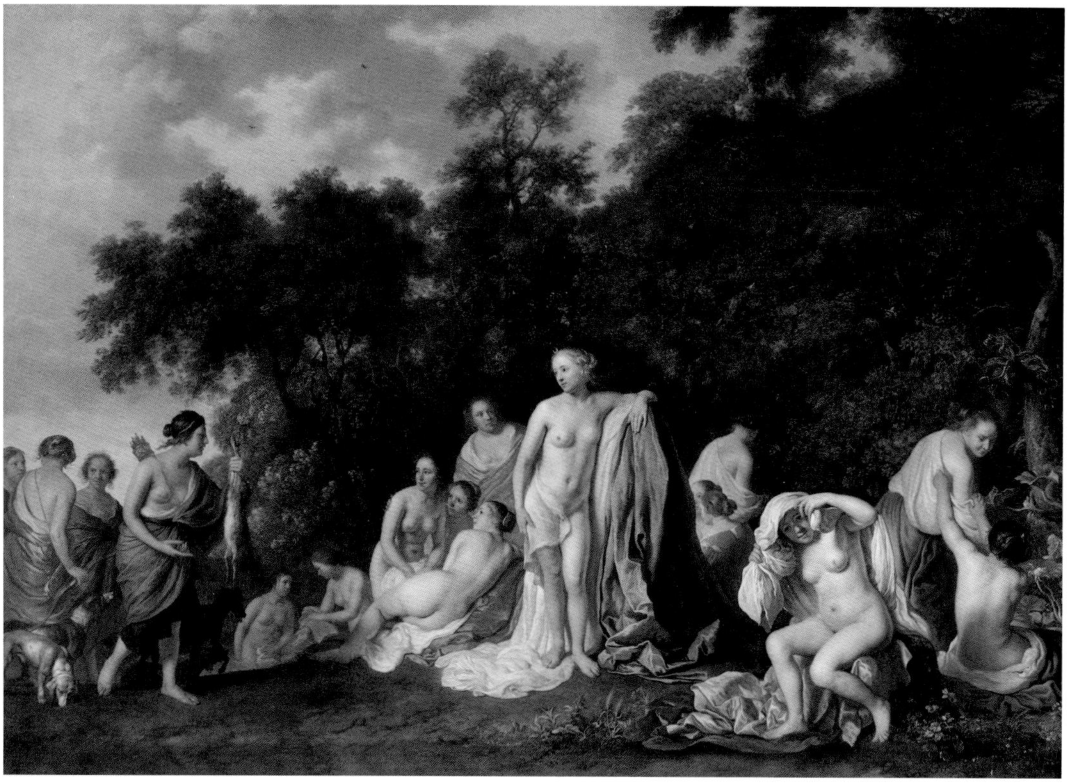

(Edinburgh, Scottish National Gallery), all of which include men looking at the sleeping women, the role the viewer of *Nymphs by a Fountain* replicates.[18] Jacob van Loo's *Diana and her Nymphs* (fig. 34) includes a recumbent, naked woman similar in posture to the sleeping nymph at the bottom of Lely's composition, demonstrating an apparent migration of poses between artists who were painting similar themes at this time.

Lely's *Nymphs bathing* (fig. 40) again enables the study of the female nude, and once again its specific subject is now unclear. It is, however, the only subject picture to be dated, although tantalisingly the last figure is illegible, making it impossible to be certain whether it is a late Dutch work, painted before Lely travelled to England, or an early English work. It is reasonable to presume it shows the Bath of Diana, as it has been called in the past, as the composition conjoins the bathing and hunting stories from the goddess's mythology: two seated women appear to be drying themselves by the side of a lake or river, in which another woman teaches a child to swim and a fourth, standing woman holds a bow in her left hand, while three leashed greyhounds and a spaniel, all hunting dogs, sniff the ground and air, with one being toyed with by a group of three naked children. Yet another scene

FIG. 34
Jacob van Loo (1614–1670)
Diana and her Nymphs, 1654
Oil on canvas, 99.5 × 135.5 cm
Statens Museum for Kunst, Copenhagen

of nymphs bathing (figs. 18 and 19) was previously thought to depict the Finding of Moses, but the baby and bulrush basket have turned out to be later additions. In the earlier twentieth century the picture was attributed to Benjamin Cuyp, despite being signed by Lely.[19] The theme of beautiful women bathing or near to fountains continues with a recently discovered subject picture by Lely (fig. 17), showing a girl sitting next to a fountain and resting one hand on the head of a greyhound whose collar is held by a naked putto. As well as the water from the fountain, the background shows a waterfall and tumbling stream below a grey sky. The naked child may represent Cupid, and there are further figures of naked children on the fountain itself. The woman may have originally been topless, and her right arm, which rather incongruously disappears in the basin of the fountain, may have first been painted resting on her lap.[20]

Lely's *Pair of Lovers in a Landscape* (cat. 2) shows an amorous couple sitting on the ground, holding hands and deep in conversation. The man has often been considered a self-portrait (which may or may not have been the artist's intention); his shirt and cloak suggest a rural occupation.[21] To the right of the composition is a naked putto, encouraging a pair of satyrs to watch the couple, in a somewhat sinister fashion, from the shadows. In the distance, to the left, is a circular, pilastered building reminiscent of the Vestal temple in Rome – possibly, through the association with the group of virgins who kept alive the sacred flame inside the temple, an allusion to the ruin of the female lover's chastity. The subversive, pleasure-loving satyr from Greek mythology can be seen again in Lely's destroyed *Idyll* (fig. 21), in which a bare-breasted woman sits at the edge of a forest, with a second woman kneeling before her, while a swarthy satyr, partly covered with an animal skin, sits behind the first woman, pawing at her shoulder and staring at her nakedness with obvious lascivious intent.[22]

A more romantic image is the enigmatic *An Allegory of Love* (fig. 35), identified by Oliver Millar as an autograph Lely picture, which was once thought to represent Elizabeth Stuart, Queen of Bohemia, and William Craven, 1st Earl of Craven, thus serving as a commemoration of their supposed relationship.[23] It was later called *The Crowning of a Poet*, which better captures its mood, as a woman is seen holding a wreath of laurel leaves above a man's head, while he has a blue ribbon tied around his wrist by a female putto, next to two other putti holding a helmet and a sword respectively.

A Boy as a Shepherd (cat. 12), painted perhaps as late as 1660, showing a long-haired youth leaning on a stone ledge before a rocky outcrop and a wooded glade, has been described as "the

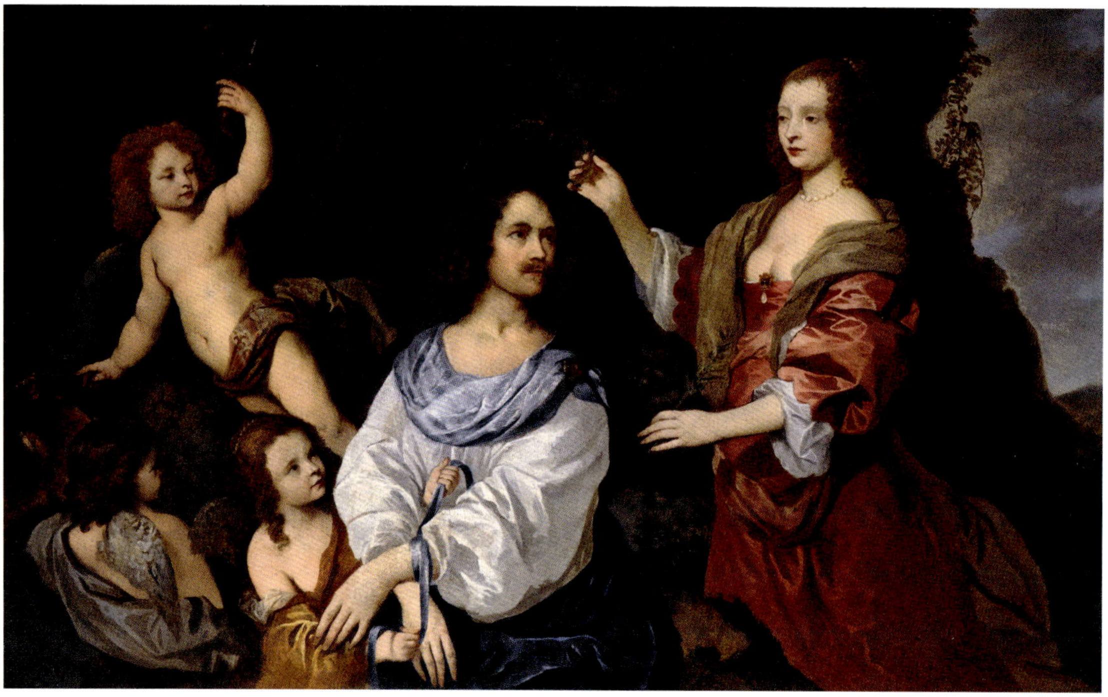

most romantic and accomplished of all Lely's Arcadian portraits".[24] In this highly lyrical image the sheep-less shepherd boy holds a recorder in his right hand, and in his other we see the shaft of a shepherd's crook or *houlette*. Clearly this is a portrait of a real individual, though not the poet Abraham Cowley as was suggested by Horace Walpole, who owned the picture and displayed it at Strawberry Hill, since Cowley would have been too old, and possibly not Mary Beale's son Bartholomew, who has also been suggested.[25] However, the fact we do not know the identity of the sitter does not detract from the power of this image as a portrait of a musical swain resting from his duties and about to play his recorder to pass the time. The boy was described by Walpole as showing "The impassioned glow of sentiment, the eyes swimming with youth and tenderness".[26]

MUSICAL SUBJECT PICTURES

An interrelated group of paintings of musicians, painted by Lely in the 1650s, adds another layer of 'types' to the wider output of his subject pictures: here images of one or two figures dominate the canvas, in paintings that fall somewhere between the clear subject pictures and Lely's early portraits, among other hybridised portraits such as the young shepherdess, the so-called *Little Girl*

FIG. 35
Peter Lely (1618–1680)
An Allegory of Love, *c.* 1650–60
Oil on canvas, 122 × 185.5 cm
Formerly Ashdown House

in Green, at Chatsworth, and Henry Sidney, the future Earl of Romney, as a shepherd, after the Apollo Belvedere (fig. 60). These figures are set in some of Lely's best and most lyrical landscapes, reminding us of the backdrops of the 'landscapes with small figures' pictures in their portrayal of the "Sweet Groves . . . wanton Brookes, and solitary Rockes"[27] of Arcadia, where "the setting effectively removes the sitter from the real world to place [them] in the context of the pastoral poetry of the day".[28]

The majority of Lely's pictures of musicians show him continuing the genres of various Netherlandish painters who had travelled to Italy and been influenced by Italian artists, especially Caravaggio and his followers, including Bartolomeo Manfredi and Orazio Gentileschi. These artists, notably the Utrecht Caravaggisti Dirck van Baburen, Hendrick ter Brugghen and Gerrit van Honthorst, produced pictures of music-makers in the dimly lit interiors that brought into play their individual powers of *chiaroscuro* painting.

Of Lely's pictures of musicians, the best known are the group of a *Man playing a Pipe* (cat. 6), a *Boy playing a Jew's Harp* (cat. 5), a *Girl playing a Theorbo-Lute* (fig. 49), a *Man playing a Violin* (fig. 45) and a *Man playing an Eleven-Course Lute* (fig. 48).[29] The five pictures were in the Craven collection by 1739,[30] and were displayed together by at least 1768, at Coombe Abbey in Warwickshire (where Lely's *An Allegory of Love* was also hung), where, for a time, they were thought to have been painted by Frans Hals (they were later thought to have been painted by Soest).[31] The picture of the eleven-course lute-player is smaller than the other four canvases, and has sometimes been read as a self-portrait, as has the sitter in another musician picture of similar dimensions, showing a man playing a violin, which could be from the same series (formerly Sarah Campbell Blaffer Foundation, Texas, fig. 47).[32] The boy playing a Jew's harp reveals several discrepancies from the rest of the group: he is the only child in the series, the only musician who is painted with a prop other than a musical instrument (the stone pedestal that he leans upon) and the only figure in an outdoor setting. The musicians were nevertheless presumably painted to be displayed as pendants: of the four large works, the sitters in the two Tate pictures (cat. 5 and 6) face towards their right, and those in the two ex-McDonald collection pictures (figs. 45 and 49) face towards their left. Similarly, the men in the two smaller pictures (figs. 47 and 48) (who are depicted with their mouths open, suggesting they are the singers for the larger group) both face in different directions, hinting at the intended hang for the six pictures, centred three to each side around a fireplace or another, larger picture.[33]

The making of music was a common theme in Dutch painting, often carrying reference to or connotations of love and amorous pursuits. Anticipating Cesare Ripa's statement that "music was invented to make the spirits happy",[34] Giorgio Vasari, in his *Lives of the Most Eminent Painters, Sculptors and Architects*, suggested that "Love is born from Music, or rather, Love is always in company with Music".[35] At the very least, the portrayal of men and women in the act of playing musical instruments suggests that their music was intended to be listened to, implying an audience within their painted world, further to our viewership. They are regarded as subject pictures because, despite that fact they clearly depict real people, they were presumably not intended as portraits, but rather as images of anonymous music makers.

The Concert (cat. 7) is one of the most intriguing of Lely's subject pictures. In common with other works here considered it is both musical and pastoral, but the specific story being told, if indeed one was intended, is unknown. In his 1978 Lely exhibition catalogue, Oliver Millar described it as "the most beautiful and (iconographically) elusive of all the 'Historical Compositions' painted by Lely in London", underlining the difficulty of the picture's subject-matter.[36] Dodsley and Walpole, in the eighteenth century, both believed the music-making group to be Lely's family, which is now thought not to be the case, although it is currently held to be possible that the man to left of centre playing a viola de gamba is a self-portrait.[37] The bare-breasted female figure to the right of the picture may represent Poetry, in accordance with the figure of Poesia in Cesare Ripa's 1611 *Iconologia*.[38] Lely painted the same woman in the small *Lady as a Saint* (fig. 39), where she sits in a landscape, being crowned with a laurel wreath by a putto that hovers above her. What she represents in this second picture – with one breast fully exposed, her left foot resting on a helmet – is also unclear, although the fact she holds a martyr's palm would indicate she is a saint.

The long, horizontal format of *The Concert* suggests it was painted for a specific site, presumably above a fireplace in a room in which music was played. As an allegorical work it emphasises the harmonious, edifying nature of music, showing a viol and flute accompanied by a singer (or two – the woman whose naked back faces us at the centre of the canvas is holding sheet music) performing a concert at the edge of a forest, essentially an Arcadian site. Iconographically, its direct sources must surely be the open-air concerts represented in Venetian painting, a subject depicted by Giovanni Cariani, Titian and Tintoretto in the previous century, and the conventional language of allegory, for example such figures as the putto dressed as a shepherd, again in Ripa's *Iconologia*, with a scroll at his feet reading *Pastorum carmina ludo* (I play the songs of shepherds).

The busiest of all Lely's subject pictures, once again with no precisely identifiable theme, is the provisionally named *Scene from History*, sometimes called *Trial by Fire* (St Petersburg, Hermitage Museum), in which a young woman walks on hot coals next to a statue of Justice and before an enthroned ruler, who wears a turban and holds a sceptre (fig. 36). From the later eighteenth century, when the picture entered the Russian imperial collection, it was thought that it represented a scene from the life of the Empress Kunigund, who, after being accused of infidelity, proved her innocence by walking on heated ploughshares before her husband, the Holy Roman Emperor Henry II. This is now seen as unlikely to be the subject. The picture has not always been well regarded: Baron Munnich's 1774 Hermitage catalogue entry described it as a painting with "nothing that places it higher than mediocre".[39]

Numerous images of Bacchus as a child, playing with other young figures, had been produced in the earlier seventeenth century, by the time Lely painted his *Infant Bacchus* (cat. 3).[40] Lely's playful picture, which, as Sir Oliver Millar noted, is reminiscent of the subject pictures painted in England by Franchoys Wouters, shows a group of young children, including a drowsy and chubby

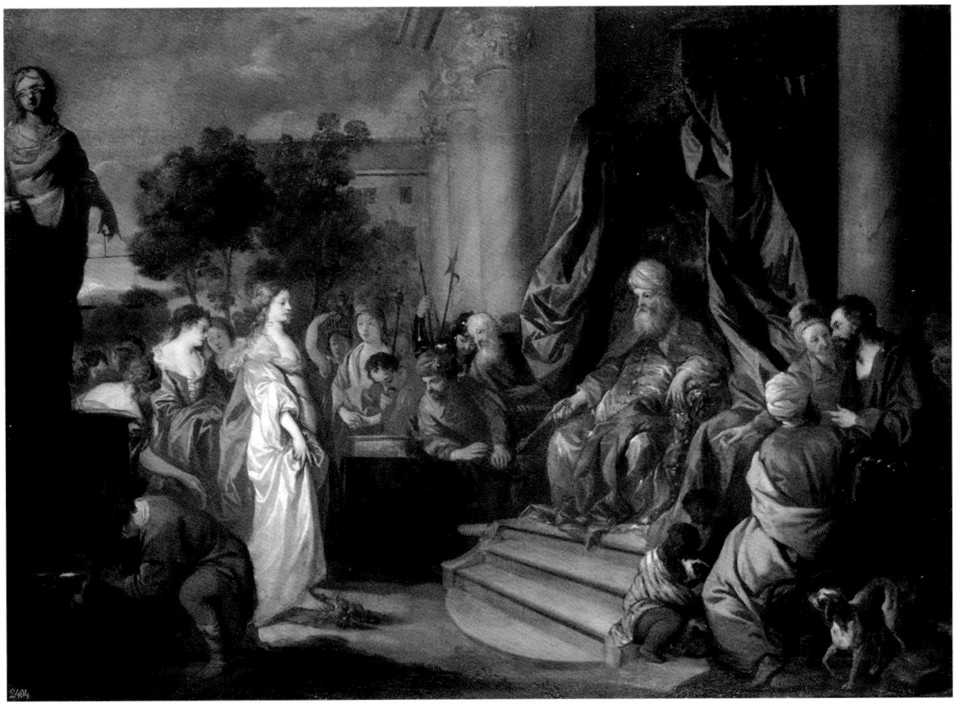

FIG. 36
Peter Lely (1618–1680)
Trial by Fire, *c.* 1645–55
Oil on canvas, 115.5 × 156.5 cm
The State Hermitage Museum, St Petersburg

Bacchus, identifiable by the wreath of vine leaves on his head, who is being helped off a wine barrel (signed on its end with Lely's monogram).[41] The accompanying children are probably meant to be infant satyrs, the young Bacchus's companions: the bagpipe-playing figure to the left of the dolphin fountain would support this reading, as would the figure holding up a wine glass, referring to both music-making and drinking as part of Bacchanalian rituals. Likewise, as already noted, the dolphin fountain recalls Bacchus's transformation of sailors into dolphins. The goat, common in Bacchanalian imagery, is associated with lust and with the general lasciviousness of the satyrs and revellers that accompany the adult Bacchus. The theme of cavorting infants, usually in the guise of putti, was popular with artists, and, in turn, with collectors, including Lely himself. His collection of almost 10,000 works on paper included several drawings of putti, including one by Giulio Romano now in Edinburgh.[42]

Lely's *Rape of Europa* (cat. 10) shows the story from Ovid's *Metamorphoses* of the abduction of the king of Tyre's daughter by Jupiter in the form of a beautiful white bull. As noted above, Lely's *Rape of Europa* is similar in attitude to Veronese's earlier one

FIG. 37
Cornelis van Poelenburgh (1593–1667)
Cimon and Efigenia, *c.* 1650
Oil on panel, 26 × 33 cm
Jean-François Heim, Paris

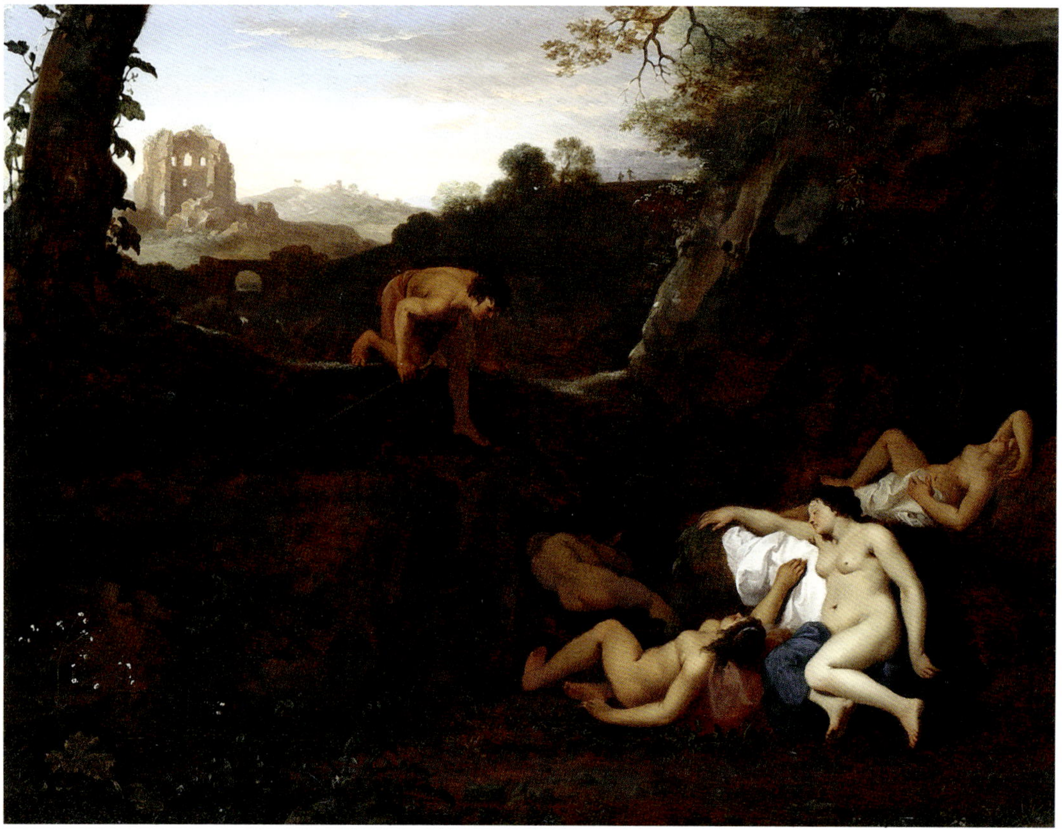

FIG. 38
Peter Lely (1618–1680)
Vertumnus and Pomona
(*A Lady and her Duenna*), *c.* 1650
Oil on canvas, 108 × 85.7 cm
Institute of Art, Detroit

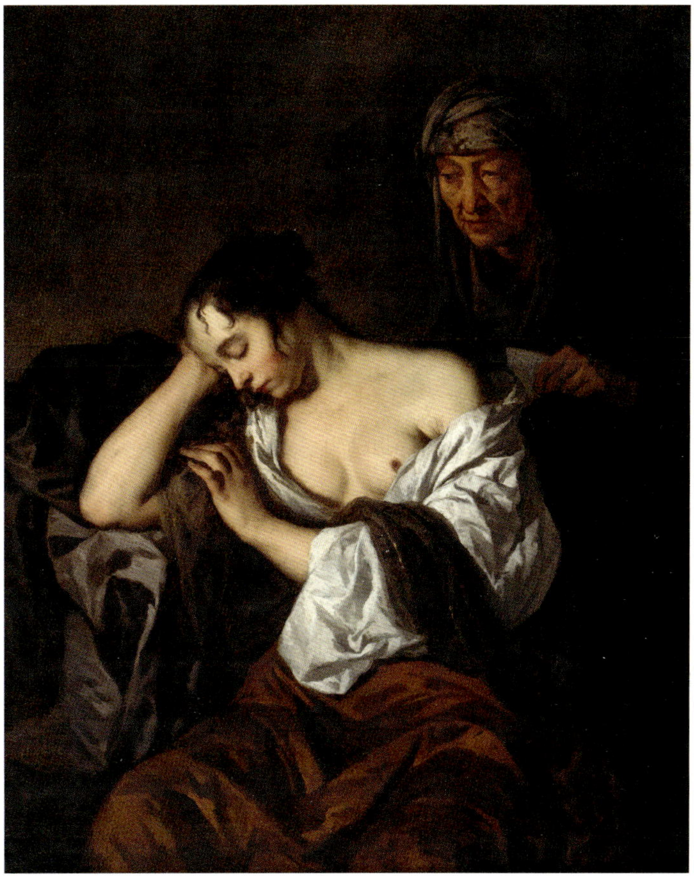

(fig. 30), rather than to works by painters such as Titian, who chose to portray the protagonists at sea. The *Rape of Europa* stayed in Lely's possession and was bought for the Devonshire collection from his executors. We also saw that the model he used for Europa plays a guitar in *The Music Lesson* (formerly Lord Dulverton) and posed for the Kingston Lacy *Mary Magdalen* (fig. 55) and for two surviving drawings.[43]

The two *Cimon and Efigenia* paintings by Lely (fig. 58 and cat. 11) capture the moment in which, in Boccaccio's story (as noted above), the shepherd Cimon comes across the sleeping Efigenia, and is transformed by the power of her beauty, and his love for her, from a rustic oaf into a civilised gentleman whom she eventually marries. This patently voyeuristic subject was the subject of many paintings, by artists such as Rubens, Abraham Bloemaert and Van Poelenburgh. Like Lely, Van Poelenburgh painted the story more than once, with Cimon either approaching the sleeping Efigenia and her women or watching her from a distance (fig. 37), by contrast to Lely's Cimon, who stands next to her. A surviving drawing by Lely (fig. 57) appears to be a study for the naked woman at the front left of the Doddington picture (cat. 11), a figure similar to that of the nymph at the front of the Dulwich *Nymphs by a Fountain*, but in reverse.[44]

The story of Vertumnus and Pomona, from Ovid's *Metamorphoses*, was a tale of erotic deception and virtue, in which Vertumnus changed his body into that of an old woman to gain access to the maiden Pomona. In Lely's *Vertumnus and Pomona* (Detroit Institute of Art, fig. 38, and a version at Hatfield House, fig. 24) the young, bare-breasted Pomona sleeps with her head propped upon one hand, while the old woman that Vertumnus has transformed himself into steals up behind her, out of the shadows. The letter that Vertumnus holds gave the picture one of its previous titles, *The Letter*, and it has likewise been called *A Lady and her Duenna*, which presumes the less sinister theme of a girl about to be awoken to read a love letter. In comparison to other contemporary paintings of the same subject, Lely's picture presents an unusual depiction of the seduction. Pomona's pose of her head on her hand, traditionally associated with melancholy, in fact shows slumber, and she is normally shown awake (and fully dressed), conversing with the old woman that Vertumnus has transformed himself into.[45]

ET IN ARCADIA EGO

The various subjects of Lely's subject pictures are in many ways quite predictable, in so far as the themes and types we can group them into are mostly of the sort that one would expect a Dutch painter making a living as a painter in England in the earlier to mid seventeenth century to undertake. The figures of unknown subjects can be assumed either to be mythological or biblical characters that would in fact have been identifiable or to be generic pastoral types – shepherd and shepherdess, nymphs or lovers. Despite oddities (such as *Reuben presenting Mandrakes to Leah*, cat. 4) and the fact that some of the subjects represented are unknown, the majority of Lely's 'landscapes with small figures' are bucolic theatrical sets upon which actors perform rustic tableaux. The pictures of single musicians link to Lely's true portraiture, while the landscapes in his subject pictures anticipate those of Lely's more pastoral portraits, such as those of the early pictures of children as well-dressed country folk or the woodland setting for the triple portrait of Charles I's three youngest children (fig. 52), complete with putto and dolphin fountain and its Arcadian forest with a prominent dead tree.[46]

FIG. 39
Peter Lely (1618–1680)
Lady as a Saint, late 1640s
Oil on panel, 31.5 × 25.9 cm
Philip Mould – Private collection

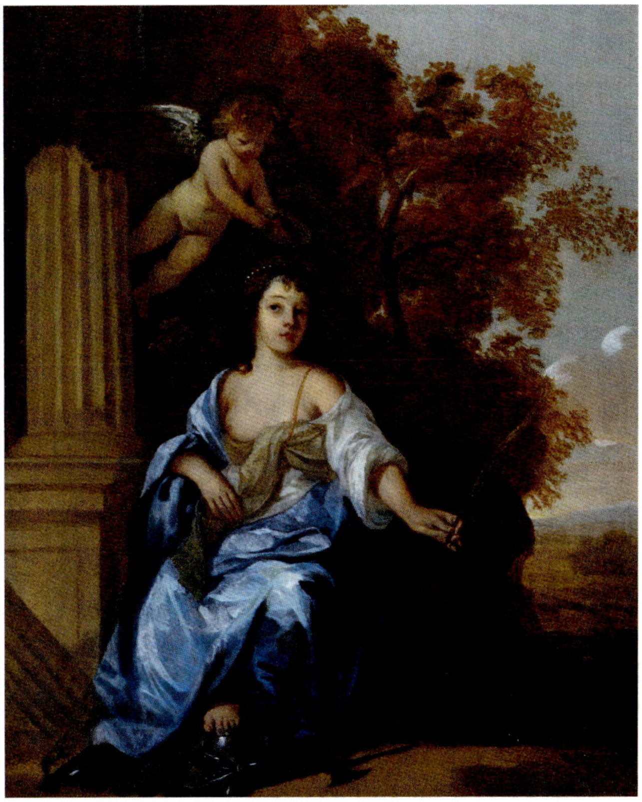

The subject pictures also reveal general traits of Lely's art during his first decades in England, with their occasionally unsure draughtsmanship and some odd positionings of figures within the composition, as well as traits typical of his middle and later career, such as the many beautiful and surprising colour schemes and the frequent touches of brilliance. The sensuous nature of the majority of the subject pictures becomes more overtly sexual in many cases, and the canvases frequently show the nude female form, often explicitly as the object of a male gaze. The pictures abound with stories of transformation, whether physical or spiritual, usually asserting the supremacy of good over evil or the strength of love. Lely not only understood the pastoral idiom, in England he contributed to it. He painted a lyrical idea of England, rather than a depiction of the actual nation, beset by political turmoil and change. By offering a fashionable vision of a poetic, pretend, once-was world, a playground made familiar through drama and poetry as much as painting, Lely has left us with the false memory that he and his anonymous sitters were also to be found in Arcadia.

NOTES

1 Richard Graham, *A Short Account of the Most Eminent Painters, both Ancient and Modern, down to the Present Times*, 2nd edn, London, 1716, p. 384.

2 The precise date of Lely's arrival in England is unknown, but was presumably *c.* 1641/42. The earlier assumption that he arrived in London in the train of William II for his marriage to Princess Mary, now disregarded, was first published by Arnold Houbraken in his *De groote schouburgh der Nederlantsche Konstschilders en schilderessen*, 's Gravenhage, 1718–21.

3 R.B. Beckett, *Lely*, London, 1951, pp. 5–6.

4 See Diana Dethloff, 'The executors' account book and the dispersal of Sir Peter's collection', *Journal of the History of Collections*, vol. 8, 1996, p. 50 n. 105.

5 C.H. Wilkinson, ed., *The Poems of Richard Lovelace*, Oxford, 1930, pp. 180–81.

6 Van Poelenburgh was invited to England by Charles I, and many of the works he painted during his three-year tenure in London remain, through descent, in British private collections.

7 Laurie B. Harwood, *Inspired by Italy: Dutch Landscape Painting 1600–1700*, exh. cat., Dulwich Picture Gallery, 2002, p. 78, no. 5.

8 Karel van Mander, *Het Schilder-Boeck*, Haarlem, 1604, f. 281r; see Albert Blankert, ed., *Gods, Saints and Heroes: Dutch Painting in the Age of Rembrandt*, exh. cat., National Gallery of Art, Washington DC, Detroit Institute of Arts and Rijksmuseum, Amsterdam 1980, p. 16.

9 See Alison McNeil Kettering, *The Dutch Arcadia: Pastoral Art and its Audience in the Golden Age*, Montclair NJ, 1983, Chapter 7.

10 See Susan J. Barnes, Nora de Poorter, Oliver Millar and Horst Vey, *Van Dyck, A Complete Catalogue of the Paintings*, London and New Haven, 2004, p. 295, no. III.60.

11 A second version, in the Royal Collection, has sometimes been taken to be the prime version, but is a copy of the Kingston Lacy picture.

12 See Alastair Laing, 'Sir Peter Lely and Sir Ralph Bankes', in David Howarth (ed.), *Art and Patronage in the Caroline Courts*, Cambridge, 1993, p. 121, appendix; document 1, no. 8.

13 See Oliver Millar, *The Tudor, Stuart and Early Georgian Pictures in the Collection of Her Majesty the Queen*, London, 1963, vol. I, pp. 126–7, no. 268; Oliver Millar, *Sir Peter Lely*, exh. cat., National Portrait Gallery, London, 1978, p. 77, no. 72 (illustrated). The second drawing was sold at Sotheby's, 10 July 1997 (lot 14).

14 Frederic Duparc and Arthur Wheelock, eds., *Johannes Vermeer*, exh. cat., National Gallery of Art, Washington DC, and Royal Cabinet of Paintings Mauritshuis, The Hague, 1995, p. 188.

15 David De Witt, *Jan van Noordt: Painter of History and Portraits in Amsterdam*, Montreal and Kingston, 2007, p. 67.

16 Horace Walpole, *Anecdotes of Painting in England*, London, 1879, p. 225.

17 Lely may have based the figure of the nymph in the background of *Nymphs by a Fountain* on Podestà's *c.* 1636 engraving of Titian's *The Andrians*, which reproduces the composition in reverse. See Giles Waterfield *et al.*, *Collection for a King: Old Master Paintings from the Dulwich Picture Gallery*, London, 1994, p. 84.

18 Van der Lisse's *Nymphs sleeping* was sold at Christie's, New York, 26 January 2001 (lot 5).

19 Sold as by Benjamin Cuyp at the comte de Caven's sale in Brussels (23 May 1935, lot 50). See also Jacques Foucart, 'Tableaux des Ecoles du Nord: un bilan d'acquisitions', *La Revue du Louvre et des Musées de France,* V–VI, Paris, 1983, p. 361, no. 21; Jacques Foucart, 'Peter Lely, Dutch History Painter', *Hoogsteder-Naumann Mercury,* vol. 8, 1989, pp. 23 and 24, no. 8; sold again, Sotheby's, 10 April 1991 (lot 13).

20 Sold Christie's, 27 April 2007 (lot 22).

21 See Albert Blankert, Jeroen Giltaij and Friso Lammertse, eds., *Dutch classicism in seventeenth-century painting*, exh. cat., Museum Boijmans Van Beuningen, Rotterdam, and Städelsches Kunstinstitut Frankfurt, 1999–2000, pp. 228–31, no. 42.

22 This picture was "destroyed by enemy action" in 1941: see Beckett 1951, p. 67, no. 584, pl. 24.

23 It was referred to as such in Avray Tipping, 'Coombe Abbey I, Warwickshire, A Seat of the Earl of Craven', *Country Life*, XXVI, December 1909, p. 803.

24 London 1978–79, p. 51, no. 28.

25 See John Ingamells, *Dulwich Picture Gallery: British*, London 2008, p. 176.

26 Horace Walpole, *Anecdotes of Painting in England: With some account of the principal artists and incidental notes on other arts, also, a catalogue of engravers who have been born or resided in England*, ed. R.N. Wornum, London, 1888, 3 vols., III, p. 29.

27 George Wither, *Ah me! Am I the Swaine* (1622).

28 Alastair Laing, *In Trust for the Nation, Paintings from National Trust Houses*, exh. cat., National Gallery, London, 1995, p. 22, no. 3.

29 The last three pictures, from the McDonald collection, were sold at Christie's, 20 November 1992 (lots 6, 7 and 8).

30 Craven Mss, Coombe Abbey Inventory, 17 September 1739, as "Five Italian Musicians by francis Halls".

31 Paget Toynbee (ed.), 'Horace Walpole's Journals of Visits to Country Seats &c.', *The Walpole Society*, vol. XVI, London, 1927–28, p. 63.

32 Tate Gallery, *Report, 1966–67*, London, 1968; Robin Gibson, *An exhibition of paintings from the collection of Dr. D.M. McDonald*, exh. cat., Leggatt Brothers, London, 1970, p. 43.

33 See London 1978–79, p. 41, no. 12, in which Millar considers the set of musicians to comprise five and not six pictures; thus he suggests, "It is perhaps not too fanciful to envisage the four canvases of uniform size hanging on either side of a fireplace, flanking the smaller canvas".

34 Translated from Cesare Ripa, *Iconologia*, Siena, 1613, vol. II, pp. 75–76.

35 Gaston Du C. De Vere, trans., *Lives of the Most Eminent Painters, Sculptors and Architects by Giorgio Vasari,* London, 1914, vol. VII, p. 240.

36 London 1978–79, p. 40, no. 11.

37 R. and J. Dodsley, *London and its Environs Described*, vol. III, London 1761, p. 85; Walpole, 1761–71 (1888), vol. II, p. 97.

38 See Aileen Ribeiro, *Fashion and Fiction: Dress in Art and Literature in Stuart England*, New Haven and London, 2005, p. 136.

39 No. 214. See Elizaveta Renne, *State Hermitage Museum Catalogue: Sixteenth- to Seventeenth-Century British Painting*, New Haven and London, 2011, p. 142, no. 69.

40 See Otto van Veen's *Putti enacting a Bacchanalian Scene* (National Trust, Ham House).

41 London 1978–79, pp. 42–43, no. 15.

42 Scottish National Gallery (D 4827).

43 The first is in the Earl of Jersey's collection: see London 1978–79, p. 77, no. 71; the second was sold at Sotheby's, 10 July 1997 (lot 14).

44 Sold at Sotheby's, Amsterdam, 18 April 1977 (lot 40); illustrated in London 1978–79, p. 11, fig. 3.

45 Pomona's pose is similar in attitude to Andrea Boscoli's drawing *A seated woman resting her head on her right arm*, which Lely owned (Scottish National Gallery, D 1515).

46 The Duke of York, the future James II, with Princess Elizabeth and Henry, Duke of Gloucester.

Catalogue

CAROLINE CAMPBELL

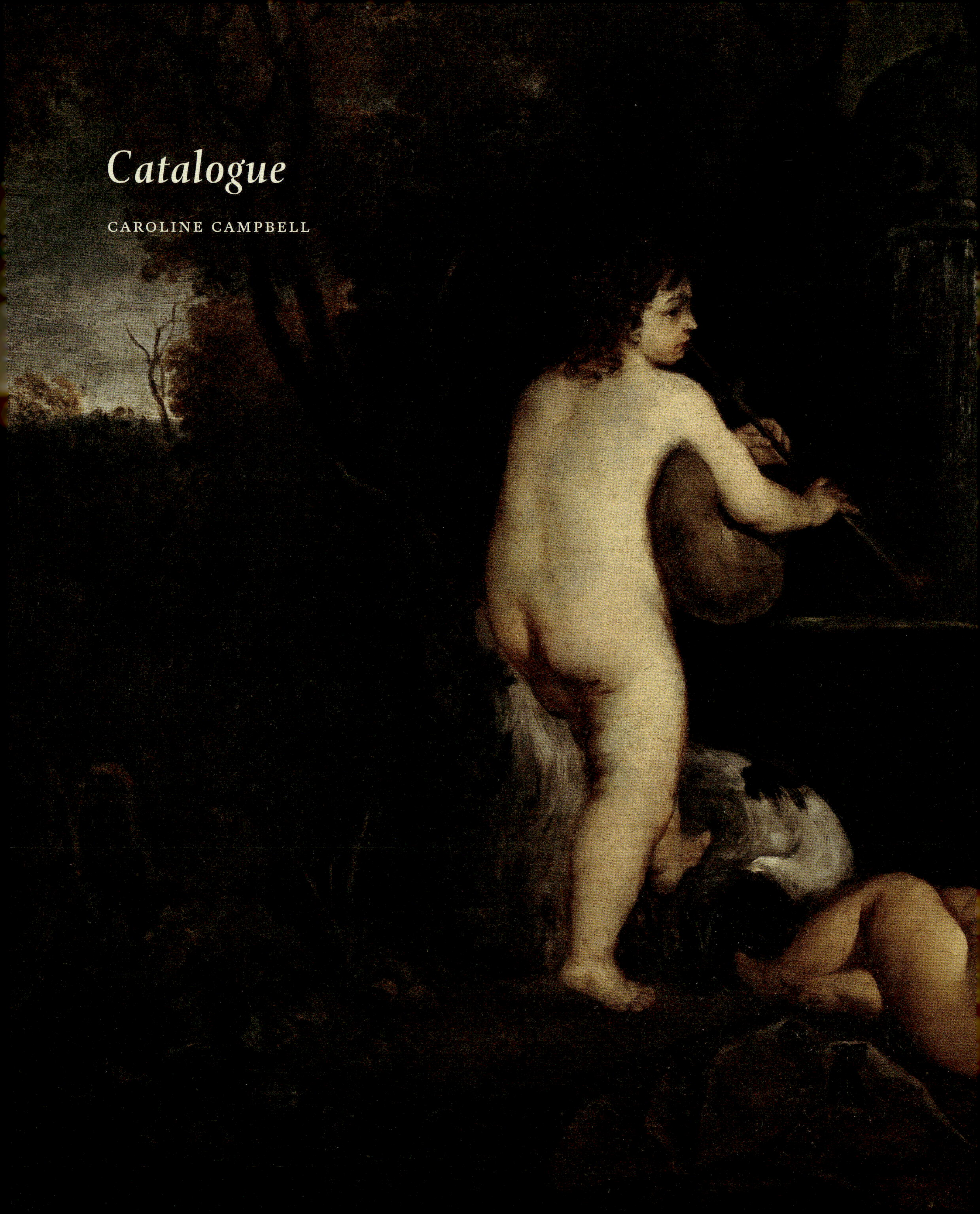

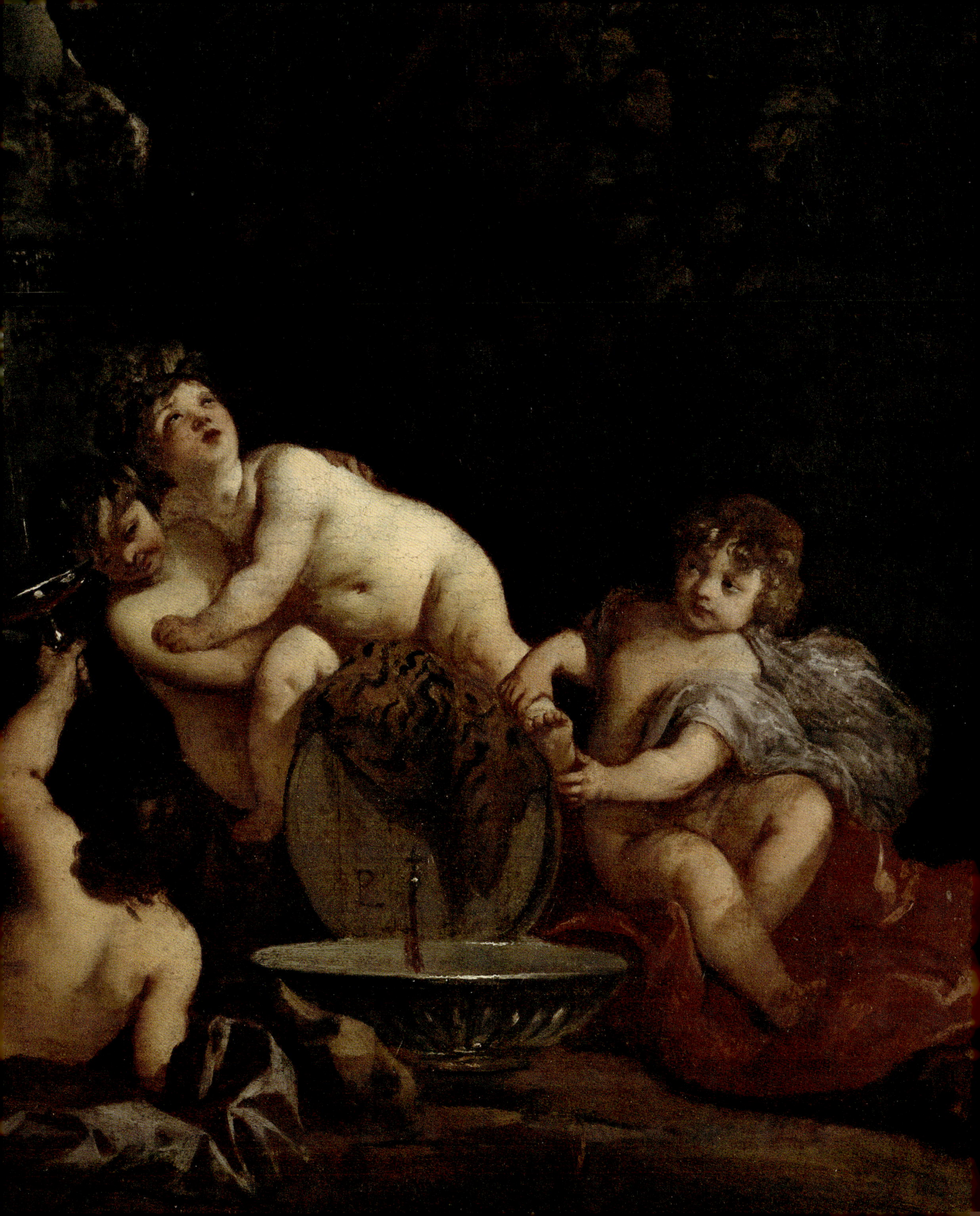

1

The Finding of Moses, c. 1641

Oil on canvas, 54 × 63 cm
Rennes, Musée des Beaux-Arts, 1979.12.1

The Finding of Moses has a very good case to be Lely's earliest surviving independent picture. Modest in scale and in composition, it is the work of a young and talented painter who has not yet managed to integrate his figures convincingly within a landscape setting. It shows Pharoah's daughter reaching out to touch the child proffered to her, who has been saved from the waters of the Nile. As narrated in the Book of Exodus (2: 1–10), the princess took pity on this child – one of the many Hebrew male children whose death her father had ordered – and gave him to an attendant to raise as if he were royal. Coincidentally, this attendant was Moses's actual mother.

This episode of Old Testament history, in which the infant Moses's salvation could be seen to prefigure the birth of Christ, appealed to both Catholics and Protestants. Together with the possibilities it offered for depicting scantily clad female beauties, it was therefore a popular subject in seventeenth-century Dutch art.[1] Artists such as Breenbergh and Poelenburgh set their minute depictions of the Egyptian princess and her entourage in impressive Italianate landscape settings, and Oliver Millar and others have pointed to the debt which Lely owed to their small-scale works and also to those of Van Loo (see figs. 37 and 34).[2] Lely was also influenced by the grander compositions of the 'Haarlem classicists' (see essays by Karen Hearn and David Taylor in this volume), in particular Pieter de Grebber, the more celebrated son of Lely's master, Frans Pietersz. de Grebber. Pieter de Grebber made several versions of *The Finding of Moses*, notably a 1634 picture (fig. 11). He favoured an approach which made the figures majestic rather than alluring, and the monumental, rather heavy female figures and the strong effects of light and shade typical of his work are found again in Lely's first subject pictures, including the present *The Finding of Moses*.

Lely, like de Grebber, developed more than one version of this subject. One of these appears to be represented in the background of two paintings by Vermeer, the *Lady writing a Letter* (fig. 32) and the *Astronomer* (Paris, Musée du Louvre).[3] Another is represented in a drawing in the British Museum formerly owned by Lely (fig. 23). Historically, this

PROVENANCE

Acquired in a public sale (*vente publique*) at the Palais d'Orsay, Paris, 7 December 1979, no. 26 *bis* (ex-catalogue)

EXHIBITION HISTORY

Rennes 1983–84, no. 4; Paris 1994, no. 31

LITERATURE

Rennes 1980, p. 68; Foucart 1983, pp. 362, 369 n. 20; Foucart 1989, pp. 21–22; Foucart 1990, pp. 4–5, fig. 5 (incomplete reproduction)

NOTES

1 Rotterdam and Frankfurt 1999–2000, p. 130.
2 London 1978–79, p. 10; Foucart 1989, pp. 18–22.
3 Foucart 1989, p. 18, figs. 2 and 3. See also the essays by Diana Dethloff and David Taylor in this volume.

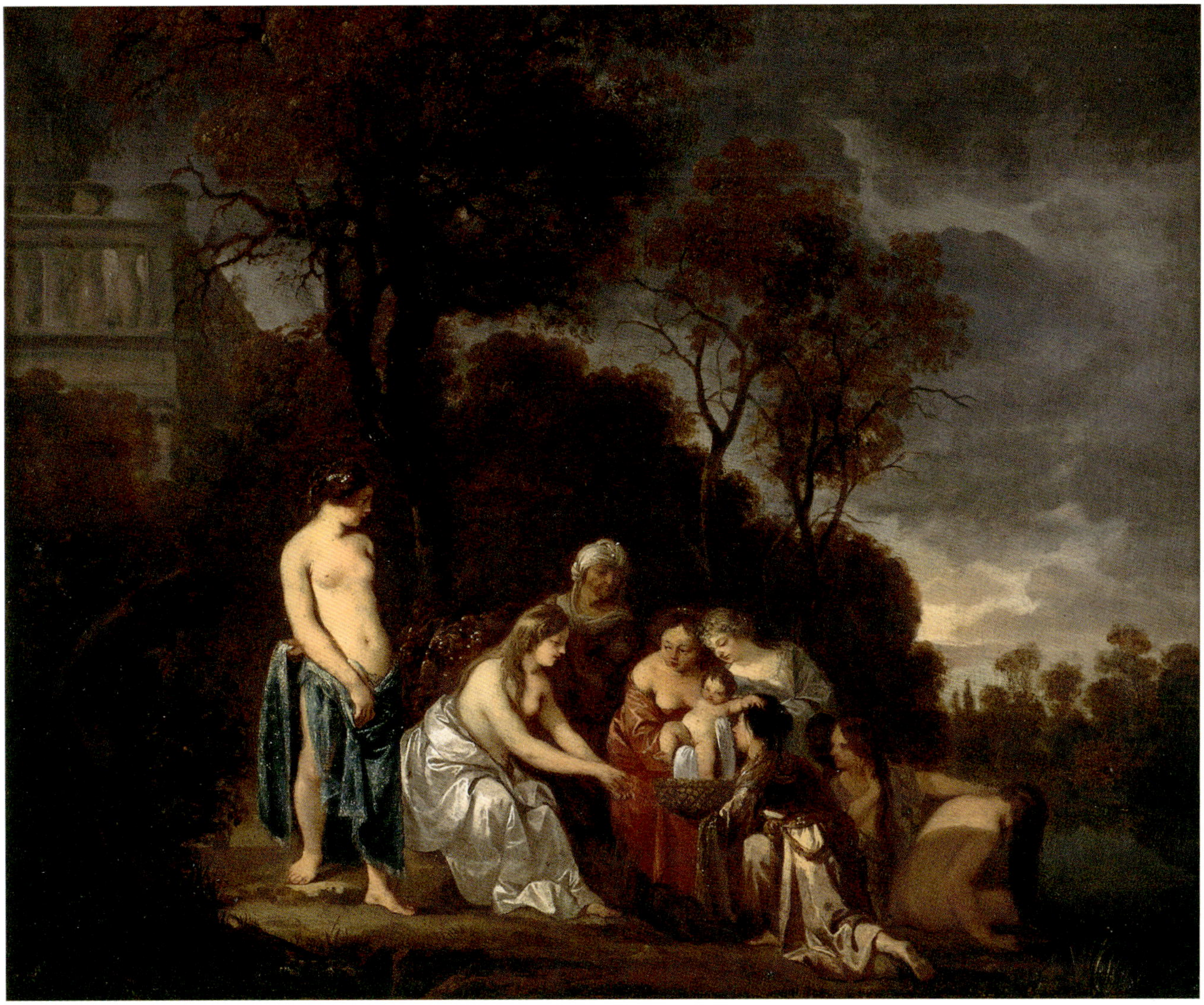

sheet has been given to Poelenburgh, but Diana Dethloff has astutely reattributed it to Lely. The scene shown is close to that found in the present painting. However, there are a few significant differences which demonstrate that the drawing is not a copy. Most strikingly, the oriental umbrella which protects the princess (and draws attention both to her exoticness and to her high status) is missing from the painting, as is the third bathing woman. The drawing may be a study for the present painting, but it is just as likely to represent a slightly different depiction of the subject.

It is notable that Lely, like Poelenburgh, made little attempt – save by introducing the infant Moses – to distinguish his depictions of the Finding of Moses from other pictures of women in landscapes that he made in the early 1640s, such as a *Nymphs bathing* in Nantes (fig. 40) and another *Nymphs bathing* formerly in the Cavens collection (figs. 18 and 19). Pharaoh's daughter is indeed dressed in virginal white, but her dress hangs round her waist, revealing her breasts, as befits someone preparing to bathe (also making Lely's composition more alluring for a potential viewer and purchaser). The ex-Cavens picture was actually for much of the twentieth century also identified as Moses saved from the waters (see fig. 19), but recent technical examination demonstrated that the baby and the basket were later additions (probably of the nineteenth century) and that Lely had painted an un-Pharaonic composition of bathing women, probably the goddess Diana and her nymphs.

The date of the present *Finding of Moses*, like that of all Lely's early subject pictures, has been much debated. Its modest scale, and also the rather ungainly female figures, with long, untidy hair and peculiarly large noses, must make it close in conception and in execution to the damaged Nantes *Nymphs bathing*. The Nantes picture is signed with Lely's monogram, *PL*, and bears a date which has been variously interpreted as 1640, 1641 or 1646. The poor condition of this area of the canvas makes it impossible to be sure about the final digit, but stylistically the *Nymphs bathing* does not resemble Lely's early English works (such as cat. 3 and fig. 52, securely dated to 1647), where there is a more assured connection between figures and landscape. For these reasons it was very probably painted in the very early 1640s. The comparable awkwardnesses and uncertainties in the present *Finding of Moses* – and its overwhelming resonances with contemporary Dutch painting – make it most likely that it too was executed in Haarlem, before Lely's departure for England.

FIG. 40
Peter Lely (1618–1680)
Nymphs bathing, *c.* 1640–41
Oil on canvas, 82 × 99 cm
Musée des Beaux-Arts, Nantes

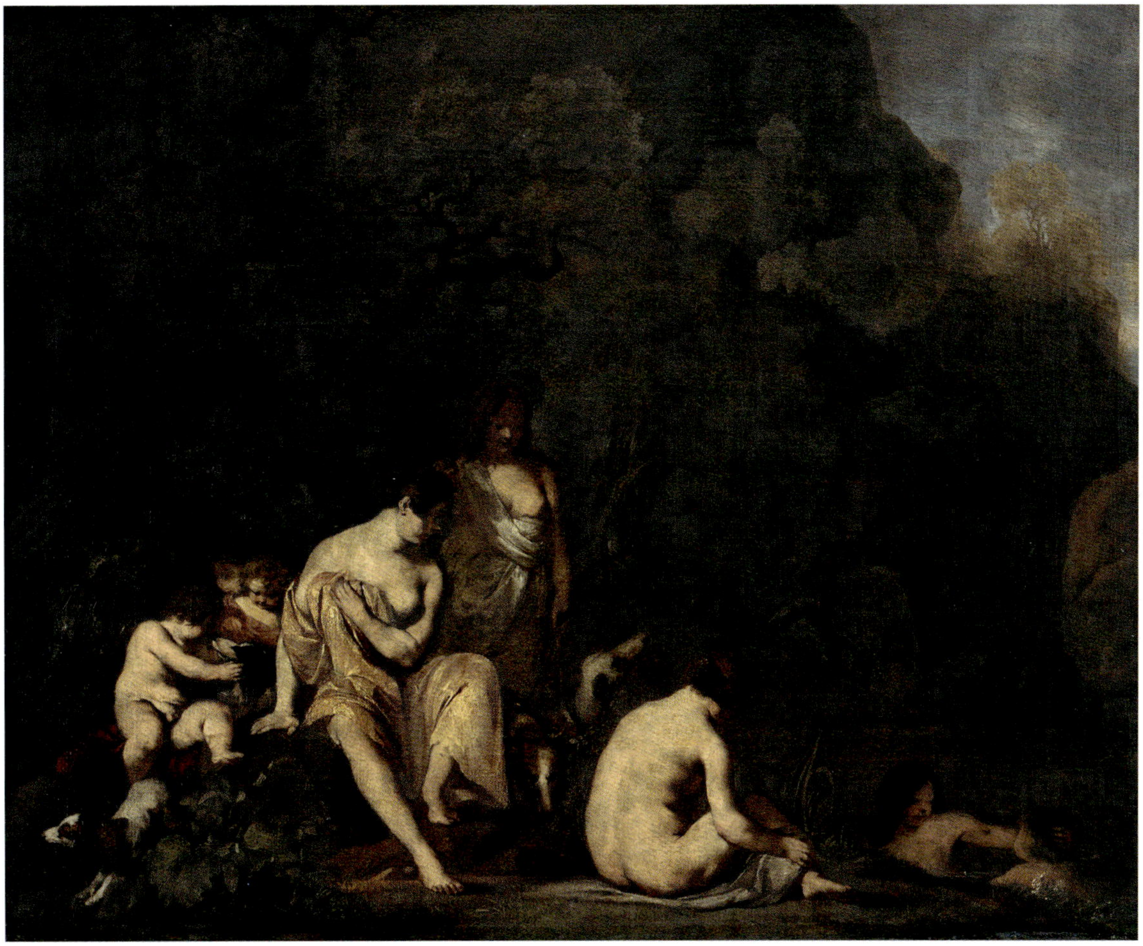

2

A Pair of Lovers in a Landscape, c. 1643

Oil on canvas, 85.5 × 95.3 cm
Valenciennes, Musée des Beaux-Arts, P.81.1

A Pair of Lovers in a Landscape shows Lely addressing a subject in more narrative and pictorial detail than in *The Finding of Moses* (cat. 1). The scale is larger, and both the figures and the landscape are described with greater care and with more precision. Nevertheless, this is the work of a young painter, and also it may have been left unfinished. The artist appears to have used his own features for those of the male lover.[1] But rather than intending to present the picture as a self-portrait, the young Lely may not have been able to pay for the services of a model.

In this picture Lely presents us with a scene of pastoral love, set in an idealised and unidentifiable setting. The round temple evokes the world of classical antiquity, as do the watching fauns or satyrs, one of whom admonishes with a raised finger the mischievous Cupid who stands between them and the pair of lovers. This warning, however, seems rhetorical and unnecessary since the young couple are oblivious to their companions. They are each lost in the sort of gaze of mutual adoration associated with the immature and all-consuming rapture of first love. The young man's dress identifies him as a shepherd, a 'type' recurrent in seventeenth-century drama and poetry throughout Europe, while the woman's costume is not specifically classical. Lely adamantly does not permit his picture to be identified with any particular subject, but rather evokes an Arcadian idyll.

Figures of this type are familiar in seventeenth-century Dutch painting, while the landscape resembles those by Franchoys Wouters,[2] and – as has been noted – there is a particularly close correlation with a painting of *Cimon and Efigenia* by Pieter de Grebber, the son of Lely's Haarlem master, Frans Pietersz. de Grebber.[3] Ultimately, however, representations of these sorts of lovers derive from the art of early sixteenth-century Venice, and it is interesting that Lely's close engagement with the Venetian Renaissance seems to have predated his exposure to original paintings then attributed to Giorgione and Titian in London in the mid 1640s. Later in his life Lely appears to have owned a sixteenth-century Venetian painting which has been identified as the *Lovers in a Landscape* in the National Gallery, London (fig. 41).[4] A more compelling comparison can be drawn with Titian's *Three Ages of Man* (fig. 42) in the Sutherland collection, on loan to the National Gallery of Scotland. By 1662 at the latest this was in the Roman collection of Queen Christina of Sweden,[5] but many engravings of the picture survive, and it seems more than possible that

PROVENANCE

Giroux collection; Giroux sale, Brussels, 11 March 1929, no. 72 (as Willem Panneels); acquired by the Hoofsteder Gallery, The Hague, by whom sold to the Musée des Beaux-Arts de Valenciennes, 1981

EXHIBITION HISTORY

Paris 1994, no. 30; Rotterdam and Frankfurt 1999–2000, no. 42

LITERATURE

Révue du Louvre 1981, p. 144; Foucart 1989, pp. 22–24, fig. 7; Foucart 1990

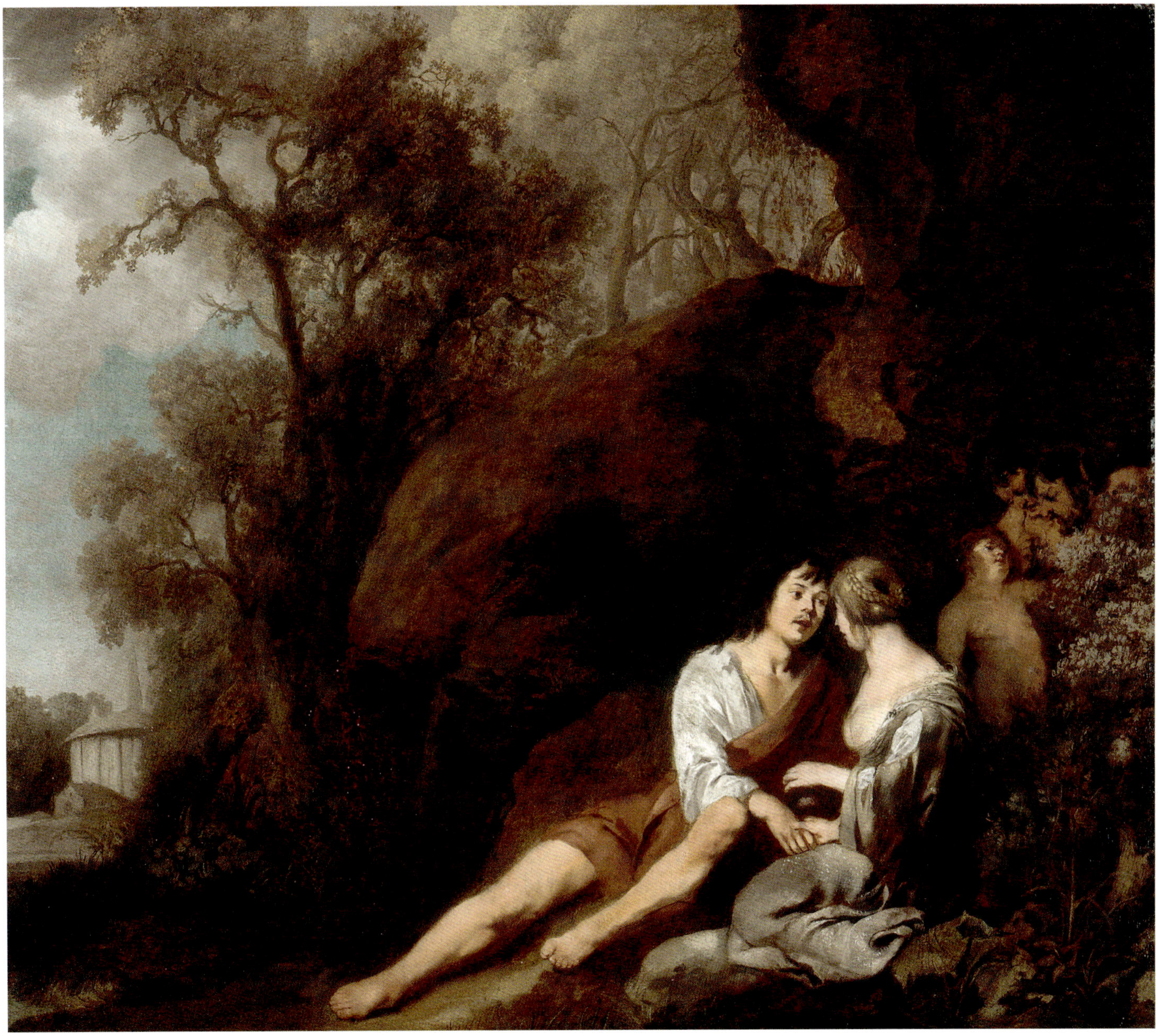

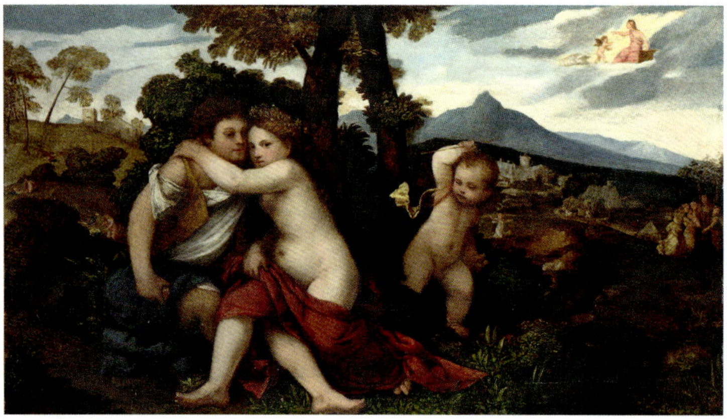

FIG. 41
Bonifazio de' Pitati (called Bonifazio Veronese) (1487–1553)
Lovers in a Landscape, *c.* 1525
Oil on panel, 76.2 × 132.1 cm
The National Gallery, London. Bought, 1882

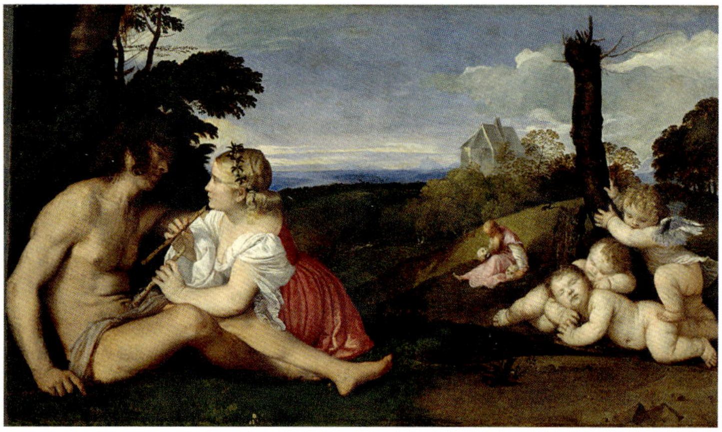

FIG. 42
Titian (Tiziano Vecellio) (active *c.* 1506–1576)
The Three Ages of Man, *c.* 1512–14
Oil on canvas, 90 × 150.7 cm
Scottish National Gallery, Edinburgh (Bridgewater Loan, 1945)

one of these was known to Lely. The paintings are not identical, but the atmosphere of young love and an unbreakable connection between the couple is closely parallel.

The *Pair of Lovers in a Landscape* has compositional and stylistic affinities with *Reuben presenting Mandrakes to Leah* (cat. 4), and they must be of similar date. The Cupid is almost (but not quite) the figure of the baby in the latter picture in reverse. Furthermore, the female lover, shown in *profil perdu* with an unusually pneumatic chest, resembles Lely's representation of Leah, who is similarly busty. Lely's subject pictures are notable for the variety of pictorial finish encompassed within one composition, and these two works are no exception to the rule. In both pictures the rocky forms at the far right of the composition are incredibly sketchy, and appear to be unfinished. Given the absence of any seventeenth-century provenance for them, this indeed may be the case. But while *Reuben presenting Mandrakes to Leah* was almost certainly painted in London (see cat. 4), the *Pair of Lovers in a Landscape* may well be Lely's final work in Haarlem.

NOTES

1 See a letter of 10 September 1995 from Oliver Millar in the painting's dossier at the Musée at Valenciennes.
2 See, for example, Wouters's *Landscape with Diana resting* (Vienna, Kunsthistorisches Museum, GG_3683), of the 1640s.
3 Lammertse in Rotterdam and Frankfurt 1999–2000, no. 42, fig. 42 b.
4 However, Peter Humfrey in his unpublished catalogue entry on the National Gallery picture demonstrates that this was not the picture owned by Lely. I am grateful to Peter Humfrey for sharing this information with me.
5 Brigstocke 1993, p. 177.

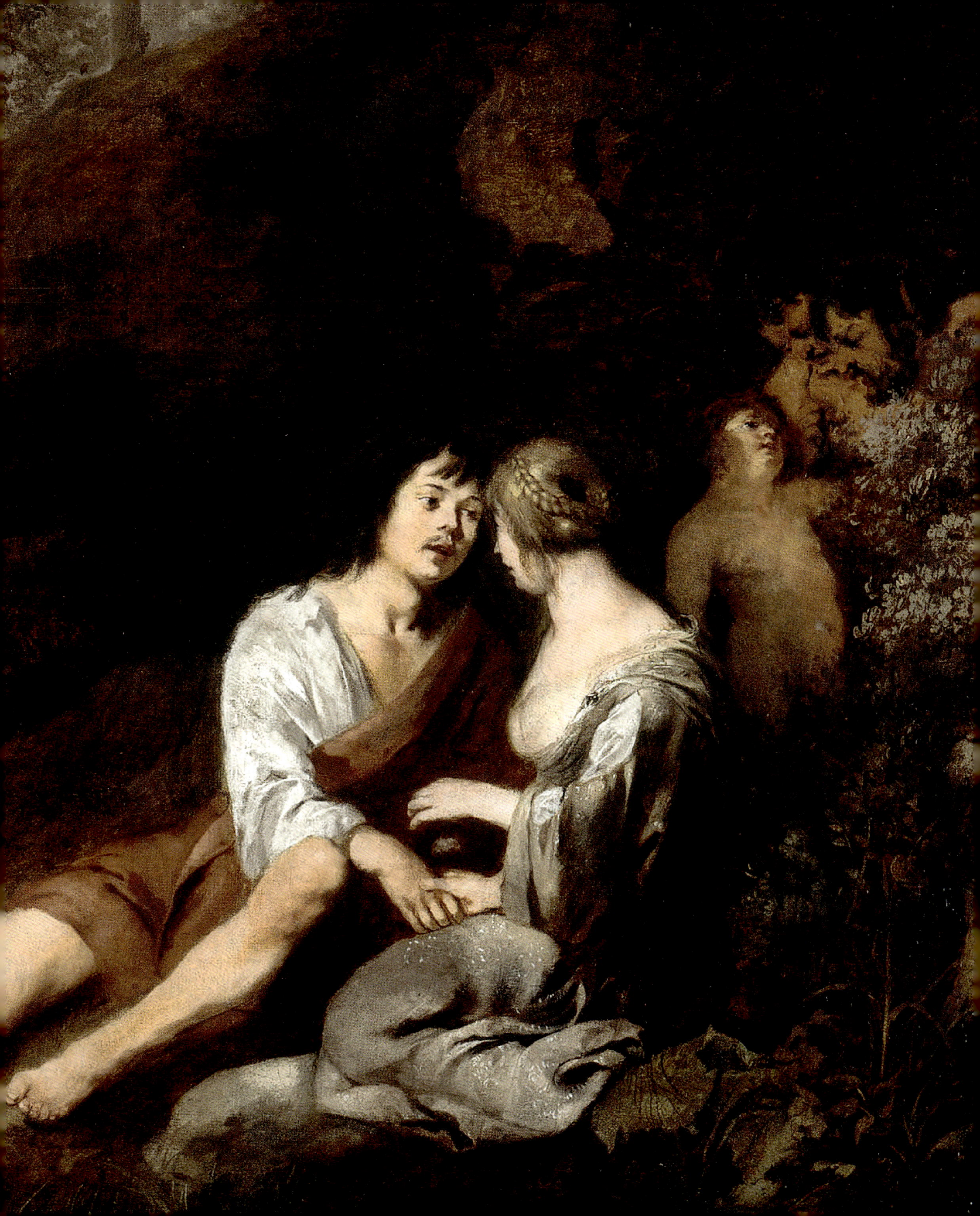

3

The Infant Bacchus, after 1643

Oil on canvas, 62.2 × 77.5 cm
Signed, with the monogram *PL*, on the wine barrel
Private collection

Bacchus, as the classical poet Ovid narrates, spent his childhood in the care of the nymphs of Mount Nysa, "bred/ in secret Caues, with milke and hony fed",[1] where he discovered a vine, and made the first wine. In Lely's picture, Bacchus looks as if he has consumed far more wine than either milk or honey. Only the support of one of his equally youthful companions enables him to remain astride the barrel of wine in the foreground, while another, lying with his back turned to the viewer, raises a wine cup towards the god. A young musician adds to the festival spirit with music from his bagpipe, while a further reveller prepares to help himself to the stream of wine pouring out of the barrel at the right. A goat lies next to the piper. Perhaps this refers to the fact that Jupiter, Bacchus's father, had been brought up by the goat Amalthea, but it is more likely an allusion to the 'goatish' sexual desires that excessive devotion to Bacchus and wine might bring. Bacchus's revels take place in a wooded glade, before a fountain topped by two nymphs sitting astride a dolphin, from which water falls. Such fountains are found in many of Lely's later subject pictures, such as *Cimon and Efigenia* (cat. 11) and Dulwich Picture Gallery's *Nymphs by a Fountain* (cat. 9), and, although the dolphin has been used as a symbol of impatient love since Ovid's day,[2] its presence here serves to make a contrast with the basin of wine in the foreground. It also alludes, as David Taylor argues elsewhere in this book, to the older Bacchus's transformation of sailors into dolphins.

The mood of Lely's painting is light-hearted and jovial rather than drunken. The mildly intoxicated children are intended to charm and delight the viewer's eye, as is the wooded landscape, unmistakably in the style of Dutch seventeenth-century painting. Narrative representations of Bacchus's early childhood are not common in seventeenth-century art, yet those that survive, such as Nicolas Poussin's *Infancy of Bacchus* in the Musée Condé, Chantilly, of around 1627, make light entertainment out of Ovid's story as Lely does.

This work must be close in date to the *Pair of Lovers in a Landscape* (cat. 2), but the painting is less precisely delineated, particularly the landscape, and the rounded forms and soft light are strongly

PROVENANCE

Probably Collivoe sale, London, 1 February 1727; in the Tollemache collection at least by 1951, and probably by 1727; by descent

EXHIBITION HISTORY

London 1964, no. 37, p. 36; London 1978, no. 15, pp. 10, 42–43

LITERATURE

Walpole 1761–71 (1879), p. 227; Vertue 1929–50, XX (1931–32), p. 23; Beckett 1951, p. 67; Waterhouse 1958, no. 60, p. 24; New York 2010, p. 41; Foucart 1989, pp. 21, 25, fig. 6

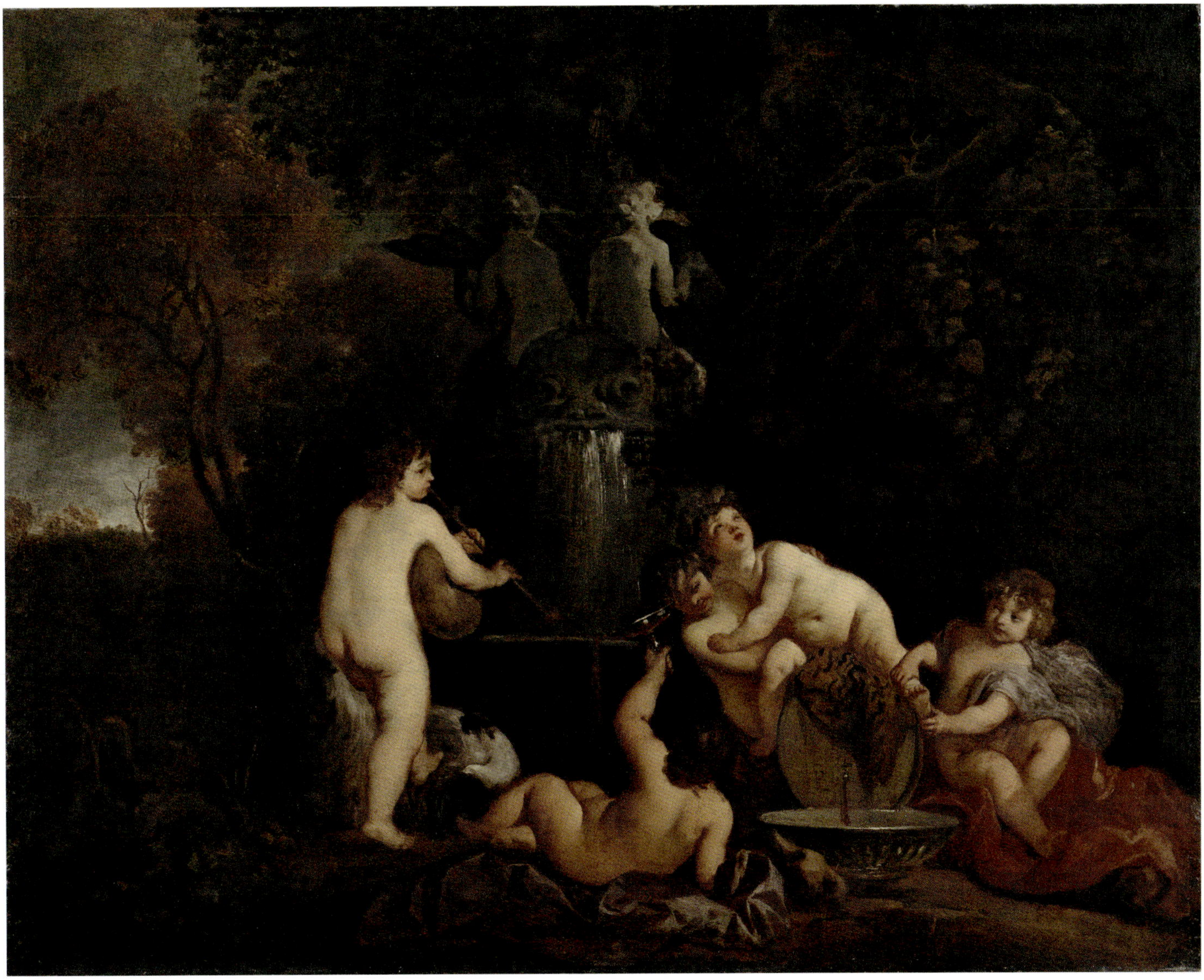

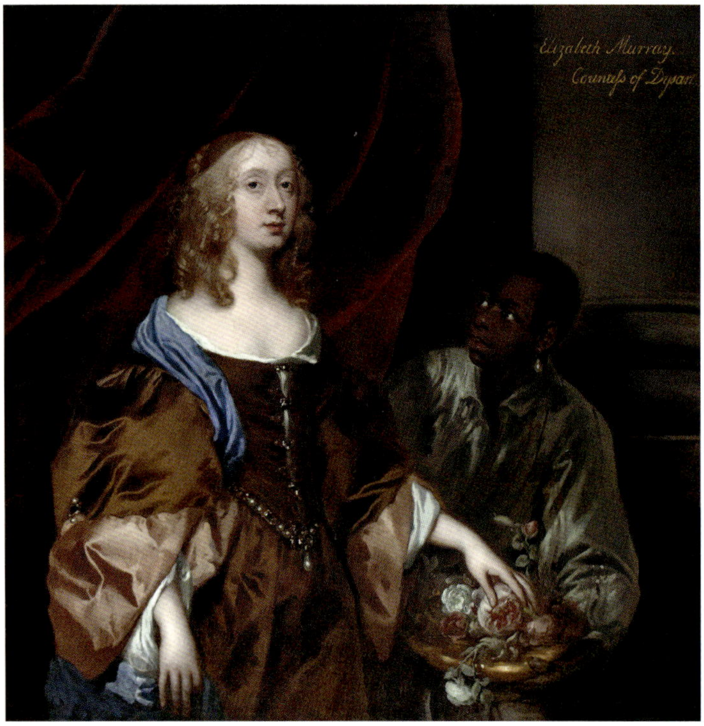

FIG. 43
Peter Lely (1618–1680)
Elizabeth Murray, Lady Tollemache, later Countess of Dysart and Duchess of Lauderdale (1626–1698) *with a Black Servant, c.* 1648
Oil on canvas, 124.5 × 119.4 cm
National Trust, Ham House

reminiscent of Titian – a feature which is common to many of Lely's earliest works.[3] The *Infant Bacchus* is particularly in the spirit of Titian's drunken musicians and lovers in his *Andrians* (fig. 29), a painting which was first engraved in 1636, and which is echoed in the works of many seventeenth-century painters, including Lely.[4] The goat and the draperies recall the work of Franchoys Wouters, a pupil of Rubens and associate of Van Dyck's who was in England between 1636 and 1641.[5] Wouters specialised in small landscapes with figures, generally drawn from mythology or the Bible, and it may have been Wouters's return to Antwerp rather than Van Dyck's death that prompted Lely to try his luck in England. The figural group is more integrated into the landscape than in the Valenciennes or Rennes paintings (cat. 1 and 2), and the innocent Bacchanalians frolic in the foreground of the pictorial space rather than being pushed somewhat back. The relative scale of the figures compared to the landscape is greater, and that also suggests greater maturity on the part of the artist. Unusually, Lely made a substantive change to his composition as he worked on it. X-radiography (fig. 44) shows that the foliage immediately above Bacchus was originally conceived as a curtain (one can make out its red colour under the leaves of the trees subsequently painted on top). In this first phase, it must have more nearly resembled *The Concert* (cat. 7) than any of Lely's other subject paintings.

The *Infant Bacchus* has an early English provenance. Its historic presence in the collection at Helmingham has led to the conclusion that it may have been commissioned by the Countess of Dysart (see fig. 43),[6] one of Lely's most important early patrons, whose first husband was Sir Lionel Tollemache of Helmingham Hall. However, it is in all probability the "Curious picture of a Bachanal. Of boys naked. 4 or five one setting [*sic*] on a Tub" which appeared in Mr Collivoe's picture sale in Covent Garden on 1 February 1727,[7] and which was noted by the eighteenth-century engraver and antiquarian George Vertue to bear Lely's monogram, as this picture does. On these grounds, it seems most likely that The *Infant Bacchus* is one of the first of the "Landtscapes with small Figures" and "Historical Compositions" made by Lely following his arrival in England in the early 1640s.[8]

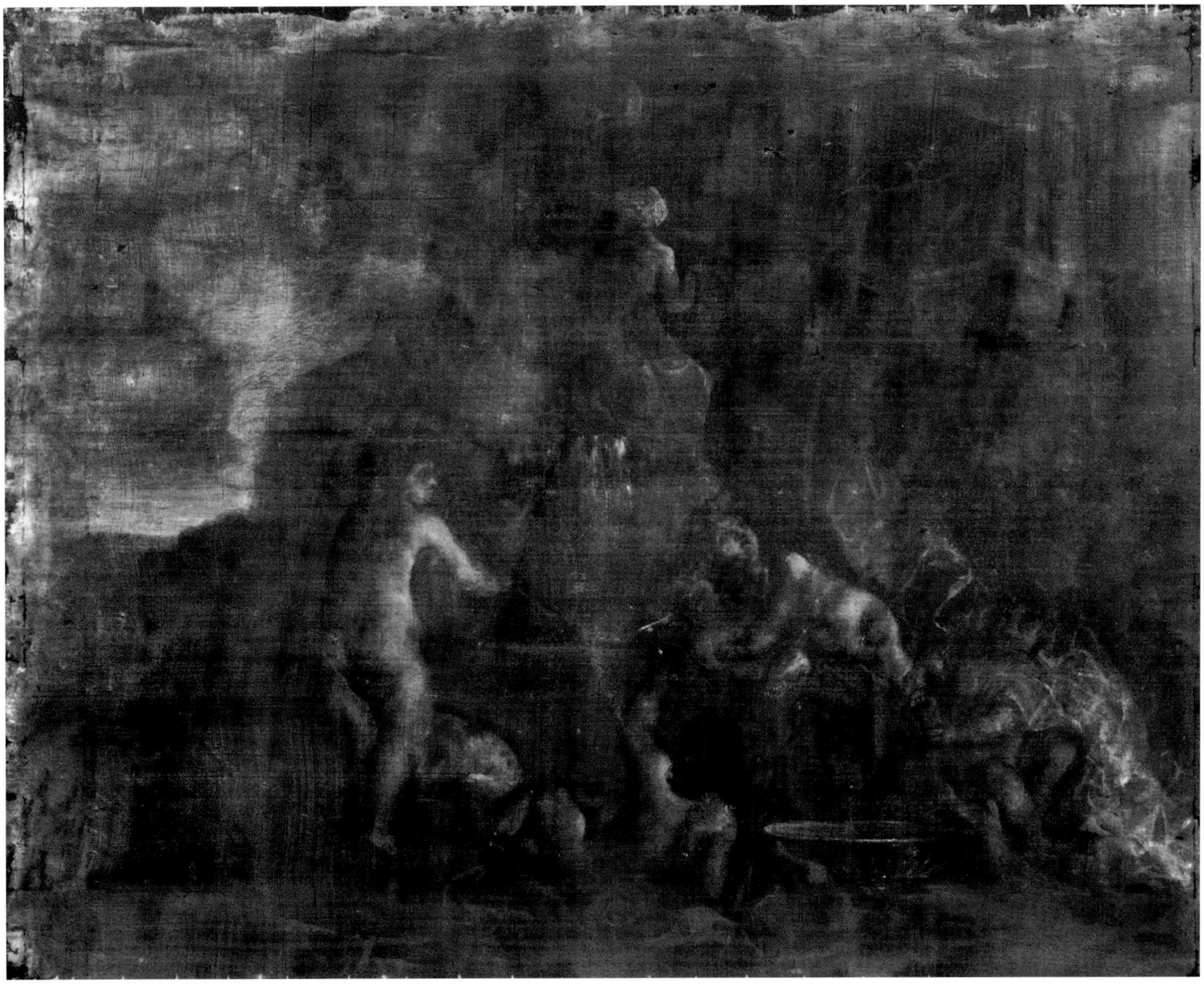

FIG. 44
X–radiograph of cat. 3

NOTES

1 Sandys 1632, Book 3, ll. 314–15.
2 New York 2010, p. 41.
3 Foucart 1989, p. 23.
4 The *Andrians* was in the Aldobrandini collection in Rome until 1638. For the best recent account of it, see Miguel Falomir's catalogue entry in Madrid 2003, no. 12, pp. 166–67.
5 Millar in London 1978, p. 43.
6 See Waterhouse 1958, p. 24.
7 Vertue 1929–50, XX (1931–32), p. 23. Vertue's note reads in full: "A Curious picture of a Bachanal [*sic*]. Of boys naked. 4 or five one setting [*sic*] on a Tub. The wine running out, the Airs of heads very gracefull. The flesh tender & well-coloured mar'd on it P. Lelly. pinx." Isaac Collivoe, a picture restorer and dealer (died 1726), lived on Charles Street near Lely in Covent Garden. Three sales were held of his collection in 1727.
8 Graham 1695, p. 343.

4

Reuben presenting Mandrakes to Leah, after 1643

Oil on canvas, 122.5 × 181 cm
The Courtauld Gallery, London
(Samuel Courtauld Trust: Lee Bequest, 1947, P.1947.LF.215)

Lely's highly ambitious but somewhat unsuccessful picture represents a biblical story which has been very rarely represented by artists. For much of the last century it was called, on uncertain grounds, *The Osborne Family in a Landscape*, and the true subject was identified by Catharine MacLeod only in 1998. It depicts the sisters Leah and Rachel, whose rivalry is recounted in the Book of Genesis. Both women were married to Jacob, in recompense for his fourteen years of servitude to their father Laban. Jacob had wished to wed the beautiful Rachel but had been tricked by Laban into marrying the older, plainer, 'tender-eyed' Leah first, and then the woman of his desire.

Rachel and Leah were regarded as an Old Testament parallel for the figures of Martha and Mary, who stood for the active and the contemplative life. Their relationship was fraught, especially as Rachel, the beloved wife, was infertile, while Leah presented Jacob with multiple progeny, and in particular sons, a divinely ordained award for being hated by her husband (Genesis 29: 31). Rachel only managed to give her husband children through the medium of a surrogate, her maid. Subsequently Leah's barrenness led her to present Jacob with her maid Zilpah. Lely takes up the story following this incident, which according to Genesis took place at the time of the wheat harvest (30: 14). Reuben, Jacob's eldest son, found mandrakes in the fields, and gave them to his mother Leah. Leah, in her turn, gave them to her barren sister.

The mandrakes held by the child Reuben are identifiable by their misshapen roots, which in the sixteenth and seventeenth centuries were supposed to mimic the human form and were associated with fertility, often being seen as sinister. Leah's fecundity is alluded to by the small, definitely male toddler wriggling out of the grip of the maidservant (presumably Zilpah) at the far right. The autocratic woman in red gesturing towards Reuben is Rachel, demanding the roots from her sister. Leah, dressed in blue, remonstrates, as it is reported in Genesis: "Is it a small matter that thou hast taken my husband? And wouldst thou take away my son's mandrakes also?" (30: 15). Rachel, as can be inferred from her haughty expression, permits Leah a rare night with

PROVENANCE

Duke of Leeds; his sale, Christie's, 20 June 1930, lot 25; Sir Henry Floyd, Bt, by 1932; purchased by Lord Lee around 1934; bequeathed by Lord Lee, 1947

EXHIBITION HISTORY

London 1932, no. 3; Worcester 1951, no. 42

LITERATURE

Beckett 1951, no. 588, pl. 23; Murray 1958, p. 21, no. 41

NOTES

1 Kirby Tally 1981, p. 53.
2 This discussion of Lely's technique is based on Kate Stonor's treatment report of *Reuben presenting Mandrakes to Leah* in the conservation dossiers at The Courtauld Gallery. I am grateful to Kate Stonor for discussing her 2007 treatment of this work with me on numerous occasions.
3 Millar in Worcester 1951, p. 26.

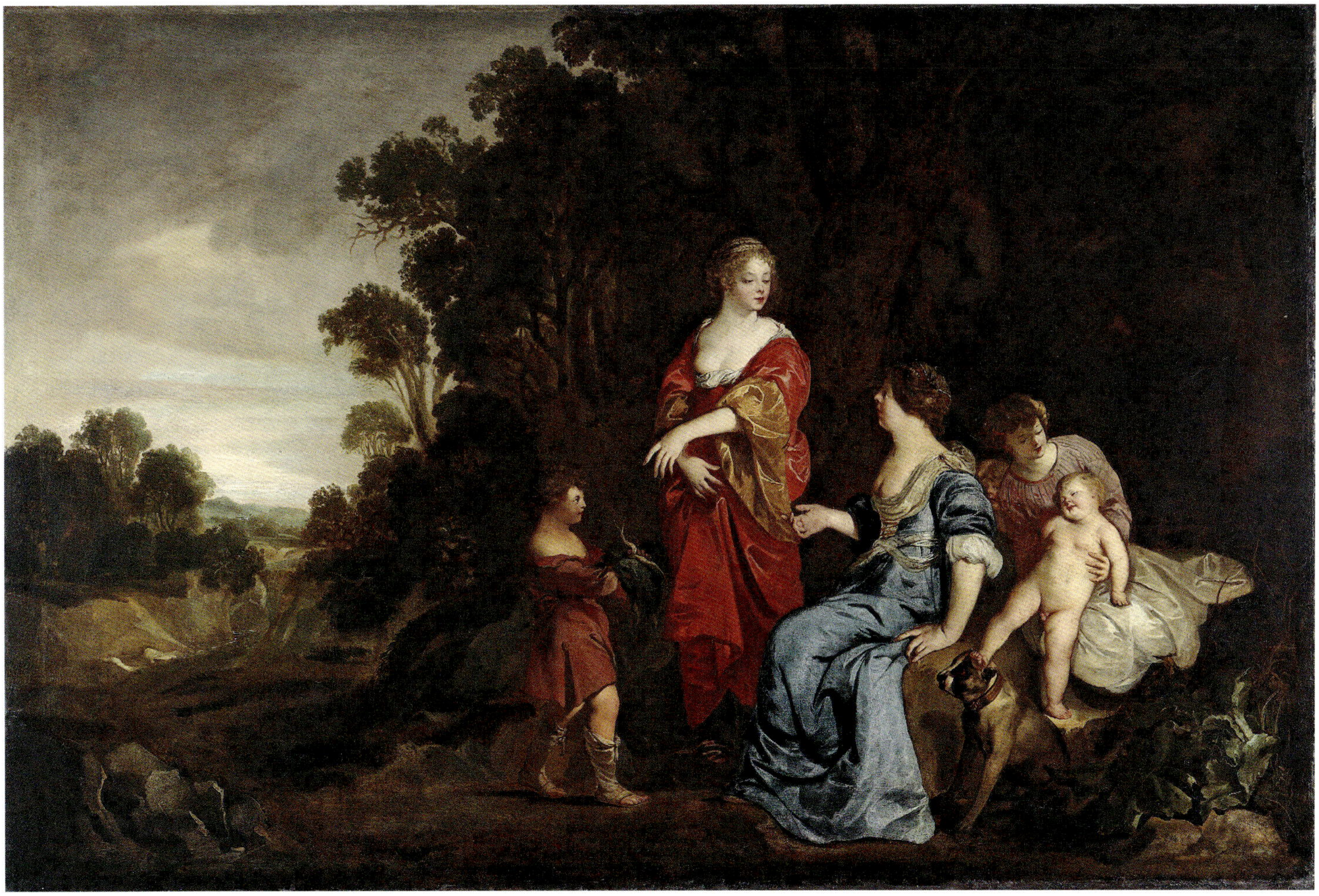

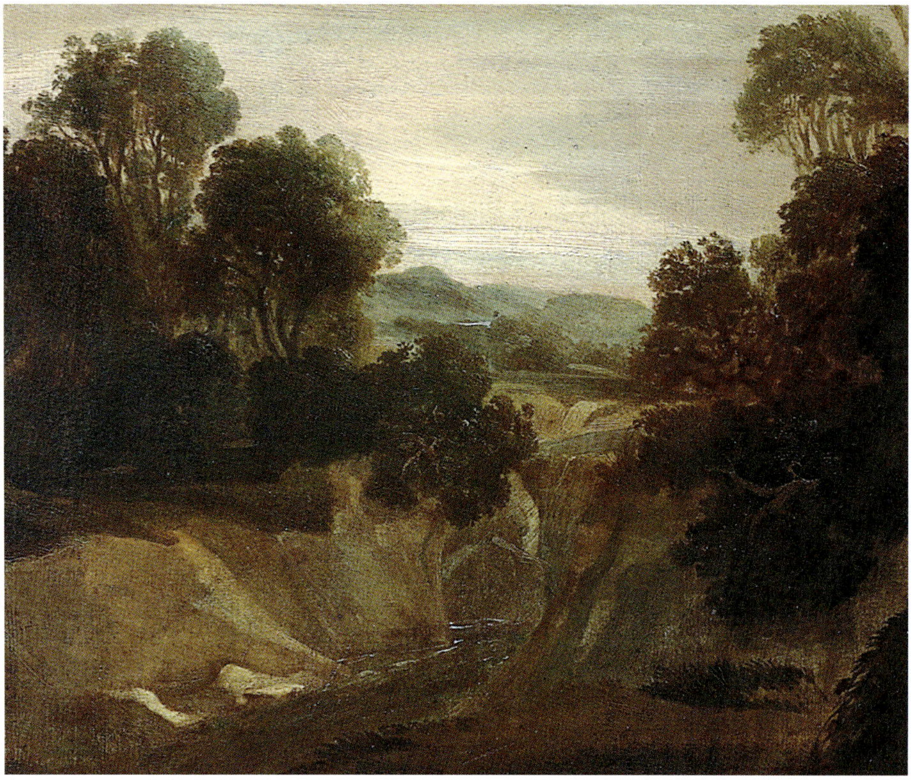

Jacob in return for the plants. The result was Leah's fifth son, Issachar.

The mandrake's association with fertility is also made in the Song of Solomon (7: 13), where the beloved entices her lover to her house with the fragrant mandrakes she has gathered for him. Well into the sixteenth century throughout Europe the mandrake was commonly placed under the bridal bed to aid conception, a custom Martin Luther mentions in his *Lectures* on the Song of Solomon and on Genesis. Such beliefs persisted into the seventeenth century, as much due to cultural norms as to the biblical tradition. Machiavelli's celebrated sixteenth-century comedy, *La Mandragora* (The mandrake), is centred round the plant's ability to make women fertile, while John Donne also refers to this tradition in his poem 'Song', which opens: "Go, and catch a falling starre,/ Get with child a mandrake roote". This root was of great and potentially evil power, feared as much as admired for its association with fertility. Treatises on witchcraft, such as the *Malleus Maleficarum*, still in print in the seventeenth century – a notorious period for the persecution of witches – described the fearful and quasi-human cry which the mandrake made when it was pulled from the ground.

Lely's painting, however, is unlikely to have had any association with unorthodox female power, and it is most probable that it was commissioned by someone to whom a long desired child had come, probably unexpectedly. Since none of the figures appear to be portraits, the painting must have had some such allegorical or commemorative significance, while the scale of the canvas and the rarity of the subject suggest that it was not made speculatively. However, parts of the picture are incomplete, and conservation treatment in 2007 revealed several unresolved passages, particularly in the figure group at the right, notably the handmaid's right arm and the partially hidden arm of the reclining child, the junction between Leah's white cuff and the child's head – which seems to float in space between Leah and Zilpah – and the area between the edge of Rachel's dress and Leah's right arm.

The presence of these unfinished passages has permitted further understanding of Lely's working method. Lely was an accomplished draughtsman, but the only type of preparatory 'graphic' work that can be seen on this canvas is a very loose laying-in of the figures with an opaque red-brown paint. He certainly worked very quickly: a contemporary painter, William Fever, wrote that "Mr Lilly works up his colours so fast that he need not keep them in Water"[1] (to prevent them drying out). In this painting, as in many of his much later works, he exploited the cool, pale grey-coloured priming, allowing it to show through in passages of flesh paint and of white draperies. For instance, he used the grey priming to create shadows in the face of the baby at the far right and in Rachel's neck.[2]

As Oliver Millar noted, the dog at the far right is taken (although on a far smaller scale) from the giant mastiff on which the future Charles II leans in Van Dyck's *The Eldest Children of Charles I* (Royal Collection) of 1637, which Lely could have seen in London.[3] The watery, wooded landscape at the far left recalls Van Dyck's English landscape drawings, while the baby held by Zilpah resembles the children in his exceedingly popular and often copied *Charity* (London, National Gallery), although he is not a direct quotation. The measurable impact of Van Dyck on this work and the large scale – far greater than Lely's earlier Haarlem paintings – together with the clumsiness of the *mise en scène* suggest that *Reuben presenting Mandrakes* belongs to the earliest period of Lely's work in England, immediately before *The Concert* (cat. 7) and *Nymphs by a Fountain* (cat. 9).

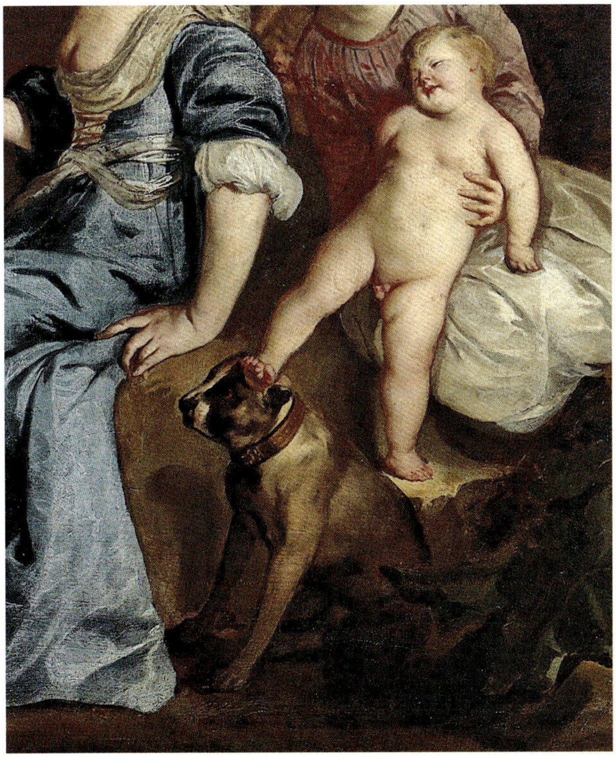

5

Boy playing a Jew's Harp, c. 1648–50

Oil on canvas, 141 × 102.9 cm
Tate, T00884. Presented by the National Art Collections Fund (Eugene Cremetti Fund), 1966

Lely's charming boy, with curling hair and bright eyes, fixes his gaze on the viewer as he makes simple music with his 'Jew's harp', one of the oldest and most rudimentary instruments in the world.[1] The name is a corruption of 'jaws' harp', as the instrument is played while it is held between the player's teeth. It consists of a metal tongue attached to a bow-shaped instrument: music is made, as Lely's boy does, by plucking the tongue with the finger.

This is one of six separate 'subject pictures' which Lely made of musicians in the late 1640s or early 1650s. Five of them, including this picture, cat. 6 and fig. 45, are recorded in 1739 at Coombe Abbey, the Warwickshire seat of William, 3rd Baron Craven, in the inventory of the house drawn up at Sir William's death. At that point they were attributed to the Dutch painter Frans Hals.[2] Horace Walpole, the earliest historian of English painting, who visited Combe in September 1768, noted "a Lady, and three [*sic*] Musicians, by Francis Halls".[3] Oliver Millar correctly reassigned them to Lely in the mid twentieth century. When the *Boy* and the *Man playing a Pipe* were bought by the Art Fund for the Tate in 1966 their

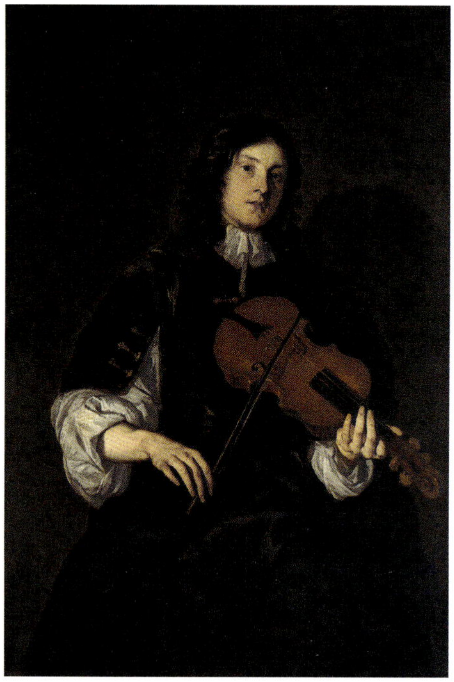

FIG. 45
Peter Lely (1618–1680)
Man playing a Violin, c. 1648–50
Oil on canvas, 142.2 × 93.3 cm
Private collection

PROVENANCE

In the collection of the Earls of Craven, Coombe Abbey, Warwickshire, by 1739; by descent to Cornelia, Countess of Craven, from whose trustees purchased by the Art Fund for presentation to the Tate Gallery, 1966

EXHIBITION HISTORY

Kenwood and Nottingham 1998, no. 1

LITERATURE

Pennant 1811, p. 247; Collins Baker 1912, I, p. 196; Toynbee 1928, pp. 10, 63; Tate 1968, pp. 16–17; Millar in London 1978–79, pp. 10, 41; Butlin 1988, p. 38

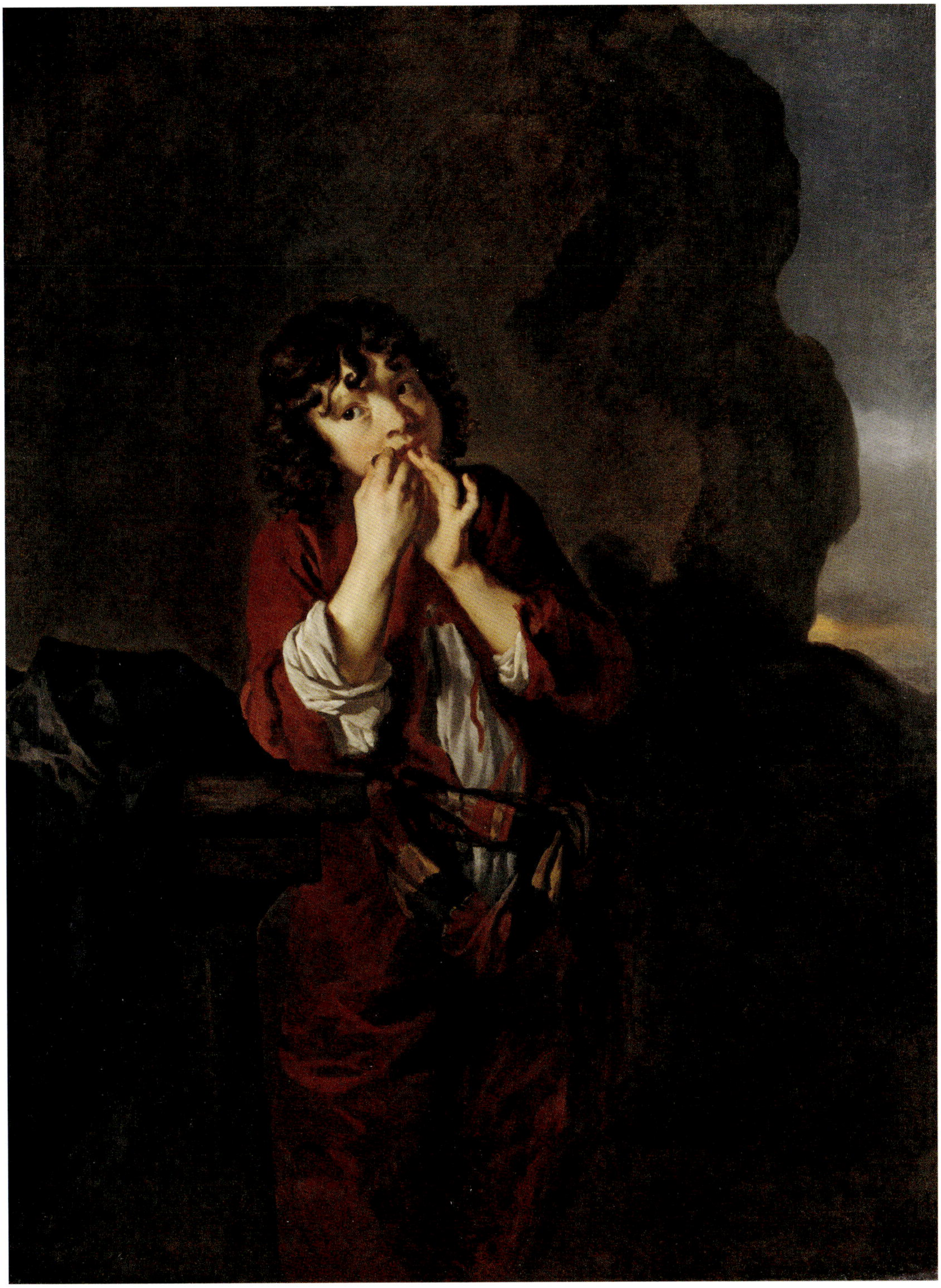

purchase was described by the institution's then director Sir Norman Reid as "the Nation's last opportunity to secure fine early Lelys of this kind", and he praised their "sombre but gracious realism".[4]

A further, sixth picture (fig. 47) was until recently in the Sarah Campbell Blaffer Foundation, Houston, Texas. It may well have been made as part of the same group as the five musicians formerly in the Craven collection, although this is uncertain. It has been suggested that it could be a self-portrait of Lely, whose enthusiasm for music is well known. However, the other pictures, including the *Boy playing a Jew's Harp*, are 'types' rather than intended portraits of a particular sitter. The same is true of Lely's somewhat later *Boy as a Shepherd* (cat. 12). Similar figures are also found in *The Concert* (cat. 7), Lely's most complex evocation of music within an Arcadian setting. It is likely that Lely's Musicians were made in the years around 1650, at about the same time as *The Concert*. As Rica Jones and Kate Stonor's unpublished research on Lely's technique has demonstrated, this group of pictures share many technical features. For example, they incorporate areas of paint which appear to have been left unfinished. The Musicians as a set have a darker, more typically Dutch palette, a characteristic which Lely gradually lost during his early years in England.[5]

Pictures of exotic, proto-Romantic music-makers were among the stock-in-trade of seventeenth-century Dutch painters, particularly the Caravaggisti of Utrecht such as Dirck van Baburen, Gerrit van Honthorst and Hendrik ter Brugghen (see fig. 46). Lely would have been exposed to some of these works during his training in Haarlem, and the 'Caravaggesque' strong lighting of the boy's face and deep contrast between light and shade are a pronounced feature both of the *Boy* and of the other pictures of this group, including cat. 6. Lely was also

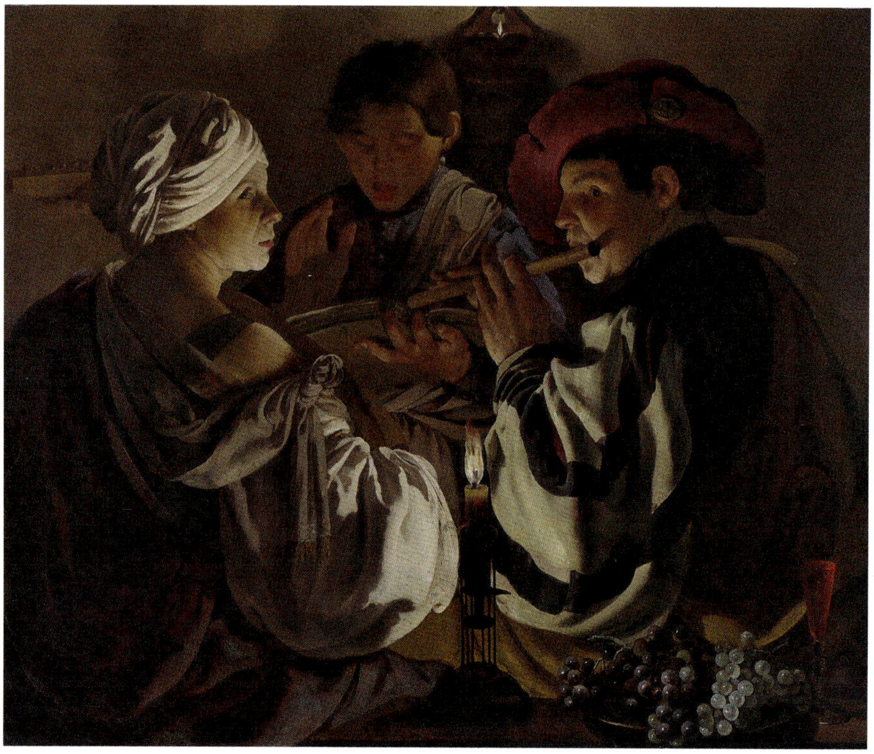

FIG. 46
Hendrick ter Brugghen (1588–1629)
The Concert, *c.* 1626
Oil on canvas, 99.1 × 116.8 cm
The National Gallery, London.
Bought with contributions from the National Heritage Memorial Fund, The Art Fund and The Pilgrim Trust, 1983

drawn to the almost theatrical and larger-than-life characters represented in earlier seventeenth-century paintings of musicians, as well as the work of Frans Hals (which explains the early attributions of these pictures to him). The *Boy*, with his loosened clothing and striped shawl tied round his waist, resembles the models dressed up as gypsies in the work of many of the Northern Caravaggisti. In this picture, Lely seems to be responding to the fashion for such images throughout Northern Europe. Interestingly, this vogue also impacted on the work of a very different painter, his Spanish contemporary Murillo, whose celebrated images of beggars and street children, such as the *Three Boys* at Dulwich Picture Gallery, were probably inspired by the tastes of the community of Flemish merchants in Seville.

An unusual feature for a genre picture of this kind is the pillar at the extreme left of Lely's painting, on which the young musician rests his arm. This sort of pictorial device, intended to impart classical dignity to the sitter, is more usually found in portraiture. Lely would of course have seen this device in the portraits by Van Dyck that he encountered in England (such as fig. 10, *The Thimbleby Sisters*). The boy in the painting evidently modelled for Lely on other occasions: he appears in the two versions of *Two Children singing* (cat. 8 and fig. 53), and his features have been further idealised for the young shepherd flautist in *The Concert* (cat. 7).

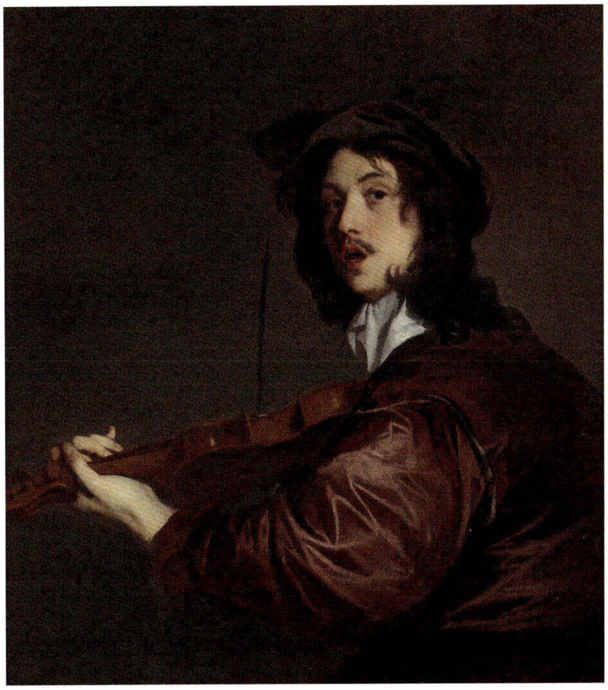

FIG. 47
Peter Lely (1618–1680)
Man, possibly the Artist, playing the Violin, c. 1648
Oil on canvas, 92 × 85 cm
Fergus Hall Master Paintings, London

NOTES

1 I am indebted to Karen Hearn for her exceptionally generous gift of copies of her draft Tate catalogue entries for the *Boy playing a Jew's Harp* and *Man playing a Pipe*.

2 "Five Italian Musicians by Francis Halls", recorded on the staircase next to the billard room at Combe Abbey, inventory of 17 September 1739 (Craven MS, cited by Millar in London 1978–79, p. 41).

3 Toynbee 1927–28, p. 63.

4 Norman Reid to Lord Crawford, letter of 3 October 1966: Tate Archive, TG 4/2/1369/1.

5 I am very grateful to Rica Jones and Kate Stonor for very kindly sharing their unpublished research on the Tate and Courtauld pictures with me.

6

Man playing a Pipe, c. 1648–50

Oil on canvas, 141 × 104.8 cm
Tate, T00885. Presented by the Art Fund
(Eugene Cremetti Fund), 1966

This painting shows a young man playing a pipe or recorder, a very popular instrument in the late seventeenth century. Recorders could be played alone, but in this picture Lely manages to convey a sense of the musician swaying to the music of companions in an invisible, accompanying ensemble. His lively eyes do not engage with us, the viewer, but rather with the musician who is keeping time for the group. The painting is one of five or six contemporary portraits of solo musicians that the artist produced, all of which are characterised by engaging informality. It is tempting to suggest that Lely's pictures of musicians are connected to his circle in Covent Garden in the late 1640s and 1650s. Another, stylistically related picture of this date represents Lely's friend the dwarf and miniaturist Richard Gibson.[1]

As has been noted in the discussion of the *Boy playing a Jew's Harp* (cat. 5), these pictures were recorded in 1739 at Coombe Abbey, in the posthumous inventory of the 3rd Earl Craven. It is likely that they had entered the family's collection through William, 1st Baron and Earl Craven (1608–1697). A friend of Prince Rupert of the Rhine, the leading Royalist commander in the Civil War, he held pictures (including works by Lely) in trust for Rupert's mistress, Margaret Hughes, and daughter Ruperta. But he also owned pictures in his own right, and it may be that the so-called Craven musicians were commissioned by him directly from Lely for himself. As a group, the pictures give an unparallelled impression of intimacy. One, and possibly two, of the musicians (figs. 47 and 48) appear to be self-portraits of Lely himself.

There were two main traditions of seventeenth-century Dutch musician paintings – those of the Northern followers of Caravaggio, centred in Utrecht, and the more domestic scenes of men and women in contemporary dress familiar from the paintings of Vermeer (such as fig. 32), Metsu and others. There are exceptions (and, in particular, the work of Frans Hals), but pictures in both traditions commonly represented more than one person (see fig. 46). This makes the Lely paintings with their single-figure compositions relatively unusual. An interesting precedent for them, however, can be found in Ter Brugghen's work (such

PROVENANCE

In the collection of the Earls of Craven, Coombe Abbey, Warwickshire, by 1739; by descent to Cornelia, Countess of Craven, from whose trustees purchased by the Art Fund for presentation to Tate, 1966

EXHIBITION HISTORY

London 1968, pp. 16–17; London 1978–79, pp. 10, 41

LITERATURE

Pennant 1811, p. 247; Collins Baker 1912, I, p. 196; Toynbee 1927–28, pp. 10, 63; Tate 1968, pp. 16–17; Butlin 1988, p. 38

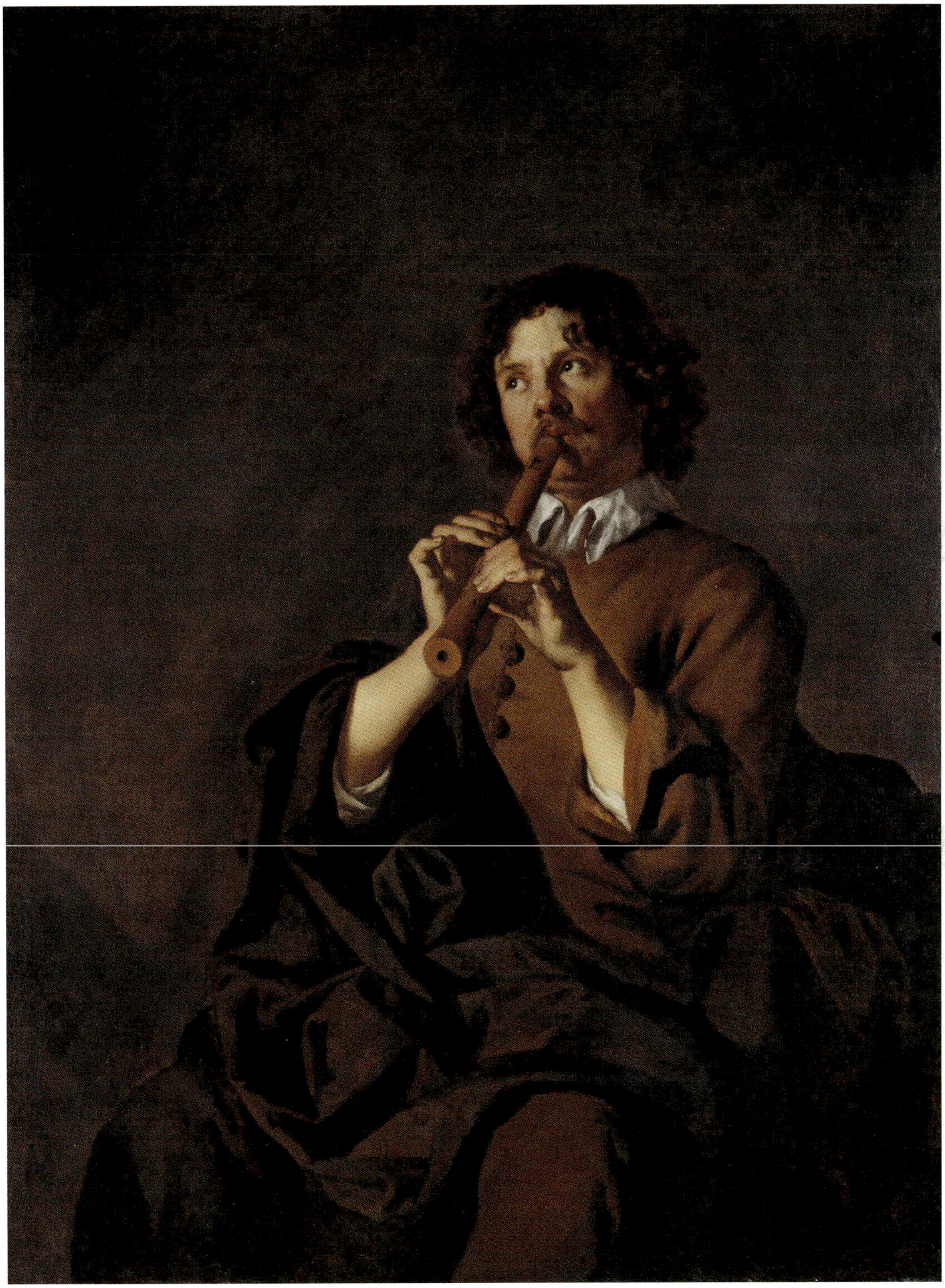

FIG. 48
Peter Lely (1618–1680)
Man playing an Eleven-course Lute, c. 1648–50
Oil on canvas, 109.9 × 88.9 cm
Private collection

FIG. 49
Peter Lely (1618 –1680)
Girl playing a Theorbo-Lute, c. 1648–50
Oil on canvas, 142.2 × 93.3 cm
Private collection

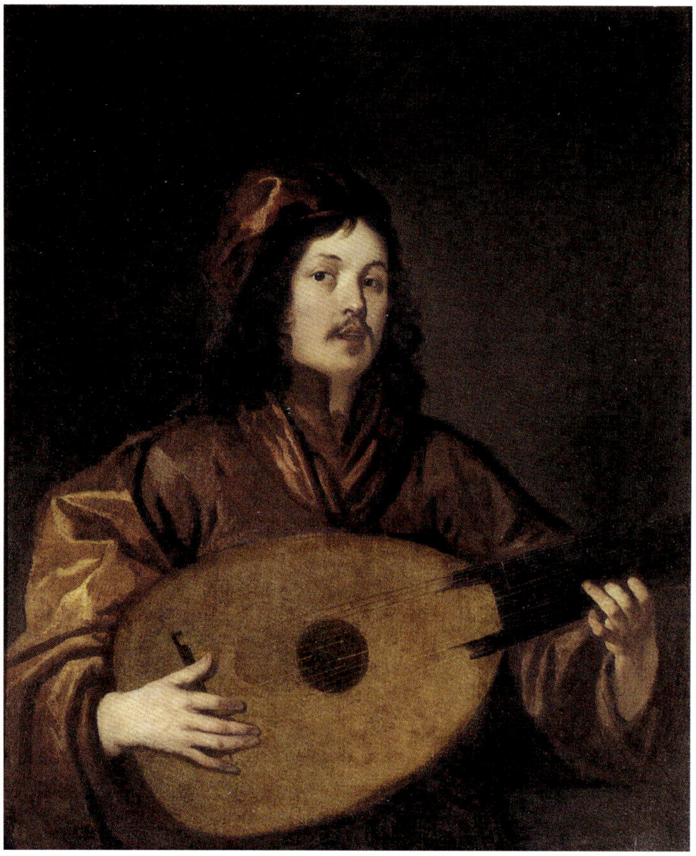

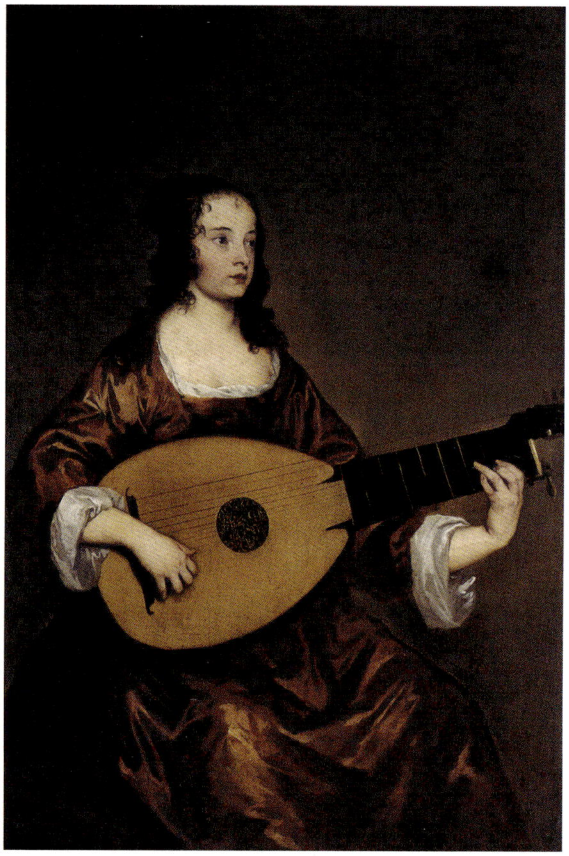

as fig. 12) and in Van Dyck's portrait of the French musician *François Langlois*, painted around 1634–37, probably in England, jointly owned by the National Gallery, London, and the Barber Institute, University of Birmingham.[2] Van Dyck showed his friend in the guise of a Savoyard bagpipe player. Lely's musicians are likewise 'types' invested with personality by the incorporation of distinctive features that are probably drawn from the study of particular models. That said, they should not be regarded as portraits. In all other respects Lely combines ideas from both pictorial traditions of musician paintings in this series. Some, such as the two Tate pictures (this and cat. 5), are dramatically lit in the manner inspired by Caravaggio, while others, notably *A Girl playing a Theorbo-Lute* (fig. 49), have the more luminous quality associated with Vermeer and Metsu.

The artist made a number of small changes to the composition as he worked. Even with the naked eye it is possible to see alterations to the man's curls (the suppressed dark hair now shows through several areas of flesh paint). Lely painted boldly – and apparently quickly. There are bravura details such as the white heightening on the nails of the slightly elongated fingers (a characteristic of Lely at this date) denoting the capture of rays of light, or the confident swathes of the drapery. This is not the work of a tentative beginner, but a mature artist who knew how to manipulate paint for his own ends.

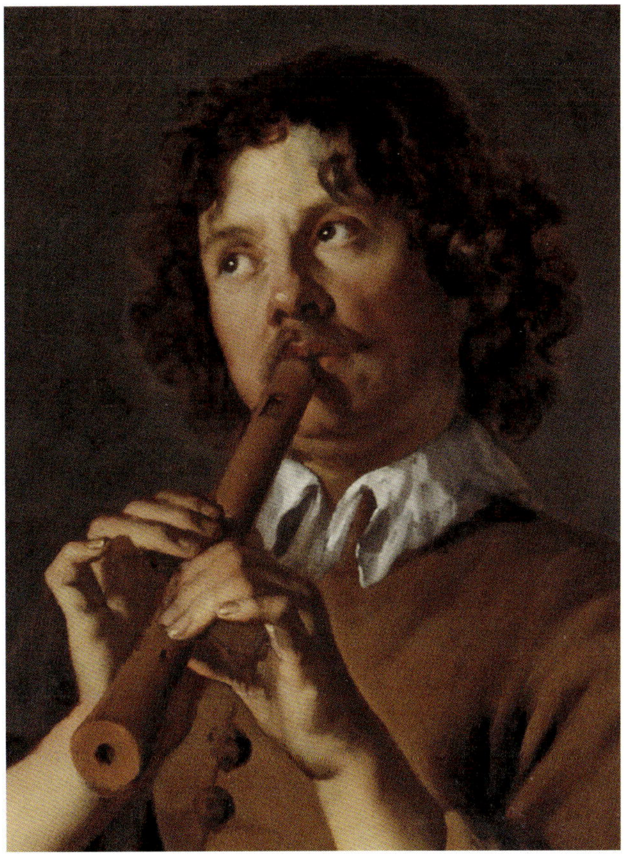

NOTES

1 London 1978–79, p. 43, cat. 16.
2 Reproduced and discussed in Antwerp and London 1999, no. 83, pp. 284–86 (catalogue entry by Judy Egerton).

7

The Concert, *c.* 1650

122.9 × 234.5 cm
The Courtauld Gallery, London
(Samuel Courtauld Trust: Lee Bequest,
1947, P.1947.LF.216)

Lely's enigmatic picture, once called *An Idyll* and now known as *The Concert*, transports its viewers into an enchanted and timeless wooded paradise, where musicians entertain beautiful women. It fully belongs among the pastoral mythologies which dominated cultural life in seventeenth-century England, from the court masques of Inigo Jones, the plays of Shakespeare and his successors and the poems of Donne, Milton, Dryden and their contemporaries. In the foreground, just to the left of the centre of the picture, is a moustachioed musician, playing a five-stringed bass viol. Just as the bass line underlies a piece of music, so this viol player unifies the two parts of Lely's composition. At the left-hand side a child sings, accompanied by another playing the flute. The young male voice is joined by that of a woman, who stands behind the viol, her mouth opened in song, and her hand raised as if preparing to beat time. She is apparently being accompanied by another woman, who has her back to the viewer. This woman reads from a sheet of music and, although we cannot see her mouth, it appears that she is also taking part in the concert.

The musicians seem to be playing for two women who are placed before a silken cloth that extends behind and above them. The woman in profile, who points with her finger to a large brooch, and whose drapery seems to be animated by a breeze, stands behind and looks towards the seated woman. Her grand chair is decorated with a cockle-shell pattern, and she looks directly, even regally, at the viewer. Her bared breasts and the fantastical dress of her companion suggest the world of the court masque. But who exactly is she, and is this a court we see around her? Lely's picture does not represent gods and goddesses at play. The seated woman, although shown in a position of honour, is neither royal or

PROVENANCE

Possibly acquired by Sir Paul Methuen, whose collection passed on his death in 1757 to his cousin and godson Paul Methuen, in whose house at 11 Grovesnor St, London, it was noted in 1761; transferred by Sir Paul Methuen to Corsham Court, Wiltshire, around 1772;[1] sold by the 3rd Lord Methuen at Christie's, London, 14 May 1920, lot 23; bought by Lord Lee of Fareham for £210; by whom bequeathed, 1947

EXHIBITION HISTORY

London 1861, no. 98; London 1934, no. 40 (reproduced); London 1972, no. 170; Sydney and Melbourne 1977–78, no. 12; London 1978–79, no. 11

LITERATURE

Dodsley 1761, III, p. 85; Walpole (1761–71) 1879, p. 227; Granger 1804, p. 116; Britton 1806, no. 203; Collins Baker 1922, p. 37 and reproduced; Borenius 1923, no. 46; Lee 1932, p. 146 and reproduced; Sitwell 1936, pp. 1–2, 89 (reproduced); Beckett 1951, no. 590, p. 13, pl. 53; Waterhouse 1953 (1994), p. 98; Murray 1958, pp. 20–21, no. 38; Rogers 1979, pp. 108–09, no. 4; Troutman 1979, p. 48, no. 3A8; Farr in Courtauld 1987, pp. 60–61 (reproduced); Courtauld 1990, p. 66; Hendriks and Groen 1994, Appendix, p. 29; White 1995–96, pp. 194–95

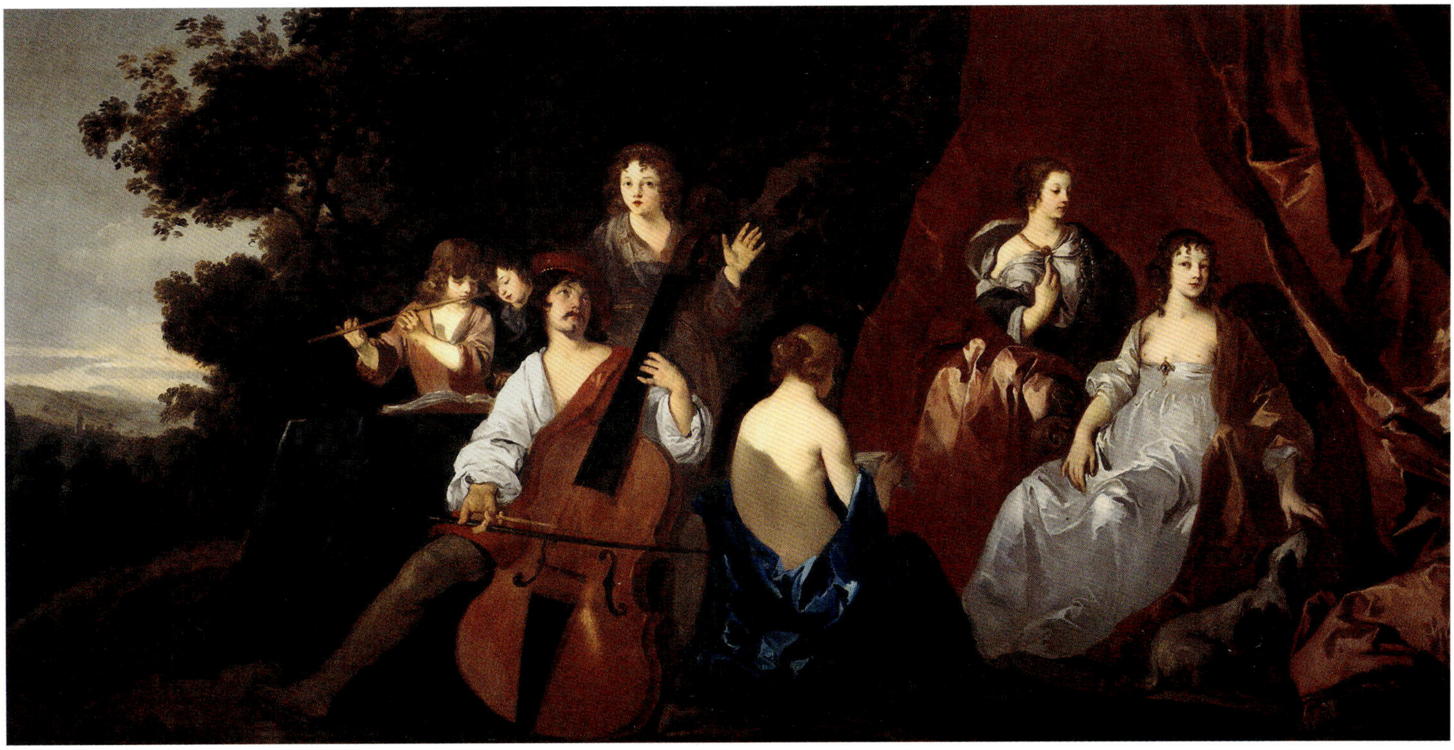

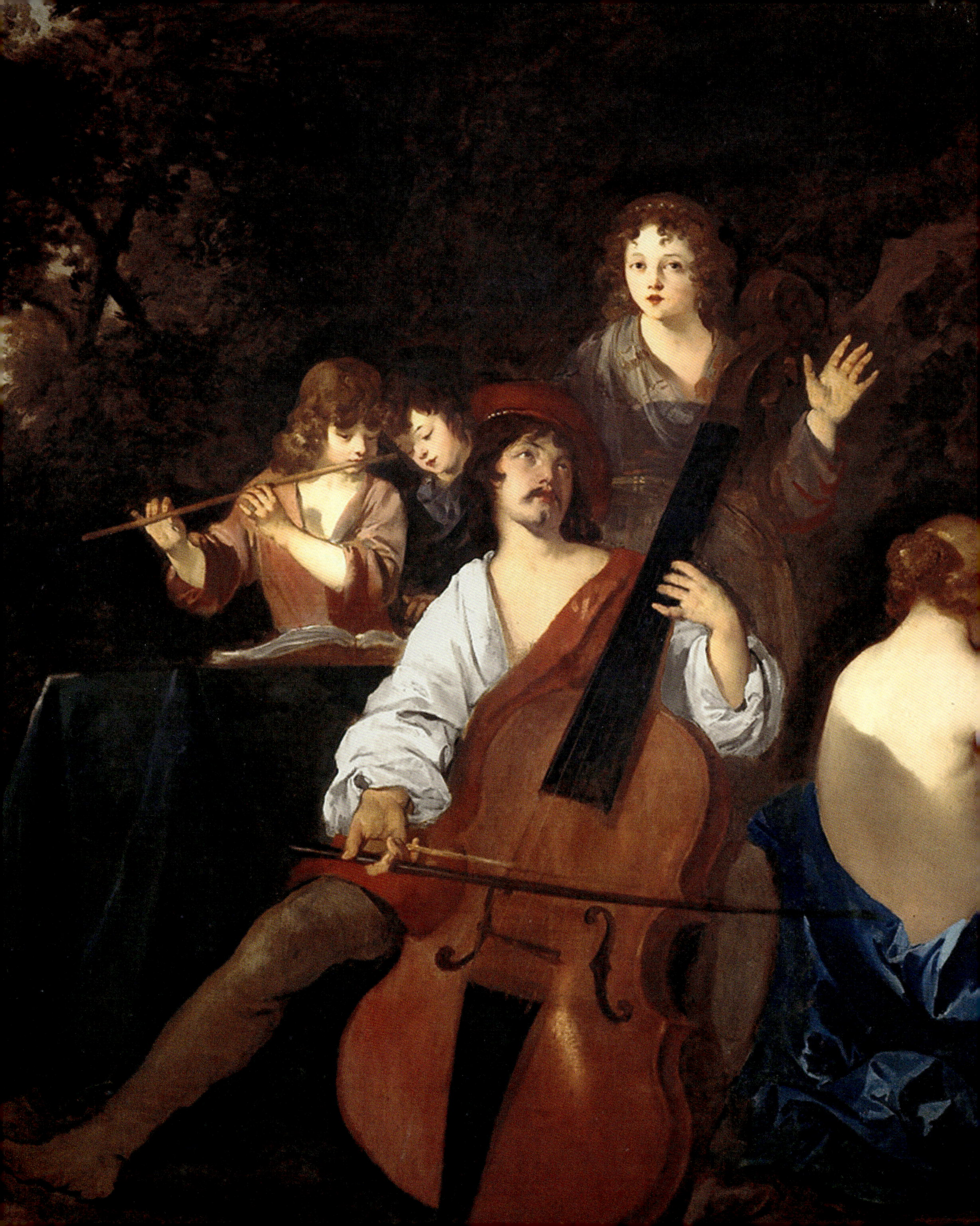

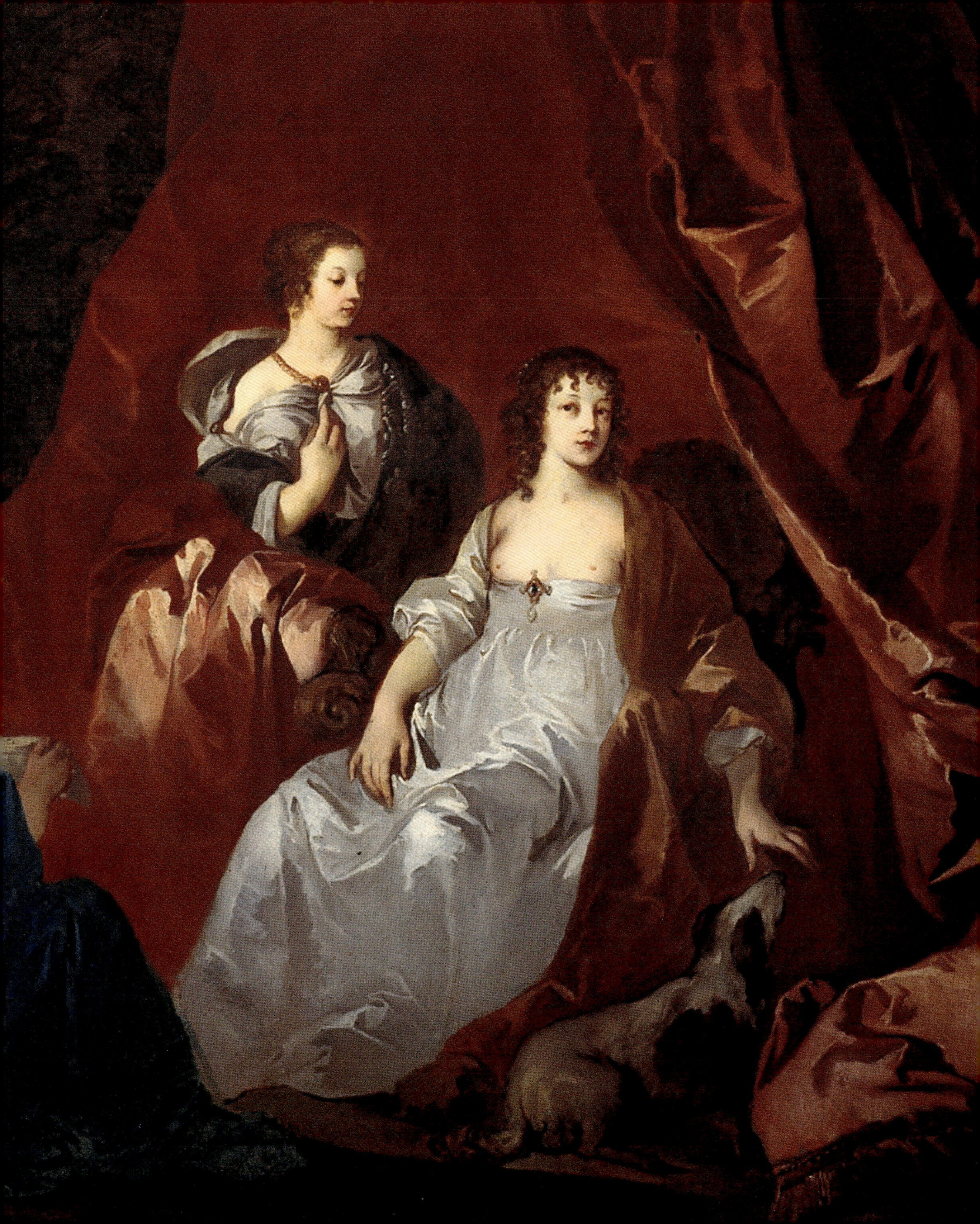

divine. She does not sit on a chair of estate, and the cloth behind her is not a canopy, but a curtain, which suggests the world of the theatre and make-believe – a world familiar from mythological paintings such as Titian's exceptionally influential *poesia* of *Diana and Actaeon*.[2] Lely's ambitious painting raises more questions than it answers.

From 1763, and possibly earlier, this picture was identified as a group portrait of Lely and his family. The viol player who seems to look over his shoulder (almost behind his instrument) to the woman seated on a chair certainly resembles Lely in those portraits we have of him, including fig. 9 and probably also cat. 2. As a result it has been suggested that the women and children are his wife and family. Such a romantic identification was favoured by Lord Lee of Fareham, who bought the painting from the Methuen family in 1920 and bequeathed it to The Courtauld Gallery in 1947. For Lee, all the women represented the same model, Ursula, Lely's mistress and subsequent wife, the mother of his children Anne (born around 1662), John and Peter. Ursula died young, shortly after Peter's birth (as did her infant son), in January 1673.[3] Lee also owned a *Portrait of a Lady*, acquired by The Courtauld Gallery in 2010 (fig. 50). This he identified as Ursula pregnant with her final child.[4] He subsequently sold the picture to Samuel Courtauld, who in his turn also developed a very personal passion for the portrait, writing a set of privately printed poems about it.[5]

Sadly there is no basis to this appealing idea. We do not know what Ursula looked like, but we can be certain on stylistic and technical grounds that *The Concert* is a painting of the late 1640s or early 1650s.[6] It cannot depict her or her children, who were born at least ten years later. What then might the picture be supposed to represent?

The picture was likely of some significance to Lely, and it reflects several of his preoccupations in the years before the Restoration, namely music and a passion for Venetian Renaissance paintings. We know that Lely loved music, and this picture and the set of single-figure musicians (two of which are included in this exhibition, cat. 5 and 6) show that he – or at least those known to him – knew how to play. Playing an instrument in a mixed consort could be a genteel pastime, and it is probably this rather than the world of professional musicians that Lely evokes, although his pictures of individual music-makers reflect a wider variety of music-making, from the Jew's harp of street children and beggars (see cat. 5) to the theorbo and lute (see figs. 48 and 49). In the *Concert* the bass viol is depicted convincingly as a playable instrument, and its player holds and moves his bow correctly.

The flute held by the boy at the far left, however, looks far too thin to be easily playable. It is indebted to the representations of bucolic pipers in paintings by Giorgione, Titian and their contemporaries. Lely was first directly exposed to these works when he came to London from Holland, and we know that they made a deep impact on him. He probably started to deal in them, and to purchase them once he could afford to do so. Not just the child with the flute, but indeed the whole picture is deeply indebted to the visual

FIG. 50
Peter Lely (1618–1680)
Portrait of a Lady (probably
Anne Booth, later Lady Delamere),
c. 1644–45
Oil on canvas, 91.4 × 76.2 cm
The Courtauld Gallery, London
Accepted by HM Government
in lieu of inheritance tax and
allocated to the Samuel Courtauld
Trust, 2010

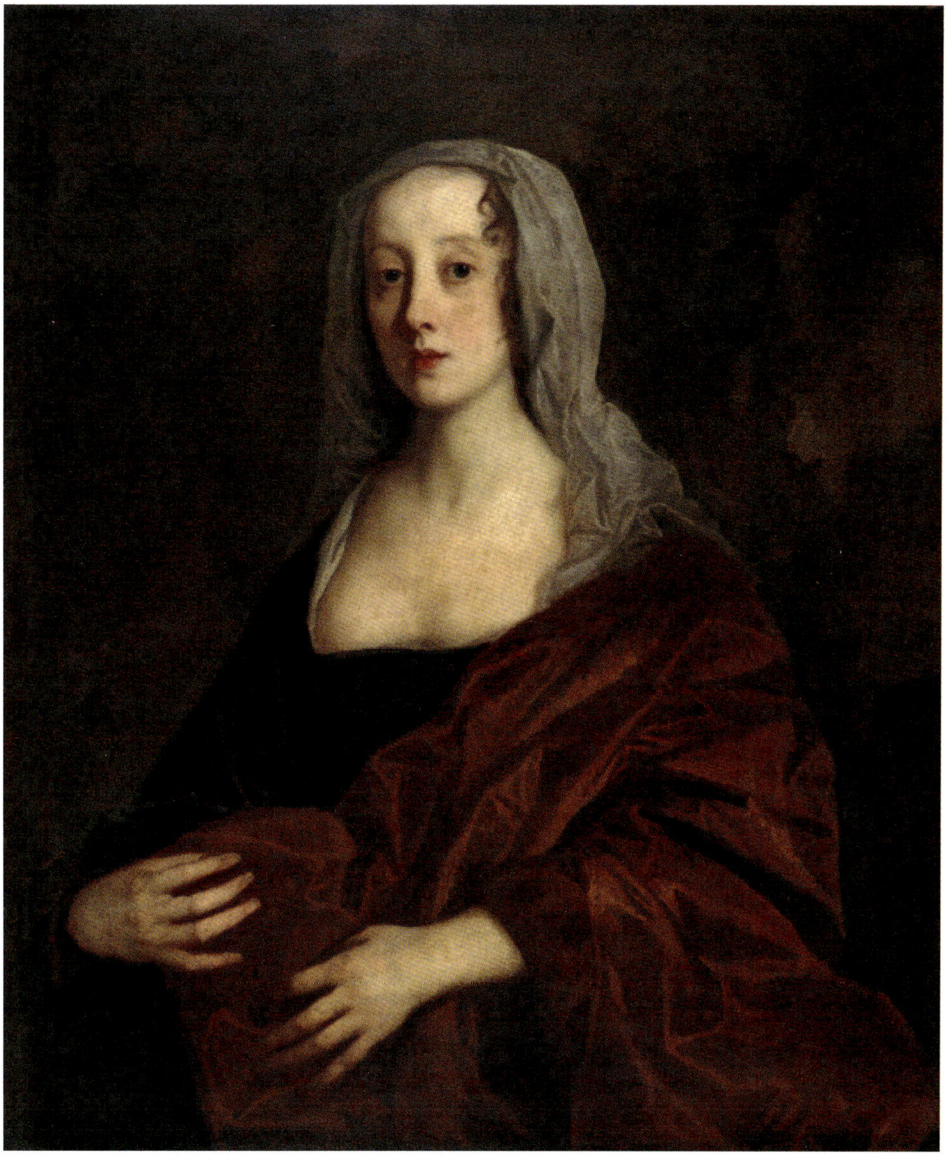

FIG. 51
Attributed to
Titian (Tiziano Vecellio)
(active *c.* 1506–1576)
and workshop
A Concert, *c.* 1510–20
Oil on canvas, 98.8 × 80.7 cm
National Gallery, London.
Bought, 1824

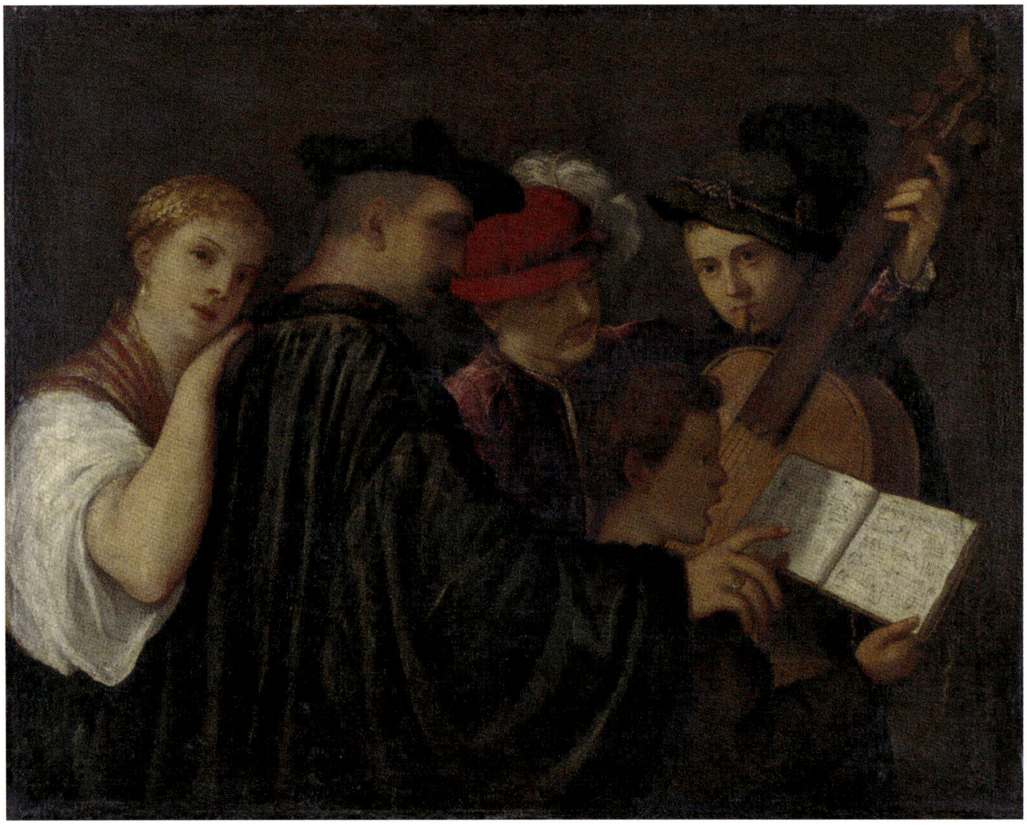

manifestations of this genre, the sixteenth-century Venetian pastorals attributed to Giorgione and Titian which Lely saw in London in the late 1640s and early 1650s, although it is a direct copy of none of these works. The beautiful, scantily clad women placed in a landscape setting recall Titian's Pardo *Venus* (Paris, Musée du Louvre), which was in the collection of Charles I. The musicans themselves resemble the groups of musicians which Titian and Giorgione painted in the first decade of the sixteenth century, and in particular it recalls the singers in a once much celebrated work, *The Concert* (fig. 51), attributed for much of its life to Titian. This was one of the star pictures which Charles I bought from the Gonzaga collection, and it was still greatly valued when it entered the National Gallery in 1824.[7]

The exceptional size of Lely's *Concert* – only equalled by *Reuben presenting Mandrakes to Leah* (cat. 4) – makes it one of Lely's most important and ambitious compositions. The painting has a similar subject (and shape) to the *Idyll* (fig. 21), destroyed in 1941, and it has been suggested that they were once a pair, although this seems unlikely given their disparity in size.[8] We do not know anything of the *Concert*'s history before the eighteenth century but it is unlikely that such a large work would have been made spontaneously, without a commission. It is also the most unusual of Lely's subject pictures. Like the Dulwich *Nymphs by a Fountain* (cat. 9) it does not illustrate some well-known narrative. Rather it tells the familiar story of Music in the service of Love and Beauty, but in a new and innovative fashion. Although in harmony with the poetic pastoral tradition, Lely reveals himself as an exceptional re-inventor of this artistic genre, which he and his contemporaries considered the apex of painterly production. What is unfortunate is that the "barbarous Trans-Alpine" land of England was so unappreciative of it that the *Concert* marks one of Lely's final attempts at a type of painting which he could have made his own. The pastoral tradition, however, did not die in England. In the late eighteenth century, Thomas Gainsborough wrote of his desire "to take my Viol da Gamba and walk off to some quiet Village when I can paint landskips and enjoy the fag End of Life in quietness and ease".[9] We cannot tell if Gainsborough knew Lely's picture. But it is fascinating that the outstanding English portraitists of two succeeding centuries considered music-making in the outdoors – and particularly playing the viol da gamba – to be the epitome of pure pleasure.

NOTES

1 Unpublished communication from James Methuen-Campbell to Ernst Vegelin and Helen Braham, 11 March 2000, in the picture's dossier at The Courtauld.

2 Now London, National Gallery, and Edinburgh, Scottish National Gallery.

3 Lee 1932, p. 146.

4 *Ibid.*

5 *Ibid.*

6 Millar in London 1978–79, p. 40; see also the unpublished technical report by Kate Stonor held in the dossiers of the Department of Conservation and Technology at The Courtauld.

7 For its subsequent history, see Penny 2008, pp. 298–99, 302–03.

8 The *Idyll*'s dimensions were 44½ × 78½ inches, while in inches the *Concert* measures 46 × 91¾. See Beckett 1951, no. 584, for the *Idyll*. Like the Tate Musicians (cat. 5 and 6), the *Idyll* also belonged to Cornelia, Countess of Craven in the 1920s. Could it have shared the same early provenance?

9 Woodall 1961, p. 115.

8

Two Children singing, c. 1650

Oil on canvas, 61 × 55 cm
Philip Mould – Private collection

Lely was an unusually sensitive portrayer of children. His earliest dated work is a portrait of a girl, inscribed 1640,[1] and thus painted before he left Holland for London. Once in England, he secured his growing reputation with two paintings of Charles I and his children (one of them fig. 52). These portrait groups were made in 1647 and 1648 for the Earl of Northumberland, in whose custody the three youngest royal children had been placed. They are among the extremely few securely dated works by Lely in England before 1660,[2] and as such are an essential reference point for understanding Lely's early career in England.

Lely's portrayals of Princes James and Henry and their sister Elizabeth have many points of comparison with this exceptionally charming and engaging study of two children singing, which has never been exhibited before. The milky tone of the flesh paints, the subtle colours and the intense characterisation and engagement of the sitters are all features in common between these three works. The strong lighting of the faces, particularly the crisp delineation of the shadows, and the very tender, wistful feel further connect these pictures with a group of early portraits including the *Portrait of a Lady* acquired by The Courtauld Gallery in 2010 (fig. 50). Oliver Millar aptly characterised these works as revealing "a restraint and a sensibility which disappeared from Lely's work when he came more directly under the influence of Van Dyck".[3]

The sitters are not known to us, but Lely conveys the impression that they were familiar with him and relaxed in his company. This informality is missing – unsurprisingly – from Lely's images of the royal children, and also of other youthful members of the elite, such as *Henry Sidney, Earl of Romney* (fig. 60) or the *Little Girl in Green* from Chatsworth, who may be one of his nieces.[4] Indeed, there are no signs of rank; the childrens' clothing is not shown in sufficient detail to be specific. However, enough can be seen to demonstrate that they wear contemporary, not historic or allegorical dress. The painting is not a fragment of a larger work, and it has not been cut down. Another version, in the Royal Cornwall

EXHIBITION HISTORY

Never previously exhibited

LITERATURE

None

NOTES

1 London 1978–79, p. 34, no. 1.
2 London 1978–79, pp. 37–38, nos. 6 and 7.
3 Millar in London 1978–79, p. 37.
4 London 1978–79, p. 45, no. 20, pl. I.

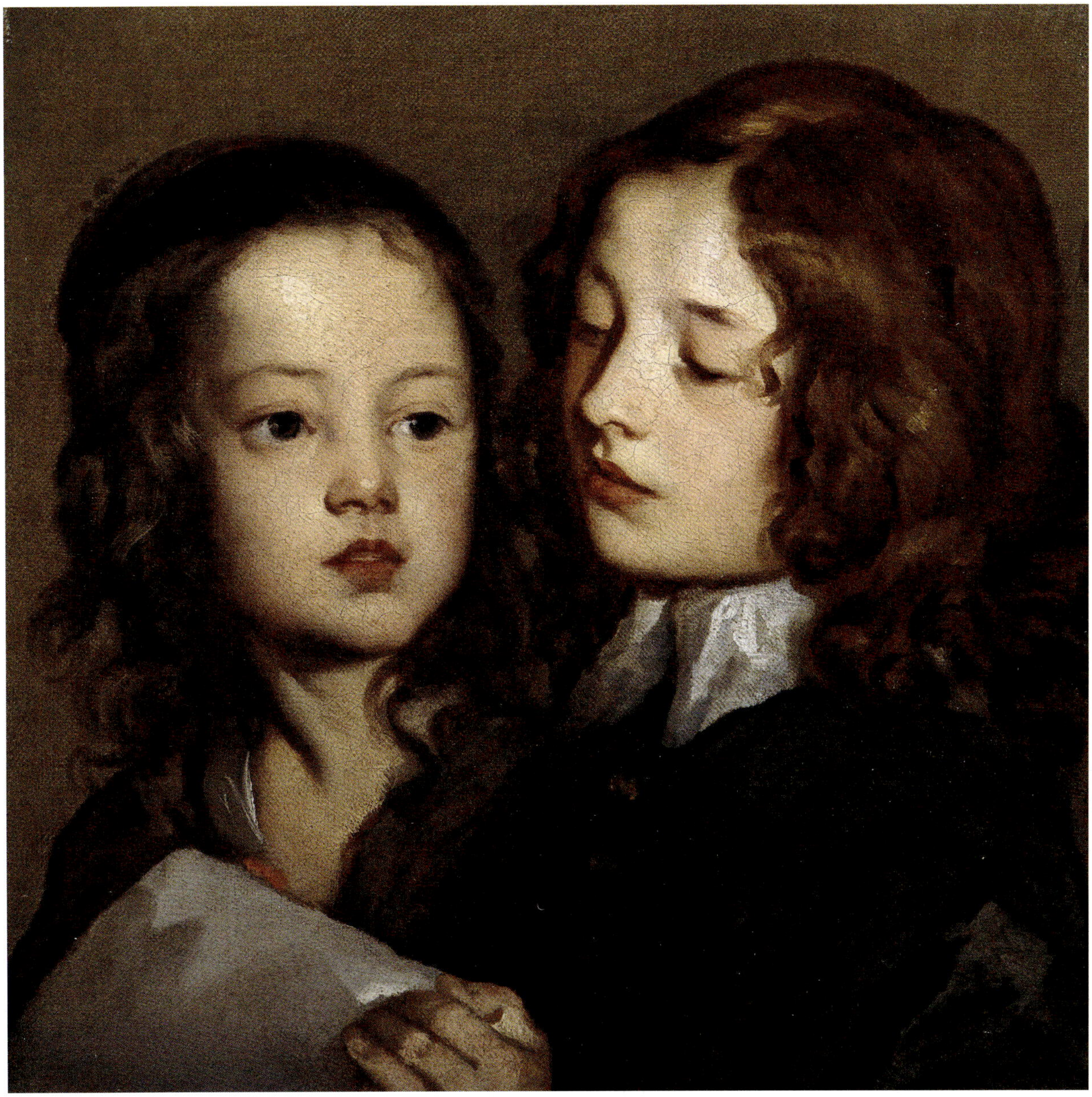

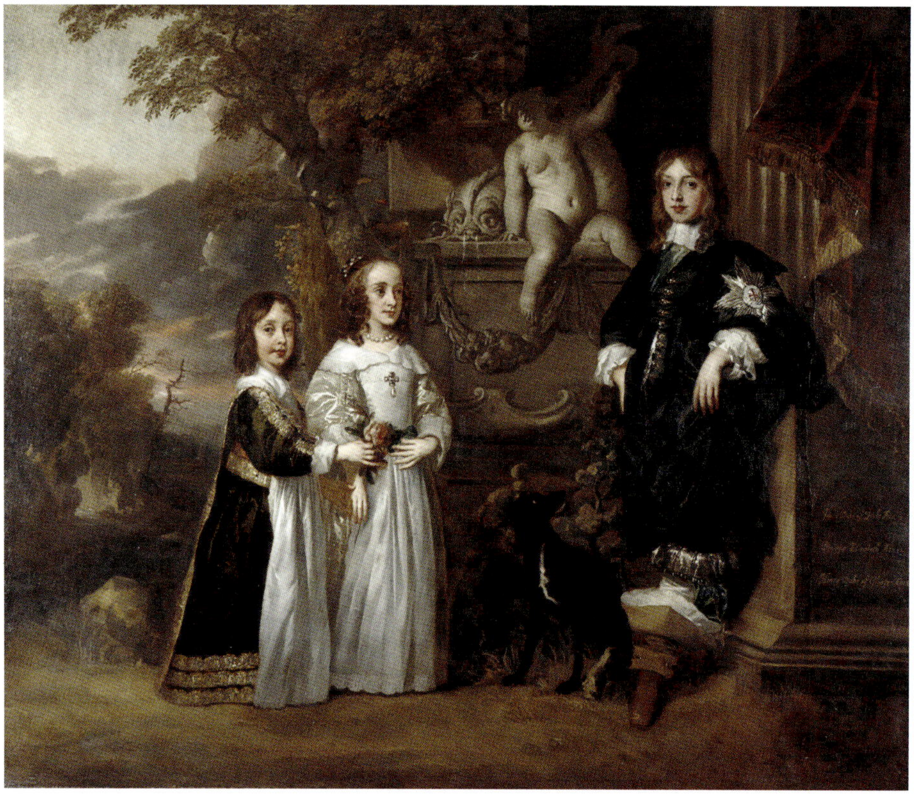

FIG. 52
Peter Lely (1618–1680)
The Three Younger Children of Charles I: James, Duke of York, Princess Elizabeth, and Henry, Duke of Gloucester, 1647
Oil on canvas, 198.2 × 233 cm
National Trust, Petworth House, Sussex

Museum in Truro (fig. 53), has almost the same dimensions, and it seems that both pictures are autograph works.

The boy holds a sheet of music in his hands. He could be reading a letter, but the tilted position of his head and his opened lips suggest rather that he is singing. This is corroborated by the action of the girl, who is probably his sister. She turns her head towards him, as if listening to his voice, and her lips are open as if she is preparing to join his song. Like the *Boy as a Shepherd* (cat. 12), the *Two Children singing* are intended as both 'real' and 'perfect' images, a 'type' or exemplar of music making, but softened and idealised. Music, of course, was a question of deep interest and importance to Lely. One of his other early English commissions was a series of portraits of musicians, two of which are included in this exhibition (cat. 5 and 6). In these, light is also powerfully cast upon figures, set against dark backgrounds, as in *Two Children singing*.

Seventeenth-century sources record that Lely liked to have musicians playing as he worked, and, although he may not have been able to afford this luxury at this early stage of his career, it cannot be coincidental that he made so many pictures of music-makers, and even went so far as to portray himself as a musician in two paintings of around 1650, fig. 47 and cat. 7. Indeed it seems that this painting of two children could have been a life study to inform the two child musicians and the older girl preparing to sing on the left-hand side of *The Concert* (cat. 7). The children are further idealised in the *Concert*, where the liveliness and sense of personality conveyed by *Two Children singing* is combined with Venetian sixteenth-century pictorial models (see the discussion in cat. 7) to produce a more timeless image of harmonious music-making.

FIG. 53
Peter Lely (1618–1680)
Two Children singing, *c.* 1650
Oil on canvas, 61.5 × 56.5 cm
Royal Cornwall Museum,
Royal Institution of Cornwall, Truro

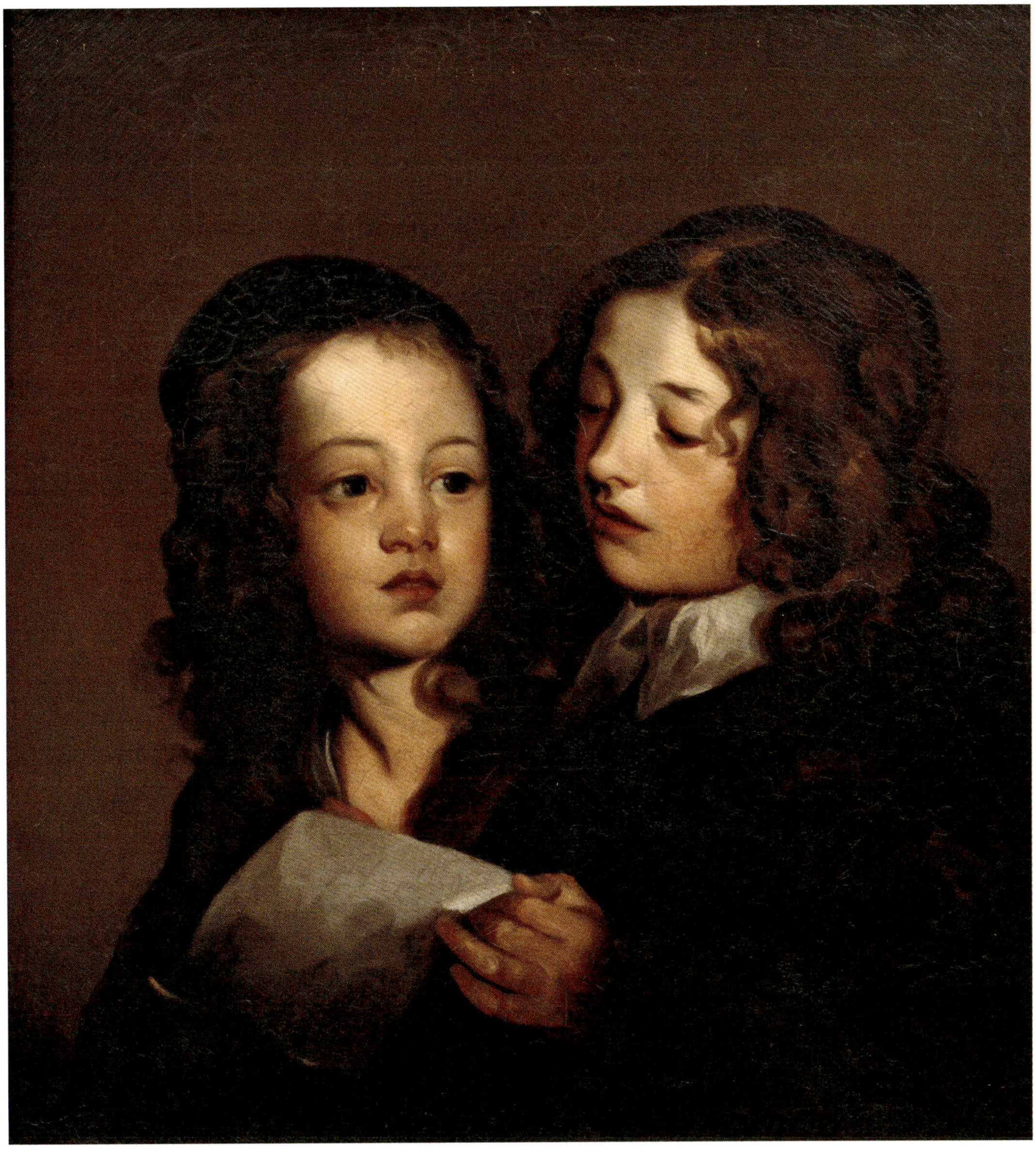

9

Nymphs by a Fountain, *c.* 1654

Oil on canvas, 128.9 × 144.8 cm
London, Dulwich Picture Gallery, DPG 555

Nymphs by a Fountain is ambitious both in scale and in conception. As in *The Concert* (cat. 7), Lely chose not to depict a familiar story; instead he was responsible both for the picture and for the narrative. Steeped in the pastoral literature beloved by the seventeenth-century elite, and deeply informed by the mythological paintings of Titian and Van Dyck – one of which he himself possessed – Lely here created a unique and enduringly compelling evocation of quiet, sensuous and sleeping beauty. It is hard to believe that the picture has not always been considered to be arousing: certainly, its potential dangers were not lost on the schoolmasters of Dulwich College, who ensured that *Nymphs by a Fountain* was kept under lock in the lumber room, "for fear it should injure the morals of the boys".[1]

Lely makes those who see his painting into voyeurs. It is as if we have stumbled into a forest glade in the gloaming, or perhaps at night, and discovered four women (and one figure of uncertain gender, whose back is turned to the viewer) in varying states of abandon and dress, all deep in sleep. They are arranged so that the viewer is able to admire the perfect youthful body from every possible angle, as if in 360° vision. The shape made by these entwined forms is echoed, deliberately, by the sculptural group of exuberant putti and a dolphin who crown the fountain at the upper right of the canvas. The combination of these naked and semi-naked beauties with a fountain would have recalled to most literate seventeenth-century viewers the Latin poet Ovid's story of Actaeon, a hunter who stumbled unawares upon the goddess Diana and her nymphs, and who suffered terrible punishments for this unwitting act. The viewer of Lely's picture has no need to worry, however, that their fate will mirror Actaeon's: none of the sleepers awake to catch the viewer's eye.

It is inconceivable that Lely should have developed this complex composition without the help of life studies. We know that he made use of male and female models, indeed he is known to have supervised drawings after living models of both sexes by the students who attended the 'academy' of *c.* 1673 in Lely's studio.[2] A drawing formerly in Lely's collection (fig. 57) which has been attributed variously to Rubens and Subleyras as well as to Lely himself,[3] and which

PROVENANCE

Charles Fairfax Murray (1849–1919), by whom "bought in Paris"; presented to Dulwich Picture Gallery, 1911

EXHIBITION HISTORY

London 1960–61, no. 17; London 1978–79, no. 25; Washington and Los Angeles 1985–86, no. 20; Nottingham and London 1991, no. 12; Bilbao 1999, no. 39; Houston and Louisville 1999–2000, no. 79; London and Amsterdam 2006, fig. 205

LITERATURE

Collins Baker 1912, I, p. 139 n. 3; Cook 1914, pp. 283–84, no. 555; Cook 1926, p. 263, no. 555; Beckett 1951, pp. 67–68, no. 594; Waterhouse (1953) 1994, p. 95; Foucart 1989, pp. 17, 24; Beresford 1998, p. 150, no. 555; Ingamells 2008, pp. 172–73, no. 555

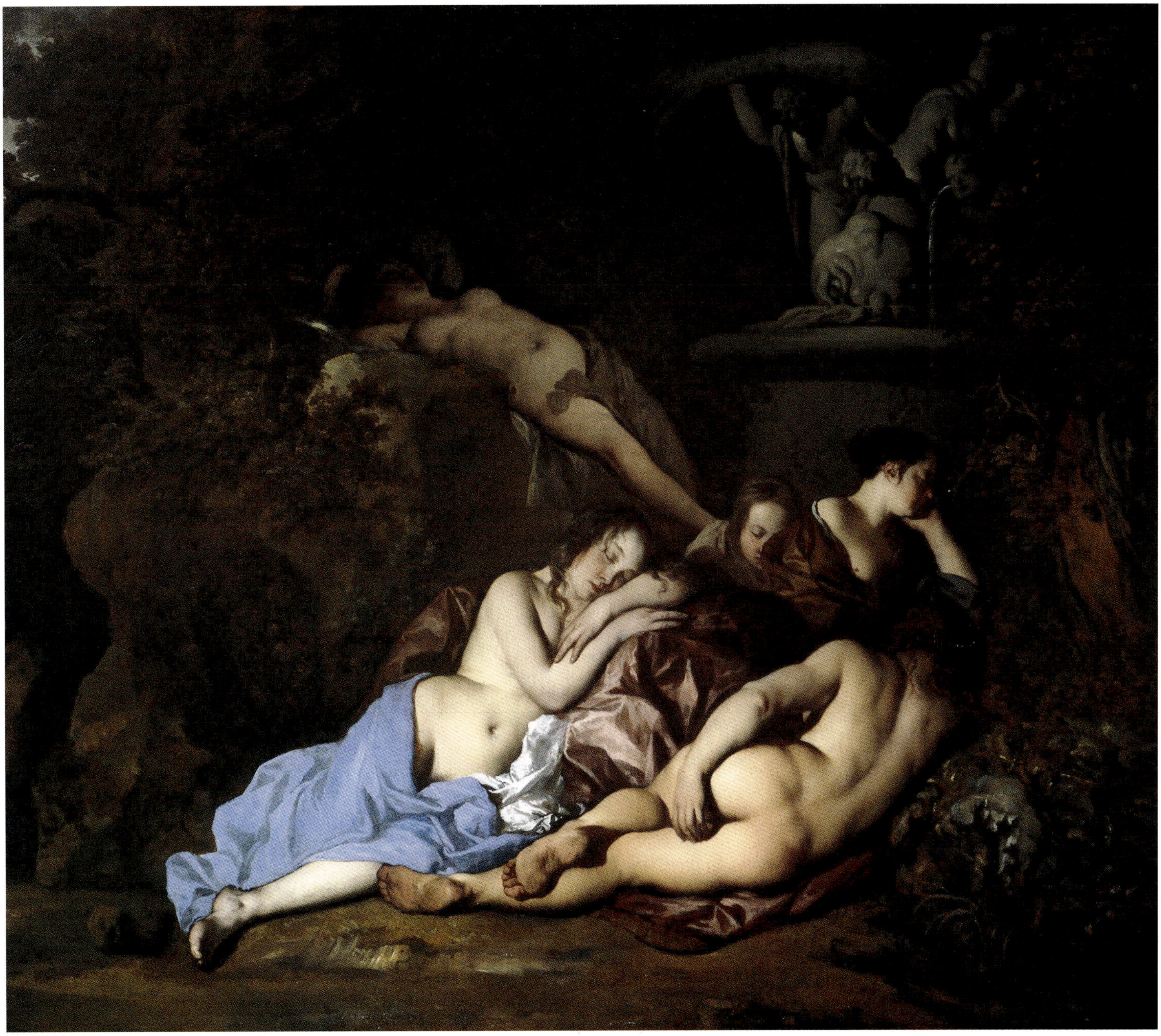

relates closely to *Cimon and Efigenia* (cat. 11), is also connected to the figure seen from behind in the foreground of *Nymphs by a Fountain*. Other figures in the composition can be recognised in more of Lely's pictures of the 1650s, and probably numbered among Lely's regular models. The dark-haired woman at the apex of the group of sleepers appears both as *Mary Magdalen* (fig. 56) and as one of Europa's attendants in the Chatsworth *Europa and the Bull* (cat. 10). The sleeping nymph at the centre of the picture is also found in the Chatsworth painting, placing a crown of flowers on the bull's head. Yet, as Ilaria Bignamini has noted, Lely also made use of antique statuary and Old Master painting in his *Nymphs by a Fountain*. The left-most nymph in Lely's painting recalls a Roman statue of the second century AD, while the boyish

FIG. 54
Jacob van Loo (1614–1670)
Diana and her Nymphs asleep, *c.* 1650
Oil on canvas, 35.6 × 45.7 cm
Private collection, London

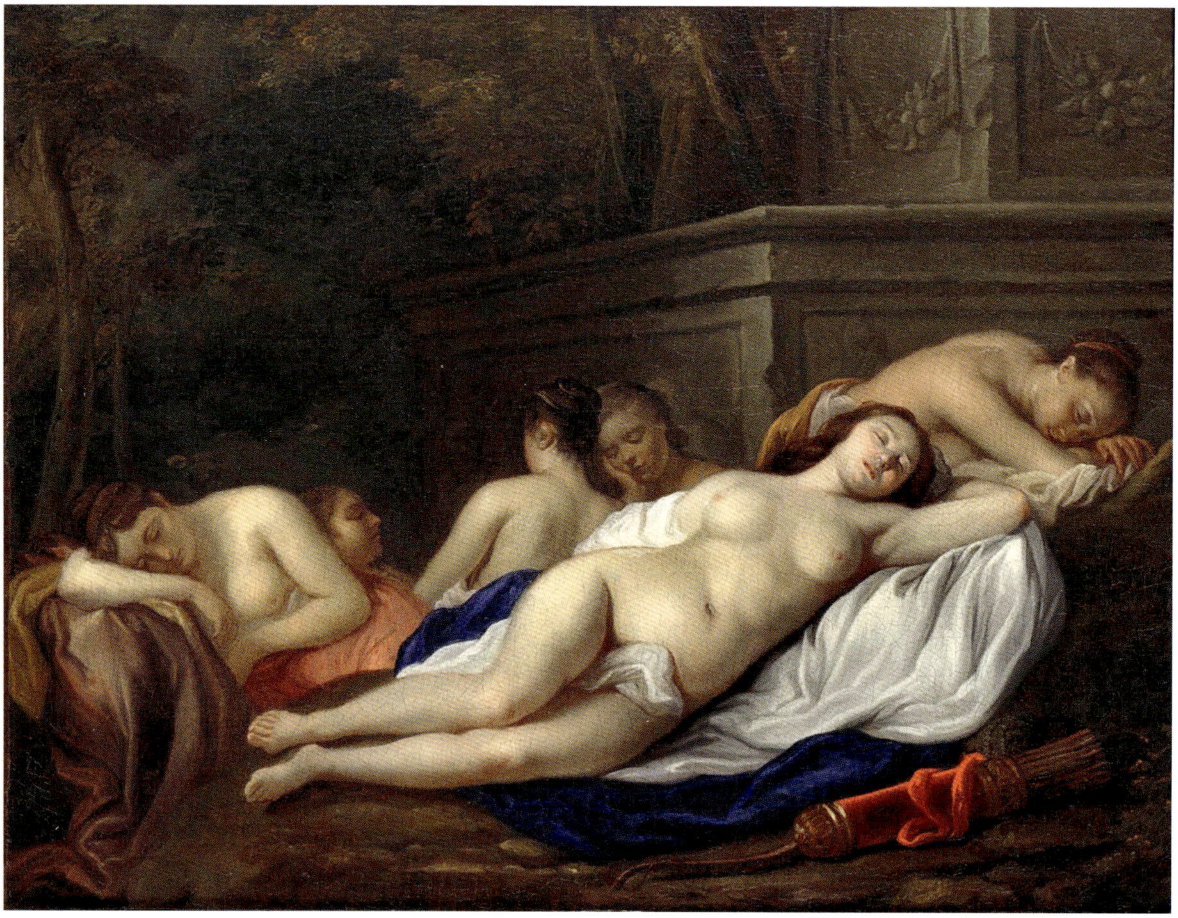

nude viewed from the back – most appropriately – resembles the sleeping *Hermaphrodite*. This latter sculpture was well known to Flemish artists and English collectors and antiquarians in the seventeenth century, such as John Eveyln, who purchased an ivory copy when in Rome in the late 1640s.[4] Lely had not seen Titian's *Andrians* (fig. 29), but he seems to have known it from the 1636 engraving by G.A. Podestà, as the nymph sprawled on a rock with her face and body lifted up for the viewer's delectation echoes the drunken woman who has lost all consciousness and self-restraint lying in the right foreground of Titian's bacchanal. A picture by Lely's contemporary Jacob van Loo depicts women sleeping in a similar fashion to the nymphs (fig. 54). Lely admired Van Loo's work, and this composition was very probably known to him, as well as Dirck van der Lisse's *Nymphs sleeping* (fig. 33).

All these factors were important in affecting Lely's artistic choices. But the single work of art which made most impact on Lely's *Nymphs by a Fountain* was Van Dyck's *Cupid and Psyche* (fig. 5), made in London in the late 1630s for Charles I, and perhaps commissioned to decorate the Queen's House at Greenwich.[5] Lely knew this painting exceptionally well: he owned it, probably from *c.* 1654, and he declared it to the House of Lords committee investigating the dispersal of the "late King's goods" shortly after Charles II's restoration.[6] There are many resonances between the two works, such as the woodland setting; the muted colours of the background, contrasting with the strong lighting of the figures; the women's heads resting on rocks; the draperies of blue, pink and white which frame the bodies; and, most evidently, the elegiac and harmonious feel of both pictures. Both pictures are alluring but un-licentious and tender depictions of what are potentially extremely erotic subjects.

Technically and stylistically, the *Nymphs by a Fountain* is undoubtedly a work of the 1650s (no trace can be found of the signature and date of 1670 mentioned in two early twentieth-century catalogues of the Dulwich collection). Since the 1970s it has normally been dated to the early 1650s, but two pieces of evidence suggest a slightly later placement in Lely's career. Technical study undertaken as part of conservation treatment in 2005–06 has demonstrated that the picture exhibits the double ground-layer which has been observed in a significant number of Lely's pictures dated between the mid 1650s and the mid 1660s (see also cat. 12).[7] Moreover, the exceptionally close connections between *Cupid and Psyche* and Lely's *Nymphs* attests to Lely's profound knowledge of Van Dyck's picture, which seems to have come into his possession only after 1654. Did Lely, therefore, have *Cupid and Psyche* before him as he worked on the *Nymphs by a Fountain*?

NOTES

1 William Spanton, cited in New York 2010, p. 41.
2 Postle 1997, p. 81.
3 For attribution of the drawing to Rubens and to Lely, see London 1978–79, p. 11, and Washington and Los Angeles 1985–86, p. 83, fig. 1; for that to Subleyras, see Rome 1987, no. 59.
4 Bignamini in Nottingham and London 1991, p. 46.
5 Egerton in Antwerp and London 1999, pp. 326–28.
6 Egerton *ibid.*, p. 326.
7 I am grateful to have had the opportunity to consult both Aviva Burnstock's and Nicole Ryder's unpublished reports on the picture at Dulwich Picture Gallery.

10

The Rape of Europa, early 1650s

Oil on canvas, 123.3 × 135 cm
The Trustees of the Chatsworth Settlement, Derbyshire, inv. PA 356

In his *Metamorphoses*, sometimes called the 'painter's bible' because of its use by generations of European artists, the Latin poet Ovid tells of Jupiter's wily deception of the beautiful North African princess Europa (II, ll. 833–75). Europa, wandering in spring meadows with her attendants, came upon a white bull of extraordinary gentleness and size. Enamoured of its charm, she proceeded to adorn it with the flowers she had been collecting, and even climbed – most unwisely – upon its back. The bull stealthily made its way, step by step, through the fields to the edge of the sea, and then, unexpectedly, took a sudden turn of speed and jumped into the water with the princess on its back. The bull, of course, was Jupiter, and he bore Europa off across the Mediterranean to the island of Crete, near to the continent which bears her name, and there she gave birth to their three sons, Minos, Rhadamanthus and Sarpedon.

This pagan creation myth was an enduringly popular subject for artists well into the eighteenth century. Lely may not have known Rembrandt's, Titian's, Rubens's and Veronese's depictions of the subject (such as fig. 30), but he did not need to; he had Ovid's text either in its original or in one of its many vernacular paraphrases to respond to. Lely, like Veronese, concentrates on the magical moments of playful and innocent repose which Europa and her companions enjoy with the bull in the spring meadows. Europa is depicted with her legs slightly akimbo as she climbs on to the bull's back to stroke his forehead and crown him with a garland of flowers. Her friends crowd round the animal, and join Europa in her attentions to the heavily disguised king of the gods.

Lely, as we have seen, started his career with "landscape and historic figures less than life" (Horace Walpole).[2] *The Rape of Europa*, however, is far removed from the little pictures of Lely's earliest years, such as cat. 1. The expansive marsh landscape which stretches out into the horizon at the left is

PROVENANCE

In Lely's possession at his death; included in his posthumous sale, 18 April 1682; bought by Roger North, the artist's executor; sold to Lely's son John (BM MS 32,504, p. 49); acquired by the 1st, or possibly future 2nd, Duke of Devonshire; recorded at Devonshire House, Little Dressing Room, *c.* 1761; in the Middle Drawing Room, 1813, 1831; [Duke's] Bedroom, south wall, 1836, marked to be taken to Chatsworth; Chatsworth, Gallery, 1854[1]

EXHIBITION HISTORY

London 1938, no. 43; Manchester 1948–49; Leeds and Sheffield 1955; Newcastle 1955–56; Manchester 1960, no. 73

LITERATURE

Dodsley 1761, II, p. 230; Walpole (1761–71) 1879, p. 227; Passavant 1836, II, p. 164; Waagen 1854–7, III, p. 348; Collins Baker 1912, I, no. 137; Beckett 1951, p. 67, no. 582, pl. 4; Waterhouse (1953) 1994, p. 95; London and New York 2010, pp. 39–49, pl. 4.1

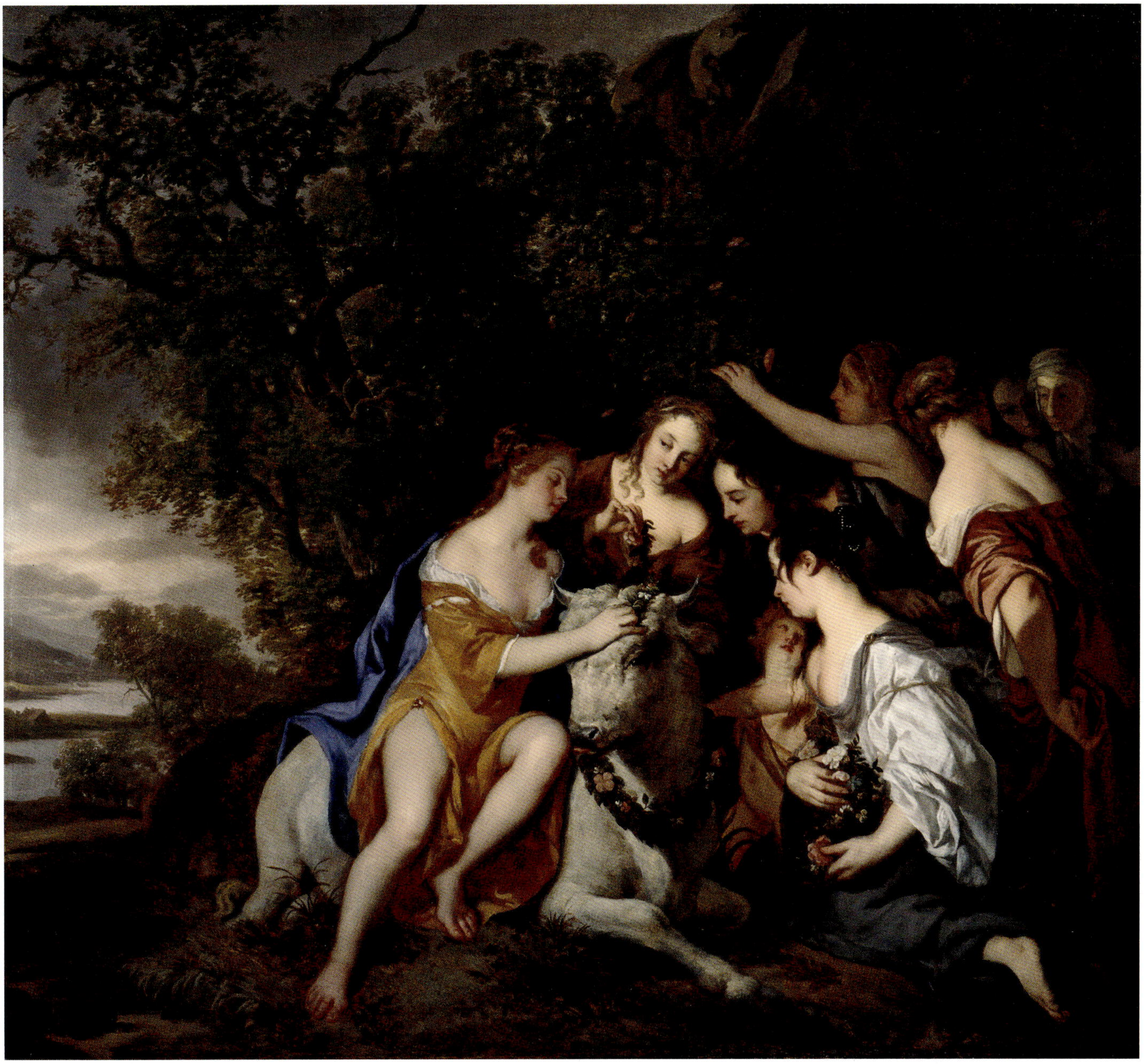

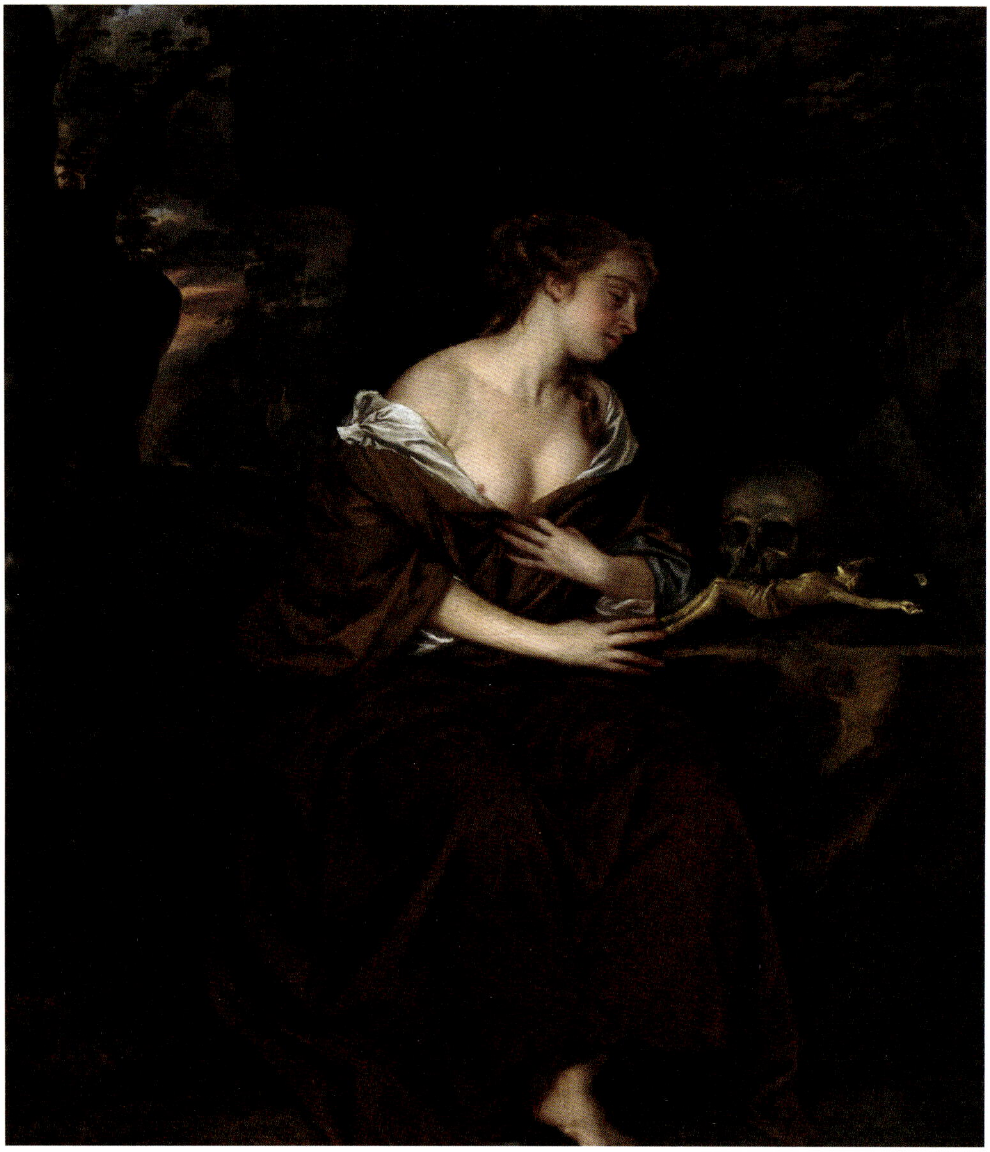

reminiscent of those of Lely's native Holland. It leads out from the figures, rather than enclosing them. In this quality it recalls *The Concert* (cat. 7) and *Reuben presenting Mandrakes to Leah* (cat. 4), but, like *The Concert* and unlike *Reuben*, *The Rape of Europa* is a successful marriage of figures and landscape. Like both these pictures, it includes passages which seem to be unfinished. The strange, almost mystical heads which loom at the far right of the composition are not fully resolved, and have been painted more thinly and less completely than the other figures.

The picture evidently belongs to the same period as several of the other large-scale and ambitious narrative paintings by Lely, particularly *The Concert* (cat. 7), *Nymphs by a Fountain* (cat. 9) and *Cimon and Efigenia* (cat. 11). A cast of familiar faces appear from among the female models whom Lely used very regularly. Europa is the same girl as the female student in *The Music Lesson* (formerly in the collection of Lord Dulverton) and the Kingston Lacy *Mary Magdalen* (fig. 55) while the attendant who has collected flowers in her lap, rather like a Saint Dorothy, appears in

FIG. 55
Peter Lely (1618–1680)
The Penitent Mary Magdalen, *c*. 1650–55
Oil on canvas, 163.2 × 141.3 cm
National Trust, Kingston Lacy, Dorset

FIG. 56
Peter Lely (1618–1680)
The Penitent Mary Magdalen, *c*. 1650
Oil on canvas, 105.5 × 91.2 cm
Private collection, on long term loan to the Barber Institute of Fine Art, Birmingham

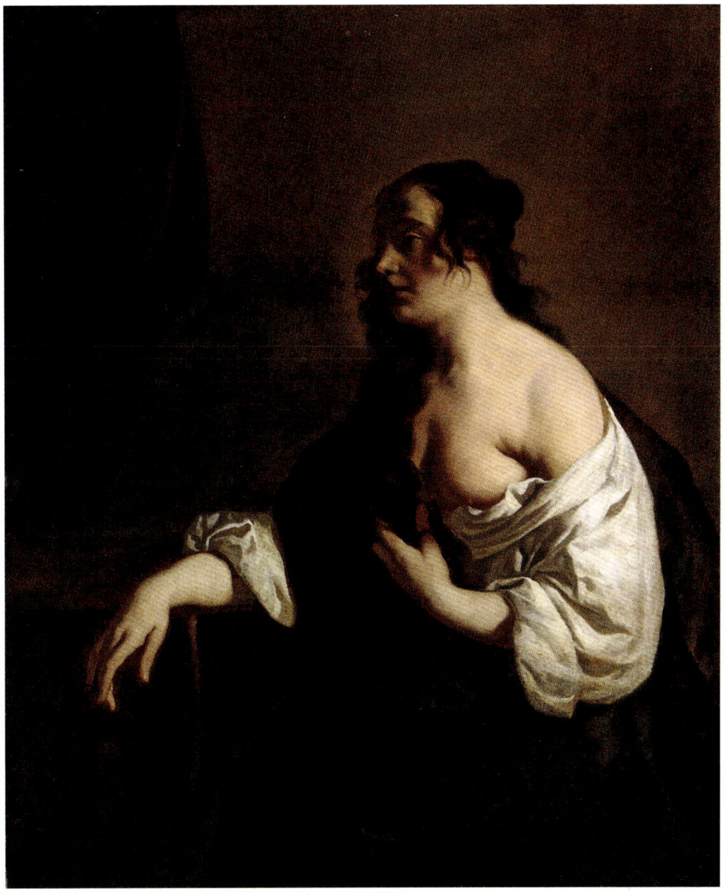

another *Mary Magdalen* (fig. 56), as the sleeper resting her hand on her chin in the *Nymphs* (cat. 9) and Pomona in fig. 38, while also resembling Leah in cat. 4. This figure is shown in the *profil perdu* which seems to have been among Lely's favourite poses at this point in his career, and can be seen additionally in the Valenciennes *Pair of Lovers in a Landscape* (cat. 2). The child who gazes up at her is somewhat uncomfortably placed, squeezed between the woman's chin and shoulder. This too is typical of Lely in the late 1640s and early 1650s, recalling the disembodied face peering out from behind Zilpah in *Reuben* (cat. 4), and the female singer at the centre of the *Concert* (cat. 7).

The *Rape of Europa* is among the minority of Lely's subject pictures which has a narrative subject drawn from literature. Its substantial dimensions make it surprising that it cannot be connected securely with a patron and that it apparently must have been made speculatively. Maybe Lely painted it for himself, but this would be surprising for a young artist making his reputation. It is far more likely that it did not find a buyer, and this, too, would explain its presence in Lely's posthumous sale in 1682. This hypothesis is further corroborated by the fact that the painting was rolled up at a relatively early date in its life.[3] It seems quite possible that it was stored for many years in Lely's studio, forgotten, and discovered after his death.

NOTES

1 I am grateful to Charles Noble for very kindly sharing with me his research into the *Rape of Europa*'s provenance and various locations while in the Devonshire collection.
2 Walpole (1761–71) 1879, p. 225.
3 I am grateful to Wilma Day and Charles Noble for allowing me to examine the painting with them at Chatsworth.

11

Cimon and Efigenia, after 1650

Oil on canvas, 131 × 150.8 cm
Mr and Mrs James Birch

In his *Decameron*, a collection of stories supposedly narrated by a group of friends who had fled the Black Death raging in Florence, the fourteenth-century Florentine writer Giovanni Boccaccio tells of Cimon's transformative love for Efigenia.[1] Cimon was a handsome youth who belonged to one of Cyprus's most noble families, but unfortunately he was an ignorant boor, who his father and friends despaired of ever civilising. As he was thought capable of nothing better, and indeed to be of very limited intellect, he went to work in the countryside on his family's estate. One summer's day, out in the fields, he came across an exceptionally beautiful girl, who was asleep and – because of the heat – almost naked. She was, however, accompanied by male and female chaperones, but they too were sleeping. Cimon was overcome with admiration for this girl, and gazed on her until she awoke. After much hesitation, she permitted him to escort her and her servants home. Cimon was encouraged by this encounter to improve himself. But the path of true love is rarely smooth and, although Efigenia was not adverse to his advances, she determined to honour her promise of marriage – given as a child – to another man on the island of Rhodes. Cimon, nothing daunted, set off for Rhodes to regain his true love. After many adventures, including imprisonment for the attempted murder of Efigenia's betrothed, Cimon regained both his beloved and his freedom, and sailed home for Cyprus.

Boccaccio's fantastical tale was well known in Northern Europe. The *Decameron* has had a long history of reception in England, beginning with Chaucer's *Canterbury Tales*, and continuing long into the eighteenth century. Shakespeare has been shown to have made considerable use of William Painter's *The Palace of Pleasure* of 1566–67, which was the most extensive collation of Boccaccio's fables until the publication of John Florio's 1620 complete translation. Lely read Italian so did not need to use any of these translations. The mood of his picture, however, is in sympathy with John Dryden's somewhat later *Fables, Ancient and Modern*, which includes a retelling of Boccaccio's Cimon and Efigenia. Dryden writes of a "crystal flood, / by which an alabaster fountain stood: / And on the margin of the fount was laid / (Attended by her slaves) a sleeping maid".

PROVENANCE

In the collection at Doddington Hall since the mid eighteenth century; probably moved to the house from Seton Delaval

LITERATURE

Millar in London 1978–79, p.10; Salomon in New York 2010, p. 41

EXHIBITION HISTORY

Never previously exhibited

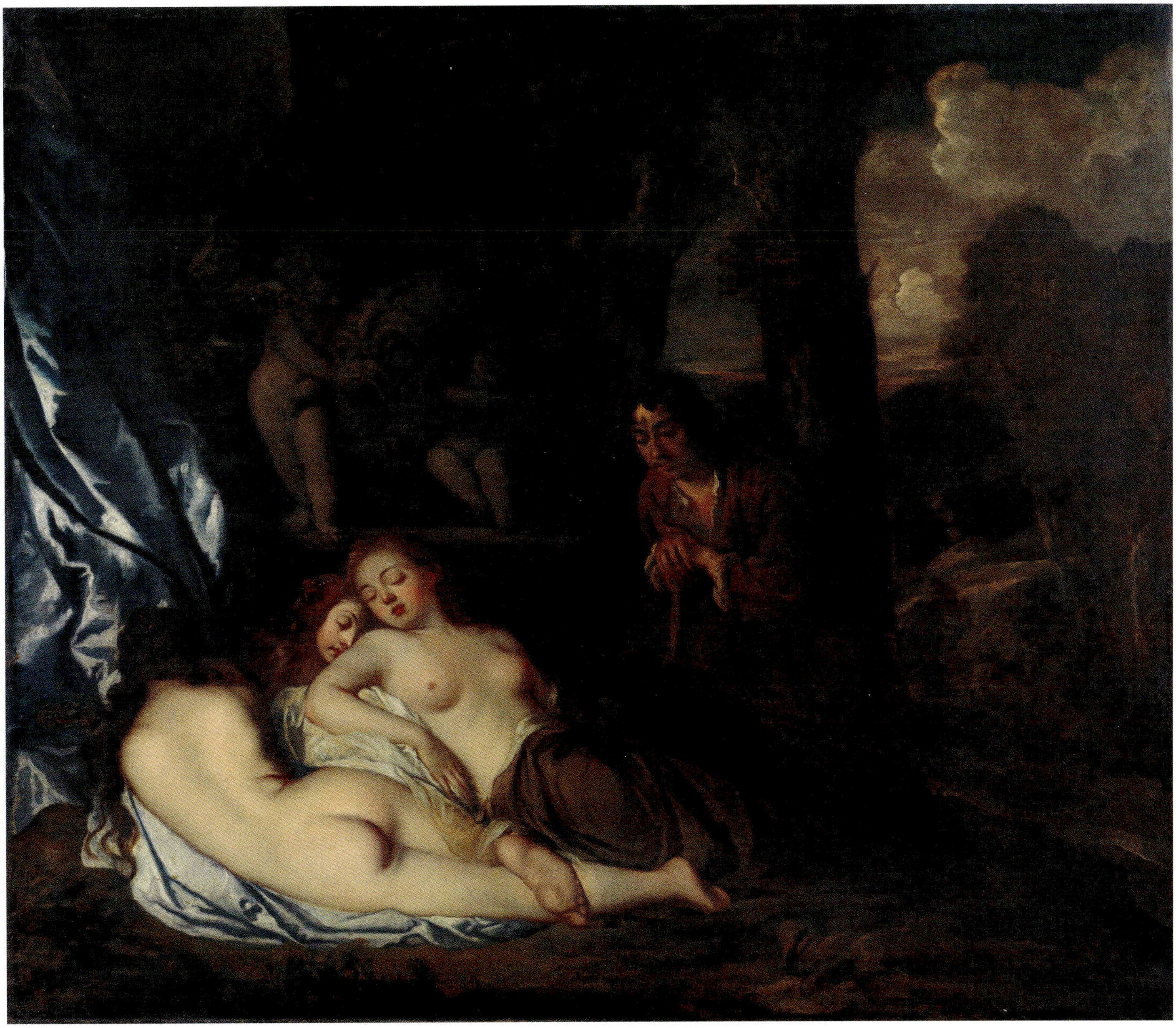

FIG. 57
Attributed to
Peter Lely (1618–1680)
Study for a reclining female figure,
c. 1650
Black chalk with white heightening
on paper, 22.2 × 51 cm
Private collection

As Lely was the outstanding artistic figure of the Restoration, so Dryden played a parallel role in the literary life of the period. Lely made at least two paintings of Cimon and Efigenia, the present work and fig. 58.[2] Either of these could be the canvas mentioned in Lely's posthumous sale, or that could be another painting again, now lost. Lely is known to have made several versions of his more popular subject paintings, such as this or *Susanna and the Elders* (figs. 25–27).

Here, Lely depicts the moment of Cimon's discovery of Efigenia. A dark-complexioned moustachioed shepherd, wearing coarse rustic clothing, clasps his staff as he kneels in awe before the marvellous sight of the innocent girl with her perfect face and body. As Dryden wrote of Efigenia, "the dame herself the goddess [Diana] well expressed". This is also true of Lely's painting. Like the *Nymphs by a Fountain* (cat. 9) this picture depicts loveliness in ignorance of itself but it is also suffused by eroticism: Efigenia is presented as an object of desire, possibly more shocking because she is wholly unaware of it. Like Giorgione and Titian's Dresden *Venus* she is lost to her dreams.

The picture is impressive in scale and in construction. Lely has balanced the sleeping nudes with a fountain, as he did in *Nymphs by a Fountain*. Another connection with the Dulwich picture is provided by Efigenia's two sleeping servants. The head of the girl nestled between her mistress and the male servant recalls the pose of the black-haired girl who rests her head on her elbow in *Nymphs by a Fountain*. The man's back is turned to the viewer, in the left foreground of the composition. The outlines of his body are identical to the drawing (fig. 57), which has also been connected with the Dulwich 'hermaphrodite'. On these grounds it seems reasonable to assume that the drawing is by Lely. Could the Dulwich and Doddington pictures

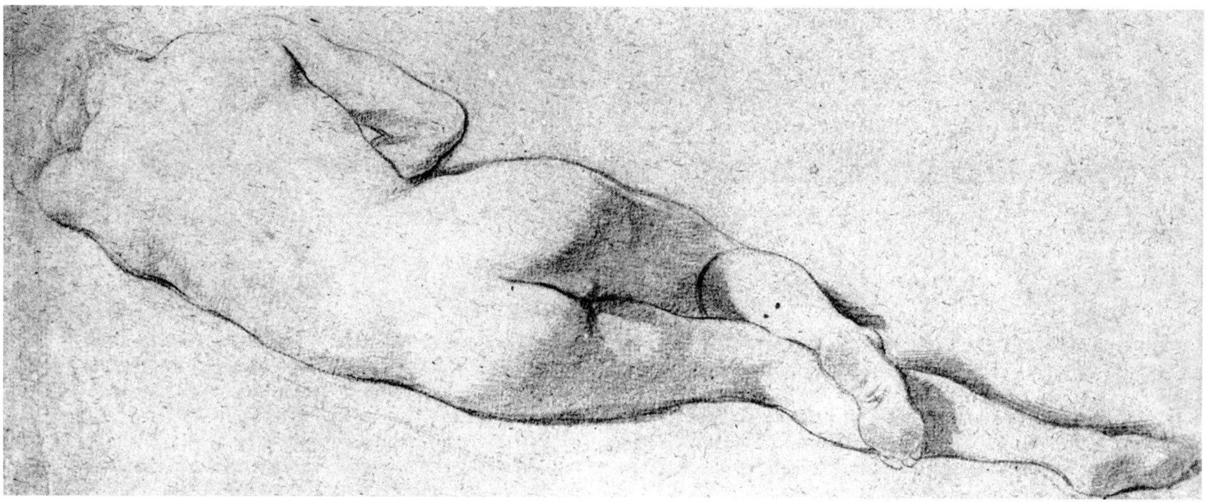

FIG. 58
Peter Lely (1618–1680)
Cimon and Efigenia, *c.* 1640–45
Oil on canvas, 103 × 164.5 cm
The Trustees of the Sackville
Estate, Knole, Kent

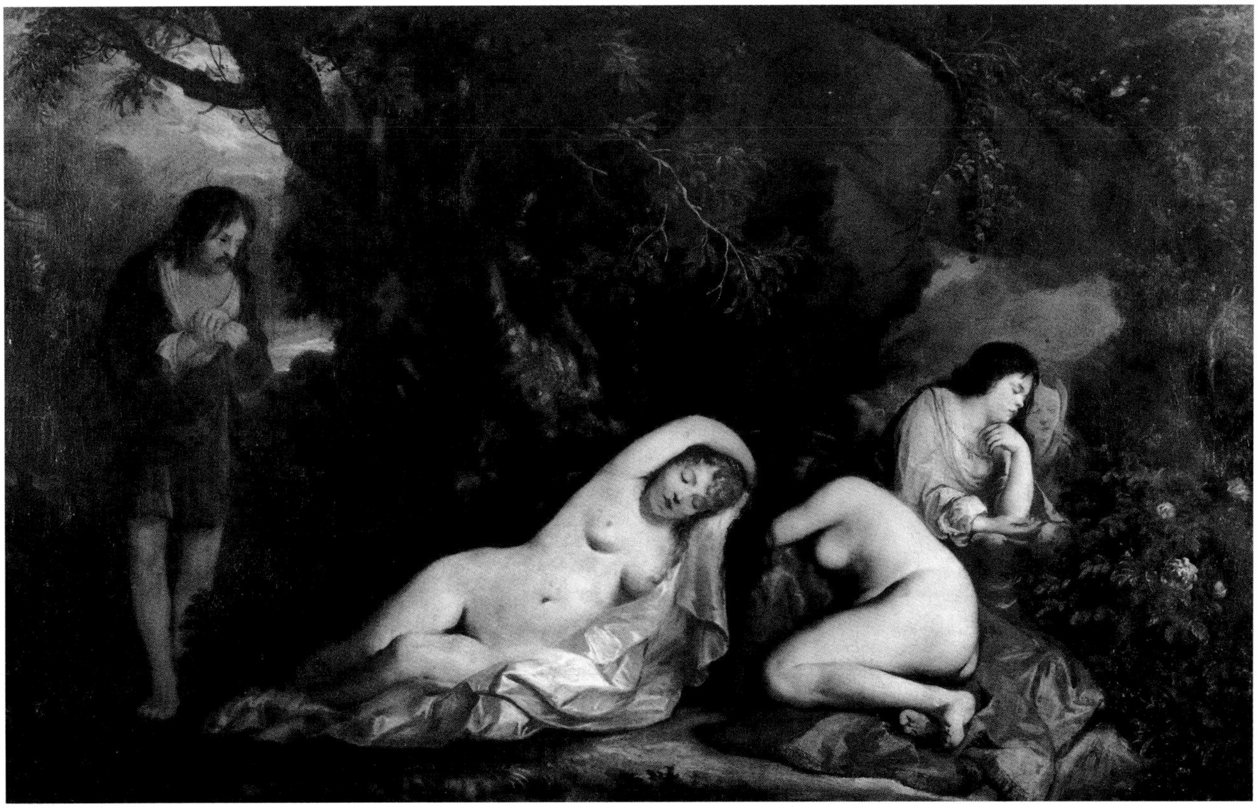

have been intended as a pair? It is tempting to suggest as much, as they are almost mirror images, each anchored by a nude, lying at opposite sides of each picture. But their dimensions are not close enough to suggest a conscious pairing. The curtain, as if it has been swept back to reveal Efigenia, both enhances the theatrical artifice of the painting and heightens the viewer's sense of the impact made upon Cimon. It recalls Lely's use of the same device in *The Concert* (cat. 7) and also his first conception of *The Infant Bacchus* (cat. 3). The landscape, as it opens up at the right behind Cimon, resembles that found in *Reuben presenting Mandrakes to Leah* (cat. 4).

NOTES

1 Day 5, Novella 1.
2 For the very damaged Knole picture, see Beckett 1951, p. 5, pl. 3.

12

A Boy as a Shepherd, *c.* 1658–60

Oil on canvas, 91.4 × 75.6 cm
Signed *PL* on the lower right
London, Dulwich Picture Gallery, DPG 563

Lely's beautiful boy is framed by a rocky niche; set in a wooded landscape. He indolently strokes a crook, called a *houlette*, which nominally denotes him as a shepherd. With his other hand he fingers a pipe, probably a recorder. It is deliberately unclear whether he is about to play, or has just put the instrument down. Lely's painting is full of these uncertainties: is it dawn or dusk; is this a portrait of an individual adopting the role of a shepherd, or a 'subject picture' with an idealised evocation of male beauty? The youth is definitely a boy, but his depiction has more in common with the conventions of alluring female portraiture which Lely did more than anyone to establish. In particular, the half-length format, the boy's profile, and his dreamy glance towards a putative companion recall Lely's various series of admired beauties at the court of Charles II, and Lely's almost total move into portraiture after 1660.

This has long been one of Lely's most celebrated and beloved pictures. Horace Walpole, the collector and early historian of English art, coveted it long before he purchased it in 1776 (he also owned a copy in enamel, by Christian Friedrich Zincke, dated 1716).[1] He eulogised the sitter's "impassioned sentimental glow, the eyes swimming with youth and tenderness".[2] Walpole believed that it represented the poet Abraham Cowley (1618–1667), but Cowley, an exact contemporary of Lely's, would have been middle-aged by the time *A Boy as a Shepherd* was painted. From at least the early eighteenth century to 1776 the picture was paired with *Bartholomew Beale* (fig. 59). The two pictures, which have recently been reunited at Dulwich Picture Gallery, share fine eighteenth-century frames, probably commissioned by the poet Edward Lovibond, who inherited them on his father's death in 1737. The elder Lovibond, a director of the

PROVENANCE

Probably painted for Mary Beale (1633–1699); before *c.* 1726 in the collection of Edward Lovibond (d. 1737); by descent to Edward Lovibond (1724–1775); bought by Horace Walpole (1717–1797) at the sale of the Lovibond collection, Skinner, 27–28 May 1776; by inheritance to Anne Seymour Damer (d. 1811), Walpole's residuary legatee; following her death in 1811, the painting reverted (as directed by Walpole's will) to the 6th Earl Waldegrave (d. 1835), grandson of Maria, Dowager Countess of Waldegrave, Horace Walpole's niece and heiress; by inheritance to the 7th Earl Waldegrave (d. 1846); his sale, Robins, Strawberry Hill, 6 May 1842 (11th day), no. 21; bought at the Waldegrave sale by Sir Robert Peel, 2nd Bt (d. 1850); by inheritance to the 3rd and 4th baronets; Peel Heirlooms sale, Robinson & Fisher, London, 10 May 1900, no. 203; bought by Agnew's, London, from whom purchased by Charles Fairfax Murray (1849–1919) by 1908; presented to Dulwich Picture Gallery by Charles Fairfax Murray, 1911

EXHIBITION HISTORY

London 1908, no. 157; Aberystwyth 1945, no. 45; London 1947, no. 27; Leeds 1947–53, no. 27; London 1978, no. 28; Washington and Los Angeles 1985–86, no. 21; Warsaw 1992, no. 15; Houston and Louisville 1999–2000, no. 80; Japan 2000, no. 45; London and Frankfurt 2007, no. 3

LITERATURE

Baker 1912, II, p. 40, p. 122, no. 6; Baker 1915, p. 101; Beckett 1952, p. 42, no. 129, pl. 38; London 1998, p. 151, no. 563; Beresford 1998, p. 79; Ingamells 2008, pp. 176–77

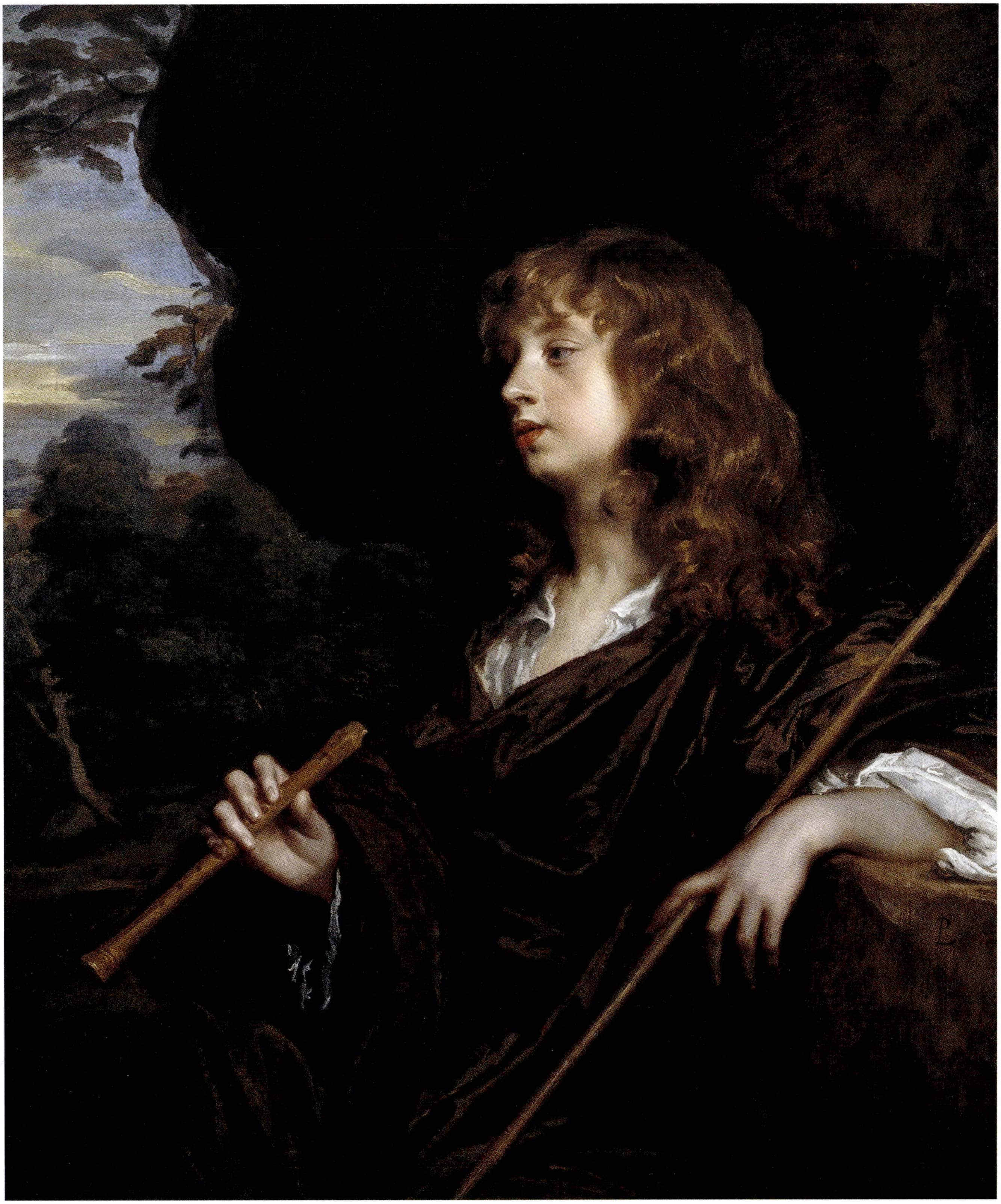

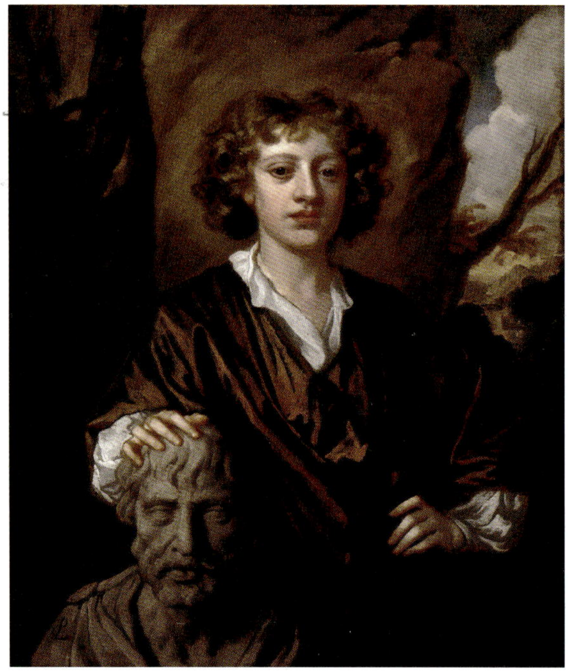

FIG. 59
Peter Lely (1618–1680)
Portrait of Bartholomew Beale, *c.* 1670
Oil on canvas, 91.5 × 76.2 cm
Dulwich Picture Gallery, London

East India Company, had acquired the pictures (in circumstances which remain unclear) from the Beale family. They seem to have entered the Beales' possession directly from Lely.[3] Mary Beale, who was probably the first professional female artist in England, was a protégée of Lely's. Her two sons, Bartholomew and Charles, are mentioned in their father's diary for 1672 as having been shown Lely's "rare collection" of pictures.[4] They were evidently well known to Lely, and he to them. Bartholomew (who died an impoverished physician in Coventry in 1709) was painted by Lely as a boy, around 1670 (fig. 59). Charles, who became a painter, training first with his mother and then as a miniaturist, made several red-chalk copies of *A Boy as a Shepherd*, one of which is in the British Museum.[5]

It has been tentatively suggested that *A Boy as a Shepherd* could also represent Bartholomew Beale.[6] However, Bartholomew would have been no more than four in 1660, which is probably the latest date one can ascribe to the Dulwich picture. Stylistically it has been dated consistently to around 1658–60.[7] Technical analysis, carried out by Libby Sheldon, has discerned a particular type of double ground or preparation layer on the canvas. This consisted of chalk beneath a pinkish or greyish upper ground[8] and was a technical feature employed by Lely from the late 1650s until the mid 1660s.[9] For these reasons the identification of the shepherd boy with Bartholomew seems unlikely. Moreover, he does not closely resemble the two extant portraits of Bartholomew at Dulwich (including fig. 59) and a later painting of *c.* 1685 by his mother, Mary.

If the *Boy as a Shepherd* is a portrait, it should be seen more in the light of Lely's depictions of children in Arcadian costume such as fig. 60, which portrays Henry Sidney, Earl of Romney as a beautiful shepherd boy, crook in hand. But, rather than representing even a highly prettified likeness like that of the young Earl of Romney, Lely's *Boy* is more probably an ideal, meant to evoke the rural paradises described by ancient poets including Theocritus, and particularly Virgil, whose *Eclogues* are frequented by handsome young shepherds. Lely was well aware of the pictorial tradition of beautiful shepherds, often playing rustic musical instruments as his shepherd boy does, and he would have been familiar with the – somewhat phallic – motif of the shepherd holding his pipe at arm's length from the Arcadian paintings associated with Titian and Giorgione, such as *The Three Ages of Man* (fig. 42). It is tempting to suggest that a Giorgionesque painting of a *Shepherd holding a Flute* (a version of which is at Wilton House, now attributed to Savoldo) which was copied by Charles Beale,[10] and which has clear resonances with Lely's *Boy as a Shepherd*, was from Lely's collection, or at least was known to Lely.

It should also be mentioned that the pastoral poetry of Theocritus and Virgil had many seventeenth-century English literary imitators. In these works honourable Englishmen could be eulogised as shepherds. Perhaps the most apposite example is Edward King, drowned in 1637 and cast by his friend John Milton as Lycidas in Milton's eponymous poem (1638,

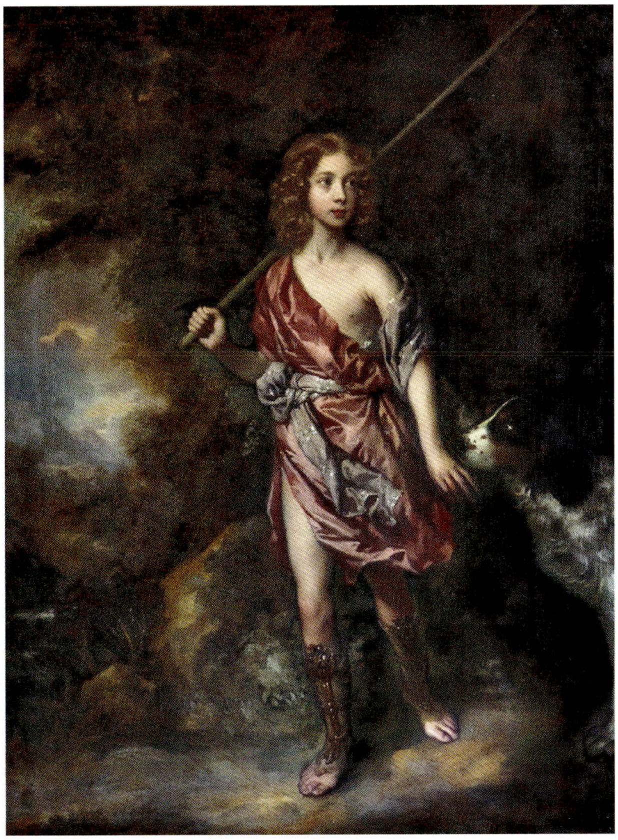

FIG. 60
Peter Lely (1618–1680)
Henry Sidney, Earl of Romney, early 1650s
Oil on canvas, 165.1 × 124.5 cm
Penshurst Place, Kent

revised 1645), in which his rustic friends – shepherds, nymphs and satyrs – mourn his passing.[11] Horace Walpole, always an astute critic, compared *A Boy as a Shepherd* to the description of the shepherd Anchises in *Brittain's Ida* by the Reverend Phineas Fletcher. This poem, first published in 1628, was believed by many readers long into the eighteenth century to be by Edmund Spenser (interestingly, Lely's library included Spenser's work).[12] Fletcher describes "a dainty Boy" with a "Nymph-like face":

> High was his Fore-head, arch'd with silver Mould,
> (Where never Anger churlish Wrinkle dighted)
> His auburn Locks hung like dark Threds of Gold,
> That wanton Airs (with their fair length incited)
> To play amongst their wanton Curles delighted;
> His smiling Eyes with simple Truth were stor'd:
> Ah! how should Truth in those thief Eyes be stor'd,
> Which thousand Loves had stoln, and never one
> restor'd?[13]

It would be foolish to suggest that Lely necessarily had these particular lines in mind. However, their resemblance to the *Boy as a Shepherd* and his striking red-gold curls draws our attention to the close links between visual and literary manifestations of the pastoral tradition in Lely's England.

NOTES

1 Fitzwilliam Museum, Cambridge, Department of Paintings, Drawings and Prints, PD.7-1949
2 Walpole 1761–71 (1888), III, p. 29.
3 London 1999, no. 27.
4 Charles Beale, diary entry for 30 September 1672, quoted in Walpole 1761–71 (1888), III, p. 29.
5 London, British Museum, Department of Prints and Drawings, Gg,5.65.
6 Washington and Los Angeles 1985–86, p. 86; London 1998, p. 151.
7 London 1978–89, pp. 51–52; London 1998, p. 151, no. 563; Beresford 1998, p. 79; Ingamells 2008, pp. 176–77.
8 Unpublished report by Libby Sheldon, dated September 2008, consulted at Dulwich Picture Gallery. I am also grateful to Sophie Plender for making available to me her treatment report on the picture.
9 Hendriks and Groen 1994, p. 32.
10 London, British Museum, Department of Prints and Drawings, Gg,5.74.
11 For an on-line edition of Milton's *Lycidas*, see http://www.dartmouth.edu/~milton/reading_room/lycidas (consulted 2 May 2012).
12 Millar in London 1978–79, p. 12.
13 Revd Phineas Fletcher, *Brittain's Ida*, first published London (Thomas Walkley) 1628 as by Edmund Spenser. See http://spenserians.cath.vt.edu/TextRecordphp?action=GET&textsid=33069, Canto 1, verse 4 (consulted 1 May 2012).

Lely's friend, the poet Richard Lovelace

Many details remain unclear about the life of Richard Lovelace, Royalist supporter, poet and soldier. One of the few undebatable facts is his friendship with Peter Lely, to whom he dedicated two poems (printed below), one entitled 'Peinture ... To the best picture of Friendship ... Mr Pet. Lilly'.[1]

LOVELACE WAS THE ELDEST SON, and second child, of a Kentish landowner, Sir William Lovelace and his wife Ann Barnes, the only daughter of a London merchant. Their marriage was far from happy, and the couple seem to have lived apart for several years before Richard's birth in 1617. Lovelace was educated at Charterhouse and Gloucester Hall, Oxford, where he matriculated in 1634, three years after he had become "gentleman wayter extraordinary" to King Charles I. When he went up to Oxford, he was accounted "the most amiable and beautiful person that ever eye beheld", according to his later biographer Anthony à Wood.[2] In August 1636, this handsome and well-mannered gentleman (fig. 28) was one of those chosen to receive the degree of Master of Arts on the occasion of the visit paid by King Charles and his consort Henrietta Maria to Oxford.

Lovelace left Oxford for London, where his comedy *The Scholars* was performed by the Queen's Players in late 1637, but also for Cambridge, where he continued his studies and met the poet Andrew Marvell, who was to commend Lovelace's later poetic production. Poetry and scholarship were combined with the life of a courtier and of soldiery: Lovelace participated in the so-called Bishops' Wars against the Scots of 1639–40, and probably achieved the rank of Captain, but by the time of outbreak of the English Civil War proper he was to be found on his estates in Kent. On 29 April 1642 he was one of a group of young Royalists who disrupted the Maidstone Quarter Sessions, and then marched at the head of a band of armed men from Blackheath (now in south-east London) to Westminster. The following day he delivered a defiant pro-Royalist petition to the House of Commons, and was sent to prison. During his seven weeks in jail he composed poetry, including probably the famous line "... stone walls do not a prison make".

On his release, Lovelace did not pay an active part in the military conflict, but appears to have remained in London, using his own wealth to help soldiers desirous of obtaining arms, and to relieve the want of "ingenious men", including scholars and musicians. Lovelace indeed only seems to have taken up arms abroad. He probably spent much of the period from 1642 to 1647 in France (fighting at Dunkirk for the French in 1646) and in Holland, which explains his poem to the abbess-painter Louisa Hollandine, cousin of Charles II and sister of Prince Rupert of the Rhine. He may also here have made the acquaintance of Peter Lely. Certainly, it was in Holland that Lovelace was exposed to contemporary Dutch painting. He was well informed about writing about the arts, mentioning in his panegyric to Lely both the Italian sixteenth-century artist and historian Giorgio Vasari and his seventeenth-century Dutch follower Karel van Mander (here called "Vermander").

By 1647, Lely and Lovelace seem to have been firm friends. They shared a love of music as well as art. Lovelace was closely associated with the musicians formerly of the court who set his poems to music.

Lely's first English pictures and drawings (including cat. 5–8) also attest to the musical nature of his London circle. Perhaps the "Mrs Gratiana" who appears in several works by Lely of the 1640s and 1650s, including cat. 10, was the same person as the lady of that name whose dancing and singing were praised in Lovelace's poetry.[3] Lely and Lovelace were given the Freedom of the Painter-Stainers' Company on the same day, 26 October 1647, in the company of two other royalist sympathisers, the sculptor Thomas Rawlins, who was Charles I's engraver of seals, and the cleric Dr George Wild.

In 1648 Lovelace probably wrote his poem (see below) on Lely's portrait of the captive Charles I and his second son, the future James II. We know that the picture was commissioned by the Earl of Northumberland, and cost £30. The poem was published in 1649 as part of *Lucasta*, the only collection of Lovelace's poems to be published during his lifetime, and delayed for several months by the author's committal to prison for involvement in another Kentish uprising. Lovelace commends Lely's ability to depict the king's "clouded majesty" with "eyes / Whose glory through their mist doth brighter rise!" Lovelace is struck by Lely's subtle portrayal of a monarch, albeit a diminished one, and concludes: "None but my Lilly ever drew a minde".

Similar ideas are expressed in 'Peinture', which asserts the superiority of painting over poetry. The former can embody imagined forms, while the latter can simply conceive them. Lovelace was aware of Lely's desire to paint more narrative pictures. The subjects he refers to in 'Peinture', including Venus and Cupid, Hercules and the Hydra, and the nymph Echo, are more likely wishful thinking and poetic license than references to any particular paintings by Lely. As the poem ends, Lovelace enjoins his "best Lilly" to "walk hand in hand / And smile at this un-understanding land; / Let them their own dull counterfeits adore, / Their Rainbow-cloaths admire and no more; / Within one shade of thine more substance is / Than all their varnish'd Idol-Mistresses".

Lovelace's association with Lely aside, the poet's movements in the last years of his life become more shadowy and difficult to discern. His second collection of verse, *Lucasta Posthume Poems*, which includes 'Peinture', was licensed for print in 1659, two years after his death. He was believed by the Parliamentarians to have been involved in several Loyalist plots, and appears to have travelled to Holland in the mid 1650s. Perhaps these travels coincided with those of Lely, who we know was also there in the summer of 1656.[4] Lovelace's biographer Anthony à Wood asserted that he died in dire need, relying on the charity of his friends. Although the sale of his estate suggests that his material circumstances were not ideal, his poetry gives the impression of a man who remained stoically attached to his beliefs in spite of imprisonment, defeat and increasing isolation.

1 This account of Lovelace's life is heavily indebted to Raymond Anselment's excellent biographical entry in the Dictionary of National Biography (henceforth Anselment 2004) and C.H. Wilkinson's edition of Lovelace's poetry (henceforth Lovelace 1930 (1953)).
2 Wood 1691, 3:460.
3 Millar in London 1978–79, p. 77, cat.71.
4 Millar in London 1978–79, pp. 14–15.

To my *Worthy Friend Mr.* Peter Lilly: *on that excellent Picture of his Majesty, and the Duke of Yorke, drawne by him at* Hampton-Court[1]

(From *Lucasta: Epodes, Odes, Sonnets,/Songs, Etc./ To which is added/Aramantha, A/Pastorall./ By /Richard Lovelace,/Esq./ London,/Printed by Tho. Harper, and are to be sold/by Thom. Ewster, at the Gun, in Ivie Lane. 1649*)

SEE! what a *clouded Majesty*! And eyes
Whose glory through their mist doth brighter rise!
See! what an humble bravery doth shine,
And griefe triumphant breaking through each line
How it commands the face! So sweet a scorne
Never did *happy misery* adorne!
So sacred a contempt! that others show
To this, (oth' height of all the wheele) below;
That mightiest Monarchs by this shaded booke
May coppy out their proudest, richest looke.

Whilst the true *Eaglet* this quick luster spies,
And by his *Sun's* enlightens his owne eyes;
He cares his cares, his burthen feeles, then streight
Joyes that so lightly he can beare such weight;
Whilst either eithers passion doth borrow,
And both doe grieve the same victorious sorrow.

These, my best *Lilly* with so bold a spirit
And soft a grace, as if thou didst inherit
For that time all their greatnesse, and didst draw
With those brave eyes your *Royal Sitters* saw.

Not of as old, when a rough hand did speake
A strong Aspect, and a faire face, a weake;
When only a black beard cried Villaine, and
By *Hieroglyphicks* we could understand
When Chrystall typified in a white spot,
And the bright Ruby was but one red blot;[2]
Thou dost the things *Orientally* the same
Not only paintst its colour, but its *Flame*;
Thou sorrow canst designe without a teare,
And with the Man his very *Hope or Feare*;
So that th' amazed world shall henceforth finde
None but my *Lilly* ever drew a *Minde*.[3]

---

1 Text from Lovelace 1930 (1953), pp. 57–58.
2 This implies the superficiality of previous painters, who only painted the external features of a sitter, not their character.
3 Lely, by contrast, draws 'a Minde', and penetrates to the 'Flame' or essence of his sitters.

Peinture
A Panegyrick to the best Picture of Friendship Mr. Pet. Lilly[1]

(From *Lucasta./Posthume/Poems/of/ Richard Lovelace Esq;/Those Honours come too late, /That on our Ashes waite./Mart. Lib.1. Epig. 26./ London/Printed by William Godbid for/ Clement Darby./1659.*)

If Pliny Lord High Treasurer of all
Natures exchequer shuffled in this our ball;
Pincture, her richer Rival, did admire,
And cry'd she wrought with more almighty fire,[2]
That judg'd the unnumbered issue of her Scrowl,
Infinite and various as her Mother Soul,
That contemplation into matter brought,
Body'd *Idaea*'s, and could form a thought:
Why do I pause to couch the Cataract,
And the grosse pearls from our dull eyes abstract?[3]
That pow'rful Lilly, now awakened, we
This new Creation may behold by thee.
    To thy victorious pencil, all that Eyes
And minds can reach, do bow; the Deities
Bold Poets first but feign'd, you do, and make,
And from your awe they our Devotion take.[4]
Your beauteous Pallet first defin'd Loves Queen,
And made her in her heav'nly colours seen;
You strung the Bow of the Bandite her Son,[5]
And tipp'd his Arrowes with Religion.
Neptune, as unknown as his Fish might dwell,
But that you seat him in his Throne of Shell.[6]
The thunders Artillery, and brand
You fancied *Rome* in his fantastick hand.[7]
    And the pale frights, the pains and fears of Hell,
First from your sullen Melancholy fell.
Who cleft th' infernal Dog's loath'd head in three,
And spun out *Hydra*'s fifty necks?[8] by thee
As prepossess'd w'enjoy th' *Elizian*[9] plain,
Which but before was flatter'd in our brain.
Who ere yet view'd Airs child invisible,
A hollow Voice, but in thy subtile skill?
Faint stamm'ring *Eccho*,[10] you so draw, that we
The very repercussion do see.

---

1 Text from Lovelace 1930 (1953), pp. 180–83.
2 A comparison between painting and poetry is here implied, although poetry is not mentioned by name.
3 Lovelace refers to the operation to remove a cataract from an eye, which enables the patient to see.
4 Poetry 'feigns' or simulates the gods; but Painting creates them.
5 The Roman deities Venus, goddess of love, and her son Cupid, who uses his bow and arrow to make his unwitting victims fall in love.
6 Neptune, the god of the oceans in the Roman pantheon.
7 'The thunders' [or thunderer] with artillery and a brand in his hand must represent Jupiter, king of the gods.
8 Here Lovelace mentions two hideous beasts: Cerberus, the five-headed dog who guarded the entrance to the Underworld in classical mythology and the Hydra, a beast with fifty necks who was slain by Hercules.
9 The Elysian Plain was the Paradise of ancient Greece and Rome.
10 The Nymph Echo fell in love with Narcissus (who pined to death out of love for his own reflection); she was unable to confess her love because she could only repeat what others said and had no voice of her own.

Cheat *Hocus-Pocus*[11] Nature an Essay
O' th' Spring affords us, *Praesto* and away;
You all the year do chain her, and her fruits,
Roots to their Beds, and flowers to their Roots.
Have not mine eyes feasted i' th' frozen *Zone*,
Upon a fresh new-grown Collation[12]
Of Apples, unknown sweets, that seem'd to me
Hanging to tempt as on the fatal Tree;[13]
So delicately limm'd I vow'd to try
My appetite impos'd upon my Eye.
You Sir alone, Fame and all-conqu'ring Rime,
Files the set teeth of all-devouring time.
When Beauty once thy virtuous paint hath on,
Age needs not call her to Vermilion;[14]
Her beams nere shed or change like th' hair of day,
She scatters fresh her everlasting Ray;
Nay, from her ashes her fair Virgin fire
Ascends, that doth new massacres conspire,
Whilst we wipe off the num'rous score of years,
And do behold our Grandsires as our peers,
With the first Father of our House, compare
We do the features of our new-born Heir;
For though each coppied a Son, they all
Meet in thy first and true Original.[15]
Sacred Luxurious! what Princesse not
But comes to you to have her self begot?
As when first man was kneaded, from his side
Is born to's hand a ready made up Bride.[16]
He husband to his issue then doth play,
And for more Wives remove the obstructed way:
So by your Art you spring up in two moons
What could not else be form'd by fifteen Suns;
Thy Skill doth an'mate the prolifick flood,
And thy red Oyl assimilates to blood.
Where then when all the world pays its respect,
Lies our transalpine barbarous Neglect?
When the chast hands of pow'rful *Titian*,
Had drawn the Scourges of our God and Man,
And now the top of th' Altar did ascend,
To crown the heav'nly piece with a bright end;
Whilst he who to seven Languages gave Law,
And always like the *Sun* his Subjects saw,
Did in his Robes Imperial and gold,
The basis of the doubtful Ladder hold.[17]
O *Charls*! A nobler monument then that,
Which thou thine own Executor were at.
When to our huffling *Henry* there complain'd
A grieved Earl, that thought his honor stain'd;
Away (frown'd he) for your own safeties, hast,
In one cheap hour ten Coronets I'l cast:

11 Lovelace means here that Nature, as conveyed by Lely's painting, is a make-believe or an illusion.

12 Collection of apples. 'Collation' is a word often used for an assembly of cold food, well into the nineteenth century.

13 The Tree of Life, from which Eve took an apple and offered it to Adam.

14 A red pigment, sometimes used, as Lovelace implies, to heighten the colour of women's lips and cheeks.

15 Here Lovelace says that paintings enable one to compare directly new-born children with their long-dead ancestors.

16 This alludes to the creation of Eve from Adam's rib, as told in the Old Testament Book of Genesis.

17 Charles V, Holy Roman Emperor, and the most powerful man in sixteenth-century Europe ("he who to seven Languages gave Law"), was alleged to have held the bottom rung of a ladder on which the Venetian painter Titian stood while he finished a picture of the *Ecce Homo* (possibly either that now in Paris or in Munich).

But *Holbeen*'s noble and prodigious worth,
Onely the pangs of an whole Age brings forth.
Henry! a word so princely saving said,
It might new raise the ruines thou hast made.[18]

O sacred *Peincture*! that dost fairly draw
What but in Mists deep inward *Poets* saw;[19]
'Twixt thee and an Intelligence no odds,
That art of privy Council to the Gods,
By thee unto our eyes they do prefer
A stamp of their abstracted Character;
Thou that in frames eternity dost bind,
And art a written and a body'd mind;
To thee is Ope the *Juncto* o' th' Abysse,
And its conspiracy detected is;
Whilest their Cabal thou to our sense dost show,
And in thy square paint'st what they threat below.

Now my best *Lilly* let's walk hand in hand,
And smile at this un-understanding land;
Let them their own dull counterfeits adore,
Their Rainbow-cloaths admire, and no more;
Within one shade of thine more substance is
Than all their varnish'd Idol-Mistresses:
Whilst great *Vasari* and *Vermander*[20] shall
Interpret the deep mystery of all,
And I unto our modern Picts[21] shall show,
What due renown to thy fair Art they owe,
In the delineated lives of those,
By whom this everlasting Lawrel grows:
Then if they will not gently apprehend,
Let one great blot give to their fame an end;
Whilst no Poetick flower their Herse[22] doth dresse,
But perish they and their Effigies.

18 This anecdote, of the earl complaining his honour has been stained, and the king replying he could create ten peers in one hour, is used to contrast with the great worth of Holbein's portraits.

19 Painting is praised as realising in a tangible form the thoughts of poetry, which are confined to the mind.

20 Giorgio Vasari (1511–1574), Italian painter, architect and writer, who produced the first coherent art historical work, the *Lives of the Most Excellent Painters, Sculptors and Architects*, and Karel van Mander (1548–1606), painter and biographer of Netherlandish artists (*Het Schilder-Boeck*).

21 A pun perhaps, referring both to painters and barbarians.

22 Hearse.

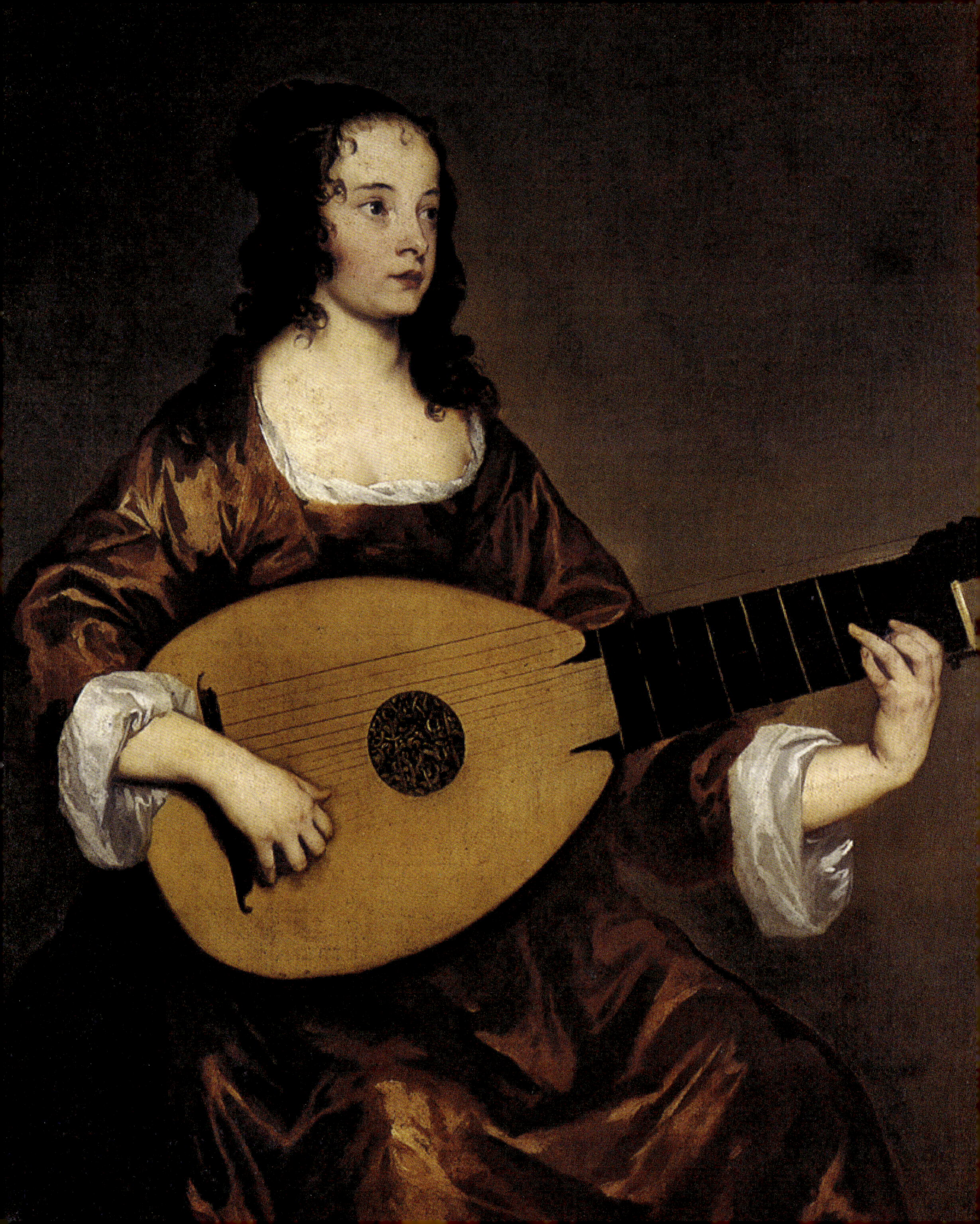

BIBLIOGRAPHY

ABERYSTWYTH 1945
An Exhibition of Sixty Pictures from the Royal, Gregynog, and Dulwich Collections, exh. cat., National Library of Wales, Aberystwyth, 1945

AILLAUD, BLANKERT AND MONTIAS 1992
Gilles Aillaud, Albert Blankert and John Michael Montias, *Vermeer*, Amsterdam, 1992

ANSELMENT 1999
Raymond A. Anselment, '"Clouded Majesty": Richard Lovelace, Sir Peter Lely, and the Royalist Spirit', *Studies in Philology*, vol. 86, no. 3, 1999, pp. 367–87

ANSELMENT 2004
Raymond A. Anselment, 'Lovelace, Richard (1617–1657)', *Oxford Dictionary of National Biography*, Oxford University Press, 2004; online edn, January 2010, http://www.oxforddnb.com/view/article/17056 [accessed 1 July 2012]

ANTWERP AND LONDON 1999
Christopher Brown and Hans Vlieghe, eds., *Van Dyck 1599–1641*, exh. cat., Koninklijk Museum voor Schone Kunst, Antwerp and Royal Academy of Arts, London, 1999

AUERBACH AND KINGSLEY ADAMS 1971
Erna Auerbach and Charles Kingsley Adams, *Paintings & Sculpture at Hatfield House*, London, 1971

BARNES, DE POORTER, MILLAR AND VEY 2004
Susan J. Barnes, Nora de Poorter, Oliver Millar and Horst Vey, *Van Dyck, A Complete Catalogue of the Paintings*, London and New Haven, 2004

BRIGSTOCKE 1993
Hugh Brigstocke, *Italian and Spanish Paintings in the National Gallery of Scotland*, Edinburgh, 1993

BECKETT 1951
Ronald Brymer Beckett, *Lely*, London, 1951

BERESFORD 1998
Richard Beresford, *Dulwich Picture Gallery : Complete illustrated catalogue*, London, 1998

BILBAO AND MADRID 1999
Carmen Giménez, *Obras Maestras de la Galería de Pinturas de Dulwich (Masterpieces of the Dulwich Picture Gallery)*, exh. cat., Banco Bilbao Vizcaya, Madrid; Museo de Bellas Artes, Bilbao, 1999

BIESBOER 1990
Pieter Biesboer, 'The Burghers of Haarlem and Their Portrait Painters', in Seymour Slive, ed., *Frans Hals*, exh. cat., National Gallery of Art, Washington DC, Royal Academy of Arts, London, and Frans Hals Museum, Haarlem, 1990, pp. 23–44

BIESBOER 2001
Pieter Biesboer, 'Collections of paintings in Haarlem 1572–1745', *Documents for the History of Collecting: Netherlandish Inventories*, I, ed. Carol Togneri, Los Angeles, 2001

BIGNAMINI 1988
Ilaria Bignamini, 'George Vertue, Art Historian, and Art Institutions in London, 1689–1768', *The Walpole Society*, vol. 54, 1988, pp. 2–18

BORENIUS 1923–26
Tancred Borenius, *A Catalogue of the Pictures at 18 Kensington Palace Gardens*, London, 1923–26, 2 vols.

BREDIUS 1915–22
Abraham Bredius, ed., with the assistance of Otto Hirschmann, *Künstler-Inventaire; Urkunden zur Geschichte der Holländischen Kunst des XVI, XVII and XVIII Jahrhunderts*, The Hague, 1915–22, 8 vols.

BUCKERIDGE 1706 (1754)
Bainbrigg Buckeridge, 'An essay toward an English school', in *The art of painting ... Translated by the French of Monsieur de Piles. To which is added, An essay towards an English school*, English translation of Roger de Piles, *Abregé de la vie des peintres*, London (Thomas Payne), 1754, 3rd edition

BRITTON 1806
John Britton, *An Historical Account of Corsham House in Wiltshire, the Seat of Paul Cobb Methuen, Esq. With a catalogue of his celebrated collection of pictures, etc.*, London and Bath, 1806

BURLINGTON MAGAZINE 1943
'Editorial: Sir Peter Lely's collection', *The Burlington Magazine*, vol. 83, no. 485, August 1943, pp. 185–91

BUTLIN 1988
Martin Butlin, *Aspects of British Painting from the Collection of the Sarah Campbell Blaffer Foundation, 1550–1800*, Houston, 1988

COLLINS BAKER 1912
Charles Henry Collins Baker, *Lely and the Stuart Portrait Painters: A Study of English Portraiture before and after Van Dyck*, London, 1912, 2 vols.

COLLINS BAKER 1922
Charles Henry Collins Baker, *Lely and Kneller*, London, 1922

COOK 1914
Edward Cook, *Catalogue of the Pictures in the Gallery of Alleyn's College of God's Gift at Dulwich: with biographical notices of the painters, revised and completed to the present time*, London, 1914

COOK 1926
Edward Cook, *Catalogue of the Pictures in the Gallery of Alleyn's college of God's Gift at Dulwich: with biographical notices of the painters, revised in 1914 by Edward Cook; and completed in 1926 by the Governors*, London, 1926

COWAN 1998
Brian Cowan, 'Arenas of Connoisseurship: Auctioning Art in Later Stuart England', in *Art Markets in Europe 1400–1800*, ed. Michael North and David Ormrod, Aldershot and Brookfield VT, 1998, pp. 153–66

COURTAULD 1987
Dennis Farr, ed., *100 Masterpieces* [from the Courtauld Collections]*: Bernardo Daddi to Ben Nicholson: European Paintings and Drawings from the 14th to the 20th Century*, London, 1987

COURTAULD 1990
Dennis Farr, ed., *The Courtauld Institute Galleries, University of London*, London, 1990

Detail of fig. 49

DETHLOFF 1996
Diana Dethloff, 'The executors' account book and the dispersal of Sir Peter Lely's collection', *Journal of the History of Collections*, vol. 8, 1996, pp. 15–51

DETHLOFF 2003
Diana Dethloff, 'Sir Peter Lely's collection of prints and drawings', in *Collecting Prints & Drawings in Europe c. 1500–1750*, ed. Christopher Baker, Caroline Elam and Genevieve Warwick, Aldershot and Burlington VT, 2003, pp. 123–39

DETHLOFF 2004
Diana Dethloff, 'Lely, Sir Peter (1618–1680)', *Oxford Dictionary of National Biography*, Oxford University Press, 2004; online edn, May 2009, http://www.oxforddnb.com/view/article/16419 [accessed 14 May 2012]

DODSLEY 1761
London and its environs described. Containing An Account of whatever is most remarkable for Grandeur, Elegance, Curiosity or Use, in the City and in the Country Twenty Miles round it, Together with a Plan of London, A Map of the Environs, and several other useful Cuts, London (R. and J. Dodsley), 6 vols.

VAN EIKEMA HOMMES 2005
Margriet van Eikema Hommes, 'Pieter de Grebber and the Oranjezaal in Huis ten Bosch: Part I: The Regulen (1649)', *Netherlands Technical Studies in Art: Art Matters*, vol. 3, 2005, pp. 20–36

VAN EIKEMA HOMMES AND SPELEERS 2005
Margriet van Eikema Hommes and Lidwien Speleers, 'Pieter de Grebber and the Oranjezaal in Huis ten Bosch: Part II: Variations in Painting Technique', *Netherlands Technical Studies in Art: Art Matters*, vol. 3, 2005, pp. 37–65

ECARTICO DATABASE
'Peter Lely, alias: Pieter van der Faes' , http://burckhardt.ic.uva.nl/ecartico/persons/4546 [accessed 12 June 2012]

FARMER 1984
Norman K. Farmer Jnr, *Poets and the Visual Arts in Renaissance England*, Austin TX, 1984

FOUCART 1983
Jacques Foucart, 'Tableaux des Ecoles du Nord: un bilan d'acquisitions', *La Revue du Louvre et des Musées de France*, vols. 5–6, 1983, pp. 359–70

FOUCART 1989
Jacques Foucart, 'Peter Lely, Dutch history painter', *Hoogsteder-Naumann Mercury*, vol. 8, 1989, pp. 17–26

FOUCART 1990
Jacques Foucart, 'Peter Lely au Musée de Valenciennes, ou la revelation d'un beau peintre d'histoire hollandais', *Valentiana*, vol. 5, 1990, pp. 2–10

DU FRESNOY 1695
Charles-Alphonse Du Fresnoy, *De Arte Graphica. The Art of Painting ... with remarks* [by Roger de Piles]*: Translated into English, together with an original preface containing a parallel betwixt Painting and Poetry. By Mr Dryden. As also a short account of the most eminent painters, both ancient and modern ... By another hand* [Richard Graham], London, 1695

DU FRESNOY 1716
Charles-Alphonse Du Fresnoy, *The Art of Painting ... with Remarks ... with an original preface ... by Mr. Dryden .... And also a short account of the most Eminent painters, both ancient and modern: By R.G. Esq; the second edition, corrected, and enlarged,* London, 1716

GIBSON 1997
Katharine Gibson, '"Best belov'd of kings": the iconography of Charles II', PhD thesis, University of London (Courtauld Institute of Art) 1997, 3 vols.

GLEISSNER 1994
Stephen Gleissner, 'Reassembling a Royal Art Collection for the Restored King of Great Britain', *Journal of the History of Collections*, vol. 6, no. 1, 1994, pp. 103–15

GOOSENS 2001
Marion Goosens, *Schilders en de Markt: Haarlem 1605–1635*, Leiden, 2001

GRAHAM 1695
Richard Graham, '... A short account of the most eminent painters, both ancient and modern', in Du Fresnoy 1695, pp. 241–404

GRAHAM 1716
Richard Graham, '... A short account of the most eminent Painters, both Ancient and Modern, down to the Present Times', in Du Fresnoy 1716, pp. 241–404

GRANGER 1804
James Granger, *A Biographical History of England, from Egbert the Great to the Revolution ... adapted to a methodical catalogue of engraved British heads, etc. ... A Supplement ... and a list of Portraits of eminent persons communicated by H. Walpole,* London, 1804

GREGORY 1986
Clive Gregory, ed., 'The Artist at Work: Restoration Image-Maker', *The Great Artists*, vol. 3, 1986, pp. 2184–89

GRIFFITHS 1990
Antony Griffiths, 'Early Mezzotint publishing in England, II: Peter Lely, Tompson and Browne', *Print Quarterly*, vol. 7, no. 2, 1990, pp. 130–45

HAARLEM AND WORCESTER 1993
Pieter Biesboer and James Welu, eds., *Judith Leyster: A Dutch Master and Her World*, exh. cat., Frans Hals Museum, Haarlem, and Worcester Art Museum, Worcester MA, 1993

HARRIS 2007
Frances Harris, 'An ambivalent image: Lely's double-portrait of Charles I and the Duke of York', *The Burlington Magazine*, vol. 149, no. 1248 (March 2007), pp. 180–82

HASKELL 1989
Francis Haskell, 'Charles I's Collection of Pictures', in *The Late King's Goods*, ed. Arthur MacGregor, Oxford, 1989, pp. 203–31

HENDRIKS AND GROEN 1994
Ella Hendriks and Karin Groen, 'Lely's Studio Practice', *Hamilton Kerr Institute Bulletin*, vol. 2, 1994, pp. 21–37

HOUBRAKEN 1718–21 (1753)
Arnold Houbraken, *De groote schouburgh der Nederlantsche konstschilders en schilderessen*, 's Gravenhage (J. Swart, C. Boucquet and M. Gaillard), 1753, 3 vols.

HOUSTON AND LOUISVILLE 1999–2000
Ian Dejardin, Desmond Shawe-Taylor and Giles Waterfield, *Rembrandt to Gainsborough: Masterpieces from Dulwich Picture Gallery*, exh. cat., Museum of Fine Arts, Houston, and Speed Art Museum, Louisville, 1999–2000

HUYGENS 1651–52 (1982)
Lodewijck Huygens. The English Journal 1651–1652, ed. and trans. Alfred G.H. Bachrach and R.G. Collmer, Leiden, 1982

INGAMELLS 2008
John Ingamells, *Dulwich Picture Gallery: British*, London, 2008

JAPAN 1986–87
Old Master Paintings from Dulwich Picture Gallery, exh. cat., Isetan Museum of Art, Tokyo; Shizuoka Prefectural Museum of Art; Daimaru Museum, Osaka; Takashimaya, Yokohama, 1986–87

KIRBY TALLEY 1978
Mansfield Kirby Talley, *Portrait Painting in England: Studies in the technical literature before 1700*, PhD thesis, University of London (Courtauld Institute of Art), 1978

KIRBY TALLEY 1978a
Mansfield Kirby Talley, 'Extracts from the executors' account book of Sir Peter Lely, 1679–1691: an account of the contents of Sir Peter's studio', *Burlington Magazine*, vol. 120, 980, 1978, pp. 745–49

KIRBY TALLEY 1981
Mansfield Kirby Talley, *Portrait Painting in England: Studies in the technical literature before 1700*, London, 1981

KULTURMANN 1990
Udo Kultermann, 'Women Asleep and the Artist', *Artibus et Historiae*, vol. 2, no. 22, 1990, pp. 129–61

KYROVA 1994
Magda Kyrova, 'Music in Seventeenth-Century Dutch Painting', in *Music and Painting in the Golden Age*, exh. cat., ed. Edwin Buijsen and Louis Peter Grijp, Hoogsteder & Hoogsteder, The Hague, and Hessenhuis Museum, Antwerp, 1994, pp. 31–62

LAING 1993
Alastair Laing, 'Sir Peter Lely and Ralph Bankes', in David Howarth, ed., *Art and Patronage in the Caroline Courts: Essays in Honour of Sir Oliver Millar*, Cambridge, 1993, pp. 107–33

LEVY PECK 2005
Linda Levy Peck, 'Luxury and War, 1640–1660', in *Consuming Splendour. Society and Culture in Seventeenth-Century England*, Cambridge, 2005, pp. 230–76

LEE 1932
Arthur Lee, 'Lely's Love Story', *Burlington Magazine*, vol. 60, no. 348, March 1932, pp. 145–47, 150

LEEDS 1954–55
Paintings from Chatsworth House, exh. cat., City Art Gallery, Leeds, 1954–55

LIGHTBOWN 1989
Ronald Lightbown, 'Charles I and the Art of the Goldsmith', in Arthur MacGregor (ed.), *The Late King's Goods*, Oxford, 1989, pp. 233–55

LONDON 1861
Catalogue of pictures by Italian, Spanish, Flemish, Dutch, French, and English masters with which the proprietors have favoured the institution, exh. cat., The British Institution for promoting the Fine Arts in the United Kingdom, London 1861

LONDON 1908
Works by the Old Masters and deceased Masters of the British School: including a collection of Watercolours, exh. cat., Royal Academy of Arts, London, 1908

LONDON 1932
E.F. Benson, ed., *The Age of Walnut: Loan exhibition in aid of the Royal Northern Hospital*, exh. cat., 25 Park Lane, London, 1932

LONDON 1934
William Llewellyn, W.G. Constable and James G. Mann, *Exhibition of British Art c. 1000–1860*, exh. cat., Royal Academy of Arts, London, 1934

LONDON 1938
Catalogue of the Exhibition of Seventeenth-Century Art in Europe, exh. cat., Royal Academy of Arts, London, 1938

LONDON 1947
Some Pictures from the Dulwich Gallery, exh. cat., National Gallery, London, 1947

London 1964
Alfred G.H. Bachrach, ed., *The Orange and the Rose: Holland and Britain in the Age of Observation, 1600–1750*, exh. cat., Victoria and Albert Museum, London, 1964

LONDON 1960–61
Oliver Millar, with a preface by Charles Wheeler, *The Age of Charles II*, exh. cat., The Royal Academy of Arts, London, 1960–61

LONDON 1960
A.E. Popham, *Italian Art and Britain*, exh. cat., The Royal Academy, London, 1960

LONDON 1970
Robin Gibson, *An exhibition of paintings from the collection of Dr. D.M. McDonald*, exh. cat., Leggatt Brothers, London, 1970

LONDON 1972
Oliver Millar, *The Age of Charles I: Painting in England, 1620–1649*, exh. cat., Tate Gallery, London, 1972

LONDON 1978–79
Oliver Millar, *Sir Peter Lely 1618–80*, exh. cat., National Portrait Gallery, London, 1978–79

LONDON 1984
Malcolm Rogers, *William Dobson 1611–46*, exh. cat., National Portrait Gallery, London, 1984

LONDON 1987
Lindsay Stainton and Christopher White, eds., *Drawing in England from Hilliard to Hogarth*, exh. cat., British Museum, London, 1987

LONDON 1995
Alastair Laing, *In Trust for the Nation, Paintings from National Trust Houses*, exh. cat., National Gallery, London, 1995

LONDON AND NEW HAVEN 2001–02
Catharine MacLeod and Julia Marciari Alexander, eds., *Painted Ladies: Women at the Court of Charles II*, exh. cat., National Portrait Gallery, London, and Yale Center for British Art, New Haven, 2001–02

LONDON 2002
Laurie B. Harwood, *Inspired by Italy: Dutch Landscape Painting 1600–1700*, exh. cat., Dulwich Picture Gallery, London, 2002

LONDON 2003
David Jaffé, ed., *Titian*, exh. cat., National Gallery, London, 2003

LONDON 2012
Lizzie Carey-Thomas, ed., *Migrations: Journeys into British Art*, exh. cat., Tate Britain, London, 2012

LONDON AND AMSTERDAM 2006
Friso Lammertse and Jaap van der Veen, eds., *Uylenburgh & Son: Art and Commerce from Rembrandt to De Lairesse, 1625–1675*, exh. cat., Dulwich Picture Gallery, London, and Rembrandthuis, Amsterdam, 2006

LONDON AND FRANKFURT 2007
Mirjam Neumeister, ed., *The Changing Face of Childhood: British children's portraits and their influence in Europe*, exh. cat., Dulwich Picture Gallery, London, and Städelsches Kunst-institut, Frankfurt, 2007

LOVELACE 1930 (1953)
Richard Lovelace, *The Poems of Richard Lovelace*, ed. C.H. Wilkinson, Oxford, 1930 (revised edition, 1953)

MADRID 2003
Miguel Falomir, ed., *Ticiano*, exh. cat., Museo del Prado, Madrid, 2003

MANCHESTER 1960
Works of Art from Private Collections: in Lancashire, Cheshire, Cumberland, Westmorland, Parts of Shropshire, Staffordshire and Derbyshire, North Wales and Anglesey, exh. cat., Manchester City Art Gallery, Manchester, 1960

VAN MANDER 1604
Karel van Mander, *Het Schilder-Boeck*, Haarlem, 1604

DE MARCHI AND VAN MIEGROET 1994
Neil B. De Marchi and Hans J. Van Miegroet, 'Art, Value, and Market Practises in the Seventeenth-Century Netherlands', *Art Bulletin*, vol. 76, 1994, pp. 451–64

MARCIARI ALEXANDER 2001
Julia Marciari Alexander, 'A Dutch "stranger … on the make": Sir Peter Lely and the Critical Fortunes of a Foreign Painter', in *From Strangers to Citizens*, eds. Randolph Vigne and Charles Littleton, Brighton and Portland OR, 2001, pp. 127–32

MASON 2009
Shena Mason, *Matthew Boulton: Selling What All The World Desires*, New Haven and London, 2009

McGRATH 1978
Elizabeth McGrath, 'The Painted Decoration of Rubens's House', *Journal of the Warburg and Courtauld Institutes*, vol. 41, 1978, pp. 245–77

McNEIL KETTERING 1983
Alison McNeil Kettering, *The Dutch Arcadia: Pastoral Art and its Audience in the Golden Age*, Montclair NJ, 1983

MILLAR 1958–60
Oliver Millar, 'Abraham van der Doort's Catalogue of the Collection of Charles I', *The Walpole Society*, vol. 37, 1958–60

MILLAR 1963
Oliver Millar, *The Tudor, Stuart and Early Georgian Pictures in the Collection of her Majesty the Queen*, London, 1963, 2 vols.

MILLAR AND DETHLOFF 1996 (revised 2004)
Oliver Millar and Diana Dethloff, 'Sir Peter Lely', *Grove Art Online, Oxford Art Online*, http://www.oxfordartonline.com:80/subscriber/article/grove/art/T050209 [accessed 12 January 2012]

MILLAR 1996 (revised 2004)
Oliver Millar, 'George Geldorp', *Grove Art Online. Oxford Art Online*, http://www.oxfordartonline.com/subscriber/article/grove/art/T031202pg2 [accessed 27 July 2012]

TER MOLEN 1983
Johannes Rein ter Molen, *Van Vianen: een Utrechtse familie van zilversmeden met een internationale faam*, PhD thesis, Leiden University, 1983

MONTIAS 1988
John Michael Montias, 'Art Dealers in the Seventeenth-Century Netherlands', *Simiolus*, vol. 18, no. 4, 1988, pp. 244–56

MURRAY 1958
Peter Murray, *The Lee Collection, Courtauld Institute of Art, University of London*, London, 1958

NEWARK 1983
Frima Fox Hofrichter, with an introduction by Egbert Haverkamp-Begemann and an essay by J.J. Temminck, *Haarlem: The Seventeenth Century*, exh. cat., Jane Voorhees Zimmerli Art Museum, Rutgers University, Newark NJ, 1983

NEWCASTLE 1955–56
Thirty-five paintings from the Devonshire Collection, Chatsworth: lent by the Trustees of the Chatsworth Settlement, touring exhibition organised by the Arts Council of Great Britain, exh. cat., Newcastle, Laing Art Gallery, 1955–56

NEW YORK 2010
Xavier Salomon, *Masterpieces of European Painting from Dulwich Picture Gallery*, exh. cat., Frick Collection, New York, 2010

NORTH 1890
Roger North, *Lives of the Norths*, ed. Augustus Jessop, London, 1890

NOTTINGHAM AND LONDON 1991
Ilaria Bignamini and Martin Postle, eds., *The Artist's Model: Its Role in British Art from Lely to Etty*, exh. cat., University Art Gallery, Nottingham, and the Iveagh Bequest, Kenwood, 1991

NOTTINGHAM AND LONDON 1998
Martin Postle, *Angels and Urchins: The Fancy Picture in 18th-Century British Art*, exh. cat., Djanogly Art Gallery, University of Nottingham, and Kenwood House, London, 1998

OGDEN AND OGDEN 1944
Henry Ogden and Margaret Ogden, 'Sir Peter Lely's collection: further notes', *The Burlington Magazine*, vol. 84, no. 495, 1944, p. 154

ORMROD 1973
David Ormrod, *The Dutch in London. The Influence of an Immigrant Community 1550–1800*, London, 1973

PARIS 1994
Olivier Meslay, Arlette Sérullaz and Barthélémy Jobert, *D'outre-Manche: l'art britannique dans les collections publiques françaises*, exh. cat., Musée du Louvre, Paris, 1994

PENNANT 1811
Thomas Pennant, *The journey from Chester to London*, London, 1811

PENNY 2008
Nicholas Penny, *National Gallery Catalogues: The Sixteenth-century Italian Paintings*, vol. II: *Venice 1540–1600*, London, 2008

PEPYS 1995
Samuel Pepys, *The Diary of Samuel Pepys: A complete and new transcription*, ed. Robert Latham and William Matthews, 1995, 11 vols.

PORTIER 1996
François Portier, 'Prices paid for Italian pictures in the Stuart age', *Journal of the History of Collections*, vol. 8, 1996, pp. 53–69

PRAK 2003
Maarten Prak, 'Guilds and the Development of the Art Market during the Dutch Golden Age', *Simiolus*, vol. 30, nos. 3–4, 2003, pp. 236–51

RENNE 2011
Elizaveta Renne, *State Hermitage Museum Catalogue: Sixteenth- to Seventeenth-Century British Painting*, New Haven and London, 2011

RENNES 1980
Bulletin des Amis du Musée de Rennes, vol. 4, 1980

RENNES 1982
Acquisitions 1979–82, exh. cat., Musée de Rennes, 1982

RÉVUE DU LOUVRE 1981
Anon., 'Les principales acquisitions des musées de province', *La Révue du Louvre et des Musées de France*, vol. 2, 1981, p. 144

RIBEIRO 2005
Aileen Ribeiro, *Fashion and Fiction: Dress in Art and Literature in Stuart England*, New Haven and London, 2005

RICHARDSON 1715
Jonathan Richardson, *Essay on the theory of painting*, London (W. Bowyer, for John Churchill), 1715

RIPA 1613
Cesare Ripa, *Iconologia di Cesare Ripa Perugino …*, Siena (Florimi), 1613, 2 vols.

ROGERS 1979
Malcolm Rogers, 'Some beauties of Peter Lely', *The Connoisseur*, vol. 200, 1979, pp. 106–13

ROOSES AND RUELENS 1898
Max Rooses and Charles Ruelens, *Correspondance de Rubens*, Antwerp (1887–1909, 8 vols.), vol. 2 (1609–25 July 1622), 1898

ROTTERDAM AND FRANKFURT 1999–2000
Albert Blankert, Jeroen Giltaij and Friso Lammertse, eds., *Dutch classicism in seventeenth-century painting*, exh. cat., Boijmans Van Beuningen Museum, Rotterdam and Städelsches Kunstinstitut, Frankfurt am Main, 1999–2000

RYNCK 2009
Patrick de Rynck, *Understanding Paintings: Bible Stories and Classical Myths in Art*, London, 2009

SANDERSON 1658
William Sanderson, *Graphice. The Use of the Pen and Pensil. Or, The Most Excellent Art of Painting: In Two Parts*, London, 1658

SANDRART 1675–76 (1925)
Joachim von Sandrart, *Academie der bau-, bild- und mahlerey-künste von 1675. Leben der berühmten maler, bildhauer und baumeister*, ed. with commentary by Arthur Rudolf Peltzer, Munich, 1925, pp. 354–55

DE SAVORIN LOHMAN 1982
R.C.C. de Savorin Lohman, 'Heeft de Engelse Sir Peter Lely (alias Pieter van der Faes) in zijn jeugd Deventer bij zijn ouders gewoond?', *De Nederlandsche Leeuw*, vol. 99, 1982, pp. 283–86

SIMON 2007–09
Jacob Simon, 'A Directory of British Picture Framemakers', http://www.npg.org.uk/research/conservation/directory-of-british-framemakers/g.php, 1st edition November 2007, 2nd edition October 2009 [accessed 18 February 2012]

SITWELL 1936
Sacheverell Sitwell, *Conversation Pieces: A survey of English domestic portraits and their painters*, London, 1936

SLIVE 1995
Seymour Slive, *Dutch Painting 1600–1800*, New Haven and London, 1995

SUTTON 1981
Denys Sutton, 'Aspects of British Collecting, Part II: London as an art centre', *Apollo*, vol. 114, no. 237, 1981, pp. 298–312

SYDNEY AND MELBOURNE 1977–78
British Painting 1600–1800, exh. cat., Art Gallery of New South Wales, Sydney, and National Gallery of Victoria, Melbourne, 1977–78

TATE GALLERY 1968
Tate Gallery, *Report of the Trustees of the Tate Gallery, 1966–67*, London, 1968

TIPPING 1909
Henry Avray Tipping, 'Coombe Abbey, Warwickshire, A Seat of the Earl of Craven', *Country Life*, vol. 26, December 1909, pp. 794–805

TOYNBEE 1927–28
Paget Toynbee, 'Horace Walpole's Journals of Visits to Country Seats, &c.', *The Walpole Society*, vol. 16, 1927–28, pp. 9–80

TOYNBEE 1946
Margaret R. Toynbee, 'The Early Work of Sir Peter Lely', *Burlington Magazine*, vol. 88, no. 516, 1946, pp. 75–76

TROUTMAN 1979
Philip Troutman, *The Paintings Collections of the Courtauld Institute of Art, with an introduction by Peter Lasko*, Chicago, 1979

DE VERE 1914
Giorgio Vasari, translated by Gaston Du C. De Vere, *Lives of the Most Eminent Painters, Sculptors and Architects by Giorgio Vasari*, London (1912–15, 10 vols.), 1914, vol. 7

VERNEY AND VERNEY 1925
Francis Verney and Margaret Verney, *Memoirs of the Verney Family during the Seventeenth Century*, London, 1925

VERTUE 1929–50
George Vertue, 'Notebooks, vols. I–IV', *The Walpole Society*, vols. 18, 20, 22, 24, 26, 29, 30, 1929–50

WALPOLE 1761–71 (1879)
Horace Walpole, *Anecdotes of Painting in England*, London, 1879

WALPOLE 1761–71 (1888)
Horace Walpole, *Anecdotes of Painting in England: with some account of the principal artists and incidental notes on other arts, also, a catalogue of engravers who have been born or resided in England*, ed. R.N. Wornum, London, 1888, 3 vols.

WAAGEN 1854–57
Gustav Friedrich Waagen, *Treasures of art in Great Britain: being an account of the chief collections of paintings, drawings, sculptures, illuminated mss., etc. etc. / by Dr Waagen*, London, 1854–57, 4 vols.

WARSAW 1992
Christopher Brown, ed., *Kolekcja dla króla: obrazy dawnych mistrzów ze zbiorów Dulwich Picture Gallery w Londynie*, exh. cat., Warsaw, Zamek Królewski w Warszawie, 1992

WASHINGTON AND LOS ANGELES 1985–86
Giles Waterfield, ed., *Collection for a King: Old Master Paintings from the Dulwich Picture Gallery*, exh. cat., National Gallery of Art, Washington DC, and Los Angeles County Museum of Art, 1985–86

WASHINGTON, DETROIT AND AMSTERDAM 1980–81
Albert Blankert, ed., *Gods, Saints and Heroes: Dutch Painting in the Age of Rembrandt*, exh. cat., National Gallery of Art, Washington DC, Detroit Institute of Arts, and Rijksmuseum, Amsterdam, 1980–81

WASHINGTON DC AND THE HAGUE 1995
Frederic Duparc and Arthur Wheelock, *Johannes Vermeer*, exh. cat., National Gallery of Art, Washington DC, and Royal Cabinet of Paintings/Mauritshuis, The Hague, 1995

WATERFIELD 1994
Giles Waterfield, ed., *Collection for a King: Old Master Paintings from the Dulwich Picture Gallery*, London, 1994

WATERHOUSE 1953 (1994)
Ellis Waterhouse, *Painting in Britain 1530–1790*, 5th edition, New Haven and London, 1994

WATERHOUSE 1958
Sir Ellis Waterhouse, *The Collection of Pictures at Helmingham Hall*, privately printed, 1958

WESTERMANN 1996
Mariët Westermann, *The Art of the Dutch Republic 1585–1718*, London, 1996

WHINNEY AND MILLAR 1957
Margaret Whinney and Oliver Millar, *English Art 1625–1714*, Oxford, 1957

WHITE 1982
Christopher White, *The Dutch Pictures in the Collection of Her Majesty The Queen*, Cambridge, 1982

WHITE 1995–96
Christopher White, 'Through Foreign Eyes: Painters from the Low Countries in Seventeenth-Century England', *The Low Countries. Arts and Society in Flanders and the Netherlands. A Yearbook*, 1995–96, pp. 190–97

WIJSENBEEK-OLTHUIS AND NOORDERAAF 1993
Thera Wijsenbeek-Olthuis and Leo Noorderaaf, 'Painting for a Living: The Economic Context of Judith Leyster's Career', in Haarlem and Worcester 1993, pp. 39–54

DE WITT 2007
David De Witt, *Jan van Noordt: Painter of History and Portraits in Amsterdam*, Montreal and Kingston, 2007

WITTENAAR 1952
J.A.C.Ab. Wittenaar, 'De Geboorteplaats en de Naam van Pieter Lely Nieuwe Documenten, *Oud-Holland*, vol. 67, no. 2, 1952, pp. 122–24

WOOD 1691
Anthony à Wood, *Athenae Oxonienses: an Exact History of all the Writers and Bishops who have had their Education in the University of Oxford from 1500 to 1690*, London, 1691–92, 2 vols.

WOOD 1994
Jeremy Wood, 'Van Dyck and the Earl of Northumberland: Taste and Collecting in Stuart England', in *Van Dyck 350*, eds. Susan Barnes and Arthur Wheelock (Studies in the History of Art, 46), Washington DC, 1994, pp. 281–324

WOOD 2000–01
Jeremy Wood, 'Orazio Gentileschi and Some Netherlandish Artists in London: the Patronage of the Duke of Buckingham, Charles I and Henrietta Maria', *Simiolus*, vol. 28, no. 3, 2000–01, pp. 103–28

WOODALL 1961
Mary Woodall, ed., *The Letters of Thomas Gainsborough*, London, 1961

WOODWARD 1951
John Woodward, *Tudor and Stuart Drawings*, London, 1951

WORCESTER 1951
Exhibition of Paintings from 1642–1651, City Art Gallery, Worcester, 1951

PHOTOGRAPHIC CREDITS

© Birmingham Museums & Art Gallery: figs. 7 and 25
Fergus Hall Master Paintings, London: fig. 47
© Trustees of the British Museum: figs. 13, 22, 23
© bpk | Staatliche Kunstsammlungen Dresden. Photo: Henrik Ahlers: fig. 11
© Dulwich Picture Gallery, London, UK/ The Bridgeman Art Library: cat. 9, 12, figs. 28, 59
© Detroit Institute of Arts, USA (Gift of Mr. and Mrs. Trent McMath) / The Bridgeman Art Library: fig. 38
© Petworth House, Sussex, UK. National Trust Photographic Library / The Bridgeman Art Library: fig. 52
Image courtesy The Burghley House Collection: fig. 26
© Devonshire Collection, Chatsworth: cat. 10
© SMK photo: fig. 34
© The Courtauld Gallery (Samuel Courtauld Trust): cat. 4, 7, figs. 15, 16, 50
© Collection Mr and Mrs James Birch: cat. 11
© National Gallery of Ireland: fig. 32
© Edinburgh, Scottish National Gallery: fig. 42
Reproduction by courtesy of the Marquess of Salisbury: fig. 24
Image courtesy Galerie Jean-Francois Heim, Paris: fig. 37
© Private collection: cat. 3
© The State Hermitage Museum. Photo: Vladimir Terebenin, Leonard Kheifets, Yuri Molodkovets: fig. 36
© National Trust Images: fig. 55
© The Photographic Survey, Courtauld Institute of Art, London: fig. 58
© The National Gallery, London: figs. 4, 10, 30, 41, 46, 51
© National Portrait Gallery, London: figs. 9, 20
© Philip Mould – Private Collection: cat. 8, fig. 39
© Ville de Nantes – Musée des Beaux-Arts. Photographie – A. Guillard: fig. 40
© The Bodleian Library, University of Oxford: fig. 3
© By kind permission of Viscount De L'Isle from his private collection at Penshurst Place, Kent, England: fig. 60
© MBA, Rennes, Dist. RMN-GP / Louis Deschamps: cat. 1
© RMN-GP / René-Gabriel Ojéda: cat. 2
The Royal Collection ©2012, Her Majesty Queen Elizabeth II: figs. 5, 12, 14
Private collection. On long term loan to the Barber Institute in Birmingham. Photo © Matthew Hollow: fig. 56
Courtesy of Sotheby's Picture Library: figs. 6, 35
© Collection of James Stunt: figs. 1, 2, 8
© Tate, London 2012: cats. 5, 6, fig. 27
Photograph reproduced with the kind permission of the Royal Institution of Cornwall: fig. 53
© Kunstammlungen Graf von Schonborn, Schloss Weissenstein, Pommersfelden: fig. 31
Image courtesy of the Witt Library, Courtauld Institute of Art, London: figs. 17, 21, 33, 45, 48, 49, 57
© Private Collection: figs. 18 and 19
© Museo del Prado, Madrid: fig. 29